# GCSE AQA

# German

When it comes to GCSE German, have no *Angst* — this splendid Revision Guide has everything you need to get top marks.

It covers every topic on the AQA course with lots of examples and practice questions, including all the vocab and grammar you'll need for the exams.

It also comes with the CGP RevisionHub, which has quick quizzes, summary tests, audio, Q&A videos and more. The Hub is all matched to your book, so you can revise exactly what you've learned, online. Don't worry, you can thank us later!

## Unlock CGP RevisionHub

Just scan a QR code in the book to access the CGP RevisionHub.
Or go to **cgpbooks.co.uk/revise** and enter this code!

1905 3360 4112 0689

By the way, this code only works for one person. If somebody else has used this book before you, they might have already claimed the code.

# Revision Guide
## with new *CGP RevisionHub*

Published by CGP

*Editors:*
Caitlin Bell
Keith Blackhall
Siân Butler
Tom Carney
Rebecca Greaves
Nathan Leach
Lorna Kimmins
Ali Palin

With thanks to Georgina Paxman for the proofreading.
With thanks to Alice Dent for the copyright research.

*Acknowledgements:*

*Audio produced by Voice Talent Online.*

*AQA material is reproduced by permission of AQA.*

*The worked solutions to questions and commentaries on questions and possible answers in this book have neither been provided by nor approved by AQA.*

ISBN: 978 1 83774 129 8
Printed by Elanders Ltd, Newcastle upon Tyne.
Clipart from Corel®

Based on the classic CGP style created by Richard Parsons.

Text, design, layout and original illustrations © Coordination Group Publications Ltd. (CGP) 2024
All rights reserved.

Photocopying more than one section of this book is not permitted, even if you have a CLA licence.
Extra copies are available from CGP with next day delivery • 0800 1712 712 • www.cgpbooks.co.uk

# Contents

How to Use this Book..................................................................................................................2

## Section One — General Stuff

Numbers and Time........................................................................................................................4
Times and Dates...........................................................................................................................6
Questions.......................................................................................................................................8
Being Polite..................................................................................................................................10
Opinions.......................................................................................................................................12
Vocabulary List............................................................................................................................14
Revision Summary Test for Section One....................................................................................18

## Theme 1: People and Lifestyle

### Section Two — Identity and Relationships with Others

About Yourself............................................................................................................................19
My Family and Friends................................................................................................................20
Describing People.......................................................................................................................22
Relationships and Partnerships...................................................................................................24
Vocabulary List............................................................................................................................26
Revision Summary Test for Section Two....................................................................................28

### Section Three — Healthy Living and Lifestyle

Food.............................................................................................................................................29
Healthy and Unhealthy Living.....................................................................................................30
Illnesses and Treatments.............................................................................................................32
Vocabulary List............................................................................................................................34
Revision Summary Test for Section Three..................................................................................36

### Section Four — Education

School Subjects...........................................................................................................................37
School Life...................................................................................................................................38
School Pressures and Difficulties................................................................................................40
Vocabulary List............................................................................................................................42
Revision Summary Test for Section Four....................................................................................44

### Section Five — Future Study and Work

Education Post–16......................................................................................................................45
Career Choices and Ambitions...................................................................................................46
Vocabulary List............................................................................................................................48
Revision Summary Test for Section Five....................................................................................49

## Theme 2: Popular Culture

### Section Six — Free-time Activities

Cinema and TV............................................................................................................................50
Music............................................................................................................................................52
Sport.............................................................................................................................................53
Going Out and Other Hobbies....................................................................................................54
Vocabulary List............................................................................................................................56
Revision Summary Test for Section Six......................................................................................58

### Section Seven — Customs, Festivals and Celebrations

Celebrations................................................................................................................................59
Customs and Festivals................................................................................................................60
Vocabulary List............................................................................................................................62
Revision Summary Test for Section Seven.................................................................................63

# Contents

## Section Eight — Celebrity Culture
Favourite Celebrities ... 64
Celebrity Life ... 66
Vocabulary List ... 68
Revision Summary Test for Section Eight ... 69

## Theme 3: Communication and the World Around Us

### Section Nine — Travel and Tourism
Where to Go ... 70
Accommodation and Travel ... 72
What to Do ... 74
Vocabulary List ... 76
Revision Summary Test for Section Nine ... 78

### Section Ten — Media and Technology
Technology ... 79
The Internet ... 80
Social Media ... 82
Vocabulary List ... 84
Revision Summary Test for Section Ten ... 85

### Section Eleven — Where People Live
The Home ... 86
The Local Area ... 88
Directions and Weather ... 90
Vocabulary List ... 92
Revision Summary Test for Section Eleven ... 94

### Section Twelve — Environmental and Social Issues
Environmental Problems ... 95
Environmental Impacts ... 96
Protecting the Environment ... 97
Social Issues ... 98
Vocabulary List ... 100
Revision Summary Test for Section Twelve ... 102

## Grammar

### Section Thirteen — Nouns, Cases and Linking Words
Nouns ... 103
Forming Plurals and Other Nouns ... 104
Cases — Nominative and Accusative ... 105
Cases — Dative and Genitive ... 106
Definite and Indefinite Articles ... 107
Subject and Object Pronouns ... 108
Relative and Interrogative Pronouns ... 110
Reflexive Pronouns ... 111
Word Order ... 112
Coordinating Conjunctions ... 113
Subordinating Conjunctions ... 114
Compound Conjunctions ... 115
Prepositions ... 116
More Prepositions ... 118
Grammar List ... 119
Revision Summary Test for Section Thirteen ... 122

# Contents

## Section Fourteen — Adjectives and Adverbs

| | |
|---|---|
| Adjective Agreement | 123 |
| More Adjectives | 124 |
| Comparative and Superlative Adjectives | 125 |
| Adverbs | 126 |
| Comparative and Superlative Adverbs | 127 |
| Grammar List | 128 |
| Revision Summary Test for Section Fourteen | 129 |

## Section Fifteen — Verbs and Tenses

| | |
|---|---|
| Verbs in the Present Tense | 130 |
| More About the Present Tense | 131 |
| More Ways to Use Verbs | 132 |
| Talking About the Past | 133 |
| The Simple Past | 134 |
| Talking About the Future | 136 |
| Negative Forms | 137 |
| Giving Orders | 138 |
| Separable Verbs | 139 |
| Modal Verbs | 140 |
| Conditional Forms | 141 |
| The Subjunctive | 142 |
| Grammar List | 143 |
| Revision Summary Test for Section Fifteen | 147 |

## Pronunciation in German

| | |
|---|---|
| Spelling and Pronunciation | 148 |

## Exam Advice

| | |
|---|---|
| The Listening and Speaking Exams | 150 |
| The Reading and Writing Exams | 151 |

| | |
|---|---|
| Answers | 152 |
| Index | 156 |

# How to Use this Book

This isn't a book. Or rather, this isn't *just* a book. It's full of online resources designed to help you get top marks. To learn how it all works, read these pages or scan the QR code for a walkthrough.

## This book follows the AQA specification

1) The content for AQA GCSE German is divided into nine topics. Each topic falls under one of three themes:

   People and lifestyle    Popular culture    Communication and the world around us

2) In this book, there is usually one section for each topic. However, some topics have been split into two sections to make things more manageable.
3) There are also three grammar sections that cover the grammar you need to know.
4) The resources on the CGP RevisionHub are split up in the same way as the book.

*There's also a 'General Stuff' topic in the book and online with content that's useful across the course.*

## The CGP RevisionHub is full of resources

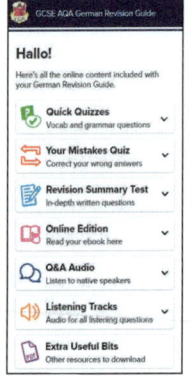

- You can use the online resources on the CGP RevisionHub alongside this book as you're revising.
- There's audio, quick quizzes and summary tests, as well as printable vocab lists and transcripts.

> There are resources for Foundation tier and Higher tier on the CGP RevisionHub. The Hub is automatically set to Higher, but you can switch to Foundation to only see Foundation content.

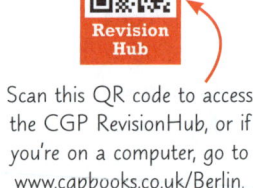

Scan this QR code to access the CGP RevisionHub, or if you're on a computer, go to www.cgpbooks.co.uk/Berlin.

## Get ready for the exams

1) In your exams, you can sit Foundation-tier or Higher-tier papers.
2) In each tier, there are four papers: Listening, Speaking, Reading and Writing. You have to choose the same tier for all four papers.

*For more about the exams, see p.150-151.*

> - In Foundation tier, there's less vocabulary and less grammar to learn and the questions are slightly easier. In this tier, you can earn up to Grade 5.
> - In Higher tier, you can achieve Grades 4-9, but you'll need to learn more vocab and more complex grammar.

3) Throughout this book, there's practice for all the key skills you'll need in the exams.
4) Most of this book is helpful for both tiers, but some vocab and questions have been marked with a bracket if they only apply to one tier.
5) If you aren't sure which tier to take, trying out the questions should help you and your teacher make a decision.

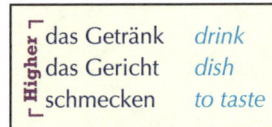

## Learn the set vocabulary

- The AQA specification contains a list of words you could be tested on in your Listening and Reading papers, depending on your tier.
- This vocab will also help you in your Speaking and Writing papers. In these two papers, you can use non-specification vocab, too.
- The key vocab is on the main pages of each section. At the end of each section, there's a list of all the vocab relevant to the topic. Every word on the specification is on at least one of these lists.
- There are printable versions of these lists on the CGP RevisionHub.

## Practise your listening skills

1) In this book, you'll find questions and example answers:

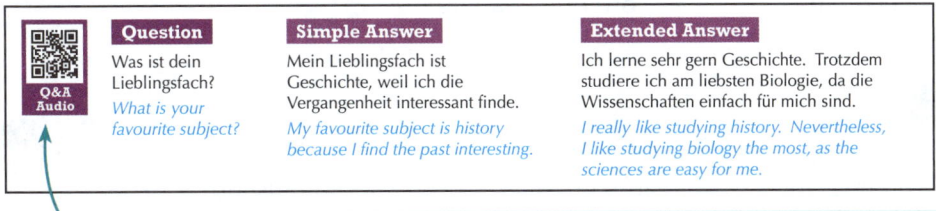

Scan the QR code to hear the sentences out loud and to practise your pronunciation.

2) There are also QR codes that take you to Listening Tracks. Each track comes with questions that test you on what you've heard.

## Test your knowledge

### Quick Quizzes

- The QR codes at the top of the page take you to a quick quiz.
- These quizzes test you on the vocab (or the grammar in Sections 13-15) on that page.
- They're a great way to keep your knowledge fresh.
- You can easily revisit questions that you answer incorrectly by doing the 'Your Mistakes' quiz.

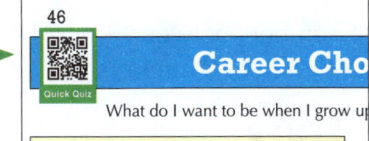

### Revision Summary Tests

- For more of a challenge, try a revision summary test. These are found at the end of each section.
- These tests cover the most important information in a topic and are a good way to see how much you can remember.
- You can do these tests on paper or you can complete them online. Online, you can find sample answers, assess your progress, and look at previous topics to see the areas you need to work on.

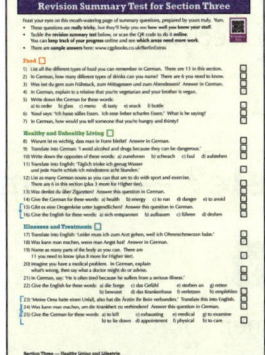

---

**Fun fact — rearrange the letters of 'RevisionHub' and you get...**
...'SnoivierUbh', which makes no sense. But do you know what *does* make sense? Using the RevisionHub alongside this book — it'll help you to get the most out of your revision and impress all those examiners.

*Find the CGP RevisionHub at cgpbooks.co.uk/Berlin*

# Section One — General Stuff

# Numbers and Time

To kick off your German revision, here are some pages about numbers and time. Get ready to begin on the count of three — eins, zwei, drei...

Head to the CGP RevisionHub for all your online content: www.cgpbooks.co.uk/Berlin

## Eins, zwei, drei — *One, two, three*

**Vocabulary**

| | | | | | |
|---|---|---|---|---|---|
| 0 | null | 13 | dreizehn | | |
| 1 | eins | 14 | vierzehn | | |
| 2 | zwei | 15 | fünfzehn | | |
| 3 | drei | 16 | sechzehn | | |
| 4 | vier | 17 | siebzehn | 21 | einundzwanzig |
| 5 | fünf | 18 | achtzehn | 22 | zweiundzwanzig |
| 6 | sechs | 19 | neunzehn | 23 | dreiundzwanzig |
| 7 | sieben | | | | |
| 8 | acht | | | | |
| 9 | neun | 20 | zwanzig | 60 | sechzig |
| 10 | zehn | 30 | dreißig | 70 | siebzig |
| 11 | elf | 40 | vierzig | 80 | achtzig |
| 12 | zwölf | 50 | fünfzig | 90 | neunzig |

The teens use numbers three to nine with 'ten' on the end — so thirteen is 'three' and 'ten' stuck together ('drei' + 'zehn'). But watch out — 16 and 17 are a bit different.

You say the in-between numbers backwards — 'one and twenty' for 'twenty-one'.

| | |
|---|---|
| 100 | hundert |
| 1000 | tausend |
| 2000 | zweitausend |
| 1 000 000 | eine Million |

BINGO!

For years before 2000, you say e.g. 'neunzehnhundert...' (*nineteen hundred...*). For a 'normal' number, not a year, you say 'tausendneunhundert...' (*one thousand, nine hundred...*).

| | |
|---|---|
| 1967 | neunzehnhundertsiebenundsechzig |
| 2005 | zweitausendfünf |

## Erste, zweite, dritte — *First, second, third*

Most numbers between 1 and 19 add '-te'. The exceptions are underlined. Numbers after 20 add '-ste'.

In German, '1st' is written '1.'.

**Vocabulary**

| | | | |
|---|---|---|---|
| 1st | das erste | 8th | das achte |
| 2nd | das zweite | 9th | das neunte |
| 3rd | das dritte | 10th | das zehnte |
| 4th | das vierte | 20th | das zwanzigste |
| 5th | das fünfte | 21st | das einundzwanzigste |
| 6th | das sechste | 70th | das siebzigste |
| 7th | das siebte | 100th | das hundertste |

The article won't always be 'das'.

**Grammar** — number endings

You might see different endings on number words. This is because the ending changes depending on the case of the noun. See p.105-106 for more on cases.

**Ich möchte den ersten Hund.**
*I would like the first dog.*
**Ich möchte die zweite Katze.**
*I would like the second cat.*

## Wie viele? — *How many?*

**Vocabulary**

| | | | | | |
|---|---|---|---|---|---|
| die Nummer | number | die Hälfte | half | viele | a lot, many |
| die Menge | quantity | einige | a few, some | ungefähr | approximately, about |

Sie hat mehrere Bücher. Sie hat ungefähr dreizehn.  *She has several books. She has about thirteen.*

Ich habe das einzige Ticket. Viele Leute wollen es.  *I have the only ticket. A lot of people want it.*

# Wie viel Uhr ist es? — *What time is it?*

## Vocabulary

| Uhr | *o'clock* | die Minute | *minute* | Viertel | *quarter* | vor | *before* |
|---|---|---|---|---|---|---|---|
| die Stunde | *hour* | die Sekunde | *second* | halb | *half* | nach | *after* |

1) There are lots of ways to <u>ask the time</u> and <u>say the time</u> in German. You'll need to get the hang of them.

| Wie viel Uhr ist es? | *What time is it?* | Wie spät ist es? | *What time is it?* |
|---|---|---|---|

2) Here are some <u>responses</u> to questions about the time. Learn to understand and use them yourself.

Something <u>o'clock</u>:

| Es ist ein Uhr. | *It is one o'clock.* |
|---|---|
| Es ist zwanzig Uhr. | *It is 8pm.* |

'<u>Quarter to</u>', '<u>quarter past</u>' and '<u>half past</u>':

| Viertel nach zwei | *quarter past two* |
|---|---|
| halb drei | *half past two* |

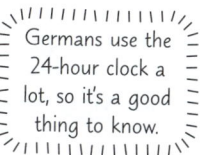

quarter to — Viertel vor

Careful — 'halb drei' means 'half to three' (i.e. half past two).

'<u>...past</u>' and '<u>...to</u>':

| zwanzig nach elf | *twenty past eleven* |
|---|---|
| zehn vor zwei | *ten to two* |

The <u>24-hour</u> clock:

| drei Uhr vierzehn | 03:14 |
|---|---|
| vierzehn Uhr fünfundfünfzig | 14:55 |

Germans use the 24-hour clock a lot, so it's a good thing to know.

## Practice Questions

**Q1** Read this text, then answer the questions.

> *Heinrich ist fünfzehn Jahre alt. Dieses Wochenende feiert er den dritten Geburtstag von seiner Schwester. Gestern hat er seine zwanzigjährige Cousine besucht.*

a) How old is Heinrich? [1 mark]
b) What is Heinrich celebrating this weekend? [1 mark]
c) How old is Heinrich's cousin? [1 mark]

**Q2** Anika is talking about her schedule for the day. What will her day look like? Write A if only statement A is correct. Write B if only statement B is correct. Write A + B if both statements A and B are correct.

Listening Track 1

a) Anika's first lesson begins at...
   **A.** eight o'clock.   **B.** nine o'clock.   [1 mark]

b) At twenty to one, Anika will...
   **A.** arrive at the doctor's.   **B.** go to the bus station.   [1 mark]

c) Anika normally gets home at...
   **A.** five o'clock.   **B.** six o'clock.   [1 mark]

*Higher*

## My favourite time of day is 6:30, hands down...

Imagine a cute German asks for the time — wowed by your German ability, they then ask for your number, which you can also give. This is why learning this stuff is important (and for passing your exams, obviously...).

Quick Quiz

# Times and Dates

Ah, times and dates — a good old examiner's classic. I mean, what's more exciting than learning the days of the week? I can't think of anything, so let's get cracking.

## Die Woche — *The week*

**Vocabulary**

| | |
|---|---|
| Montag | *Monday* |
| Dienstag | *Tuesday* |
| Mittwoch | *Wednesday* |
| Donnerstag | *Thursday* |
| Freitag | *Friday* |
| Samstag | *Saturday* |
| Sonntag | *Sunday* |

**Grammar — on Mondays**

To say 'on Monday', use 'Montag' or 'am Montag'.
To say that something happens regularly at a certain time or on a certain day, you can add an '-s' to the noun to turn it into an adverb.

Montag → montags — on Mondays
Abend → abends — in the evening(s)

| | |
|---|---|
| der Tag | *day* |
| das Wochenende | *weekend* |
| der Morgen | *morning* |
| der Nachmittag | *afternoon* |
| der Abend | *evening* |
| die Nacht | *night* |

Lina ist am Freitag ins Kino gegangen. — *Lina went to the cinema on Friday.*
Ich besuche mittwochs meine Tante. — *I visit my aunt on Wednesdays.*
Am Morgen gehe ich zur Schule. — *In the morning, I go to school.*

on Tuesday — am Dienstag
on Saturdays — samstags

## Die Monate — *The months*

**Vocabulary**

| | | | | |
|---|---|---|---|---|
| Januar | *January* | Juli | *July* | |
| Februar | *February* | August | *August* | |
| März | *March* | September | *September* | |
| April | *April* | Oktober | *October* | |
| Mai | *May* | November | *November* | |
| Juni | *June* | Dezember | *December* | |

| | |
|---|---|
| der Monat | *month* |
| das Jahr | *year* |
| der Frühling | *spring* |
| der Sommer | *summer* |
| der Herbst | *autumn* |
| der Winter | *winter* |

Mein Lieblingsmonat ist August, weil das Wetter warm ist. — *My favourite month is August because the weather is warm.*

Letzten Winter gab es viel Eis und Schnee. — *Last winter, there was a lot of ice and snow.*

My favourite season — Meine Lieblingsjahreszeit
This winter — Diesen Winter
At the end of January — Am Ende Januar

## Welches Datum haben wir heute? — *What is the date today?*

Watch out for dates in German — make sure you use the correct case. See p.105-106 for more on cases.

In German, a date is written as a number with a dot after it. Der 4. April is said 'der vierte April'.

Es ist der 4. April. — *It's the 4th April.*
Ich komme am 20. Oktober. — *I'm coming on the 20th October.*

the 8th June — der 8. Juni
on the 14th August — am 14. August

You say this as 'am vierzehnten August'. This ending is used because it's in the dative case.

Section One — General Stuff

# Gestern, heute, morgen — *Yesterday, today, tomorrow*

## Vocabulary

| | | | | | | | |
|---|---|---|---|---|---|---|---|
| gestern | *yesterday* | heute | *today* | morgen | *tomorrow* | oft | *often* |
| neulich | *recently, lately* | jetzt | *now, currently* | endlich | *finally, at last* | täglich | *daily* |
| früher | *previously* | gleich | *right away* | schließlich | *eventually* | regelmäßig | *regularly* |
| | | sofort | *immediately* | danach | *afterwards* | selten | *rarely* |

**Gestern** sind wir in die Schule gegangen. **Heute** bleiben wir zu Hause.
*Yesterday, we went to school. Today, we are staying at home.*

The day before yesterday — Vorgestern
Every day — Jeden Tag
The day after tomorrow — Übermorgen

**Dieses Mal** werde ich **gleich** kommen.
*This time, I will come right away.*

**Endlich** bin ich mit meinen Hausaufgaben fertig.
*I am finally finished with my homework.*

Mein Freund redet **ständig** über Sport. Er denkt **selten** an etwas anderes.
*My friend constantly talks about sport. He rarely thinks about anything else.*

### Grammar — time phrases

Sentences can start with a time phrase, but if they do, remember to switch the word order so the verb comes second (see p.112), e.g.

**Um zwei Uhr habe ich eine Prüfung.**
*At two o'clock, I have an exam.*

**Q&A Audio**

**Question**
Wie oft fährst du mit dem Bus?
*How often do you travel by bus?*

**Simple Answer**
Ich fahre täglich mit dem Bus.
*I travel daily by bus.*

**Extended Answer**
Ich fahre regelmäßig mit dem Bus in die Stadt. Manchmal fahre ich mit dem Bus zur Schule, aber normalerweise fahre ich mit dem Auto.
*I travel regularly by bus into town. Sometimes I travel by bus to school, but normally I travel by car.*

  *honk*

## Practice Questions

**Q1** Lisa and Jan are catching up on what they've been doing. Listen to their conversation and answer the questions in English. **LISTENING** — Listening Track 2

   a) Which day did Lisa go to the museum?
   b) When did Jan go to the birthday party?
   c) Which date will Lisa's party take place?
   d) What time of day is Lisa's party?  [4 marks]

**Q2** Write to a German friend about your typical week. You should write about 90 words in German. Make sure you cover:
   - what you normally do on each day
   - what time each activity starts
   - what you will do next week.  [15 marks]

**Top Tip for Higher Students**
✓ Explain why you do an activity by using 'um ... zu'. E.g. 'Ich lese ein Buch, um mich zu entspannen.'

---

## Why did Saturday beat Monday in an arm wrestling match?

Because Monday is a weak day. Anyway, enough of that hilarity — here's your reminder that when you start a sentence with a time phrase, you need to put the verb second. The verb won't be happy about it, but that's life.

*Find the CGP RevisionHub at cgpbooks.co.uk/Berlin*

**Section One — General Stuff**

Quick Quiz

# Questions

I've got questions about a lot of things, like why do so many question words start with a 'W'? Anyway, best get them learnt — then you'll be ready to quiz your teacher in the speaking exam.

## Fragen stellen — *Asking questions*

### Vocabulary

| | | | | | |
|---|---|---|---|---|---|
| die Frage | *question* | wie? | *how?* | wer / wen / wem? | *who / whom?* |
| was? | *what?* | wie viele? | *how many?* | welche/r/s? | *which (one)?* |
| wann? | *when?* | wohin? | *where...to?* | wieso? | *why?* |
| wo? | *where?* | woher? | *where...from?* | | |
| warum? | *why?* | was für? | *what sort / type of...?* | | |

See p.110 for when to use 'wer / wen / wem' and p.123-124 for more about 'welche'.

When you use a question word, the verb needs to come straight after it.

Wohin fährst du in Urlaub?
*Where are you going on holiday to?*

Wann wirst du ankommen?
*When will you arrive?*

Wer reist mit dir?
*Who is travelling with you?*

Mit wem fährst du?
*Who are you going with?*

Warum war dein Flug spät?
*Why was your flight late?*

Woher kommst du?
*Where are you coming from?*

### Grammar (Higher only) — Using 'wo' with prepositions

'Wo' can mean 'where', but it can also mean 'what'. You can write 'wo' in front of some prepositions to make handy question words.

Womit schreibst du? — What are you writing with?
Wofür brauche ich es? — What do I need it for?

If the preposition starts with a vowel — like 'über' or 'auf' — you need to add an 'r' between it and the 'wo'.

Worauf läuft er? — What is he walking on?
Worüber sprechen Sie? — What are you talking about?

P.116-118 have more on prepositions.

Was für ein Buch liest du?
*What type of book are you reading?*

## Swap around the word order to ask a question

To ask a question, you can also just change the word order.

Ich kann mitkommen. → Kann ich mitkommen?
*I can come along.* *Can I come along?*

'Kann' is a modal verb. See p.140 for more on modal verbs.

Sie ist zu Hause. → Ist sie zu Hause?
*She is at home.* *Is she at home?*

Dein Bruder kommt auch. → Kommt dein Bruder auch?
*Your brother is coming too.* *Is your brother coming too?*

### Grammar — questions

In English, you change 'I can go' to 'Can I go?' to make it into a question — you can in German too.

Put the verb first and then the verb's subject to show it's a question.

Section One — General Stuff

## Darf ich eine Frage stellen? — *May I ask a question?*

Here are some more examples of those handy question words from the last page in action.

Wann kommt Emilie?
*When is Emilie coming?*

Warum bist du müde?
*Why are you tired?*

Wo ist unser Lehrer?
*Where is our teacher?*

Wie sagt man das auf Deutsch?
*How do you say that in German?*

Wie viel kostet es?
*How much does it cost?*

Verkaufen Sie Käse?
*Do you sell cheese?*

Weißt du die Antwort?
*Do you know the answer?*

Hast du ein Fahrrad?
*Do you have a bicycle?*

Spielt ihr Tennis?
*Are you playing tennis?*

Woher kommen sie?
*Where do they come from?*

Müssen wir tanzen?
*Do we have to dance?*

Möchten Sie eine Tasche?
*Would you like a bag?*

Darf ich mehr Milch haben?
*May I have more milk?*

Soll sie das machen?
*Should she do that?*

Willst du Spanisch lernen?
*Do you want to learn Spanish?*

Q&A Audio

**Question**
Wie viele Schüler gibt es in deiner Klasse?
*How many pupils are there in your class?*

**Simple Answer**
Es gibt fünfundzwanzig Schüler.
*There are twenty-five pupils.*

**Extended Answer**
Es gibt fünfundzwanzig Schüler in meiner Klasse.
Es gibt zehn Mädchen und fünfzehn Jungen.
*There are twenty-five pupils in my class.*
*There are ten girls and fifteen boys.*

Demir's teacher was very proud of his pupils.

### Practice Questions

Q1  Imagine you are talking to your friend about their trip to the cinema.
Ask the following questions out loud in German.  SPEAKING

- Ask where the cinema is.
- Ask what they are going to see.
- Ask who they are going with.
- Ask how much their ticket costs.
- Ask when they are seeing the film. [5 marks]

Q2  Translate these sentences into German.  WRITING

  a) What are you happy about?
  b) What can I help you with?
  c) What do you need that for?
  d) What does she hide the gift behind?
  e) What are we waiting for? [10 marks]

*Higher*

## Swap the order word asking a if question you're...

...although you don't need to swap things around that much — just move the verb so it comes before the subject. Unlike on the last page, the verb comes first with this grammar rule. Now it can stop sulking.

Quick Quiz

# Being Polite

Hey, 'sup du- ... Oh, do pardon my manners — what I meant to say was 'Hello there, fine GCSE student. It's a pleasure to have you on this page. May I interest you in some polite vocabulary?'

## Hallo... Auf Wiedersehen — *Hello... Goodbye*

To reply to a greeting, just say it back. If someone says 'Guten Tag' to you, say 'Guten Tag' to them.

**Vocabulary**

| | | | |
|---|---|---|---|
| hallo | *hello, hi* | willkommen | *welcome* |
| guten Morgen | *good morning* | auf Wiedersehen | *goodbye* |
| guten Tag | *good afternoon* | bis bald | *see you soon* |
| guten Abend | *good evening* | tschüss | *bye* |

'auf Wiederhören' is used for ending telephone conversations.

## Wie geht's? — *How are you?*

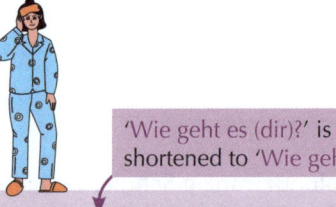

**Grammar** — formal and informal 'you'

There are four different ways to say 'you' in German:

**Informal 'you'**

1. Use 'du' for a member of your family, a friend, or someone who is your own age or younger than you.
2. Use 'ihr' for two or more people that you know well.

**Formal 'you'**

3. Use 'Sie' for someone you don't know, or someone important, or someone older than you.
4. 'Sie' is also used for a group of two or more people you don't know.

'Wie geht es (dir)?' is often shortened to 'Wie geht's?'.

| | |
|---|---|
| Wie geht es dir? | *How are you? (inf.)* |
| Wie geht es Ihnen? | *How are you? (frml.)* |
| Wie geht es euch? | *How are you? (inf. plu.)* |

| | |
|---|---|
| Es geht mir... | *I'm...* |
| ...gut. | *...fine / well.* |
| ...super. | *... super.* |
| ...schlecht. | *...not well.* |
| ...nicht so gut. | *...not so well.* |

Here's what these short forms mean:
inf. — informal
frml. — formal
plu. — plural
If you see 'sing.', it means 'singular'.

## Ich möchte — *I would like*

1) It's more polite to say 'Ich möchte' (*I would like*) than 'Ich will' (*I want*).

2) Here's how to say you would like a thing:

> Ich möchte ein bisschen Käse.
> *I would like a bit of cheese.*

See p.141-142 for more info on the grammar behind these phrases.

Whiskers would like to be removed from the bath.

3) Here's how to say you would like to do something:

> Ich möchte wandern gehen.
> *I would like to go hiking.*

**Grammar (Higher only)** — 'hätte gern' & 'würde gern'

Use 'ich hätte gern' to say you would like a thing.
**Ich hätte gern das Brot.** *I would like the bread.*
Use 'ich würde gern' to say you would like to do something.
**Ich würde gern singen.** *I would like to sing.*

Section One — General Stuff

## Darf ich — *May I*

Use 'darf ich' rather than 'kann ich' to ask for something. It's a bit more polite.

| | |
|---|---|
| Darf ich die Milch haben? | *May I have the milk?* |
| Darf ich mich hier setzen? | *May I sit here?* |

## Bitte und danke — *Please and thank you*

**Vocabulary**

| | |
|---|---|
| bitte | *please, you're welcome* |
| danke | *thanks* |
| das geht | *that's fine* |
| alles klar | *all right* |
| viel Glück | *good luck* |

Q&A Audio

**Question**
Hallo, was möchten Sie?
*Hello, what would you like?*

**Simple Answer**
Ich möchte einen Kuchen.
*I would like a cake.*

**Extended Answer**
Guten Tag. Ich würde gern einen Kuchen kaufen, bitte. Darf ich mit Karte bezahlen?
*Good afternoon. I would like to buy a cake, please. May I pay by card?*

## Es tut mir leid — *I'm sorry*

**Vocabulary**

| | | | |
|---|---|---|---|
| entschuldigen | *to excuse* | Es tut mir leid. | *I'm sorry.* |
| sich entschuldigen (bei) | *to apologise (to)* | Entschuldigung | *sorry, excuse me* |

Say this when you've done something wrong.
Say this when you want to ask someone something.

Entschuldigung, wo ist der Bahnhof, bitte?   *Excuse me, where is the train station, please?*
Ich will mich bei dir entschuldigen.   *I want to apologise to you.*

You always use the dative case with 'bei'. See p.116 for more.

## Practice Questions

**Q1** Read the following message that Mila has written, then answer the questions below.  *READING*

> Hallo Eric! Es tut mir sehr leid, dass ich deinen Geburtstag vergessen habe. Möchtest du zum Abendessen ausgehen? Als Entschuldigung werde ich zahlen! Ich möchte dir auch ein Geschenk geben. Bis bald, und viel Glück bei deiner Prüfung morgen.

a) What is Mila sorry for?
b) How does Mila want to apologise?
c) What does Mila want to give Eric?
d) Why does Mila wish Eric good luck?  *[4 marks]*

**Q2** Imagine you're in a restaurant. Act out a role-play in German between yourself and the waiter. Use as much polite language as you can. Make sure that:
- you greet each other.
- the waiter asks how you are.
- the waiter asks what you would like.
- you thank the waiter.

*[10 marks]*

---

### Sadly, saying 'please' a hundred times won't get you top marks...

In German, you need to use the correct form of 'you' to match who you're talking to. If you're ever unsure, play it safe and use 'Sie'. You can refer to the examiner as 'du', though — just maybe not 'buddy' or 'pal'*.

*\*This is 'Kumpel' in German.*

# O~~n~~inions

Fine, these pages aren't about onions. In my opinion, they *should* be, given that onions are the best vegetables. Maybe my next venture should be a recipe book — stay tuned for CGP Cooks...

## Deine Meinung — *Your opinion*

*The verb comes straight after 'Meiner Meinung nach' (see p.112), and it goes to the end after 'dass' (see p.114).*

**Vocabulary**

| | | | | | |
|---|---|---|---|---|---|
| die Meinung | *opinion, view* | denken | *to think* | diskutieren (über) | *to discuss* |
| meiner Meinung nach | *in my opinion* | finden | *to find* | von ... her | *as far as ... is concerned* |

Wie findest du Fußball? — *How do you find football?*

Ich meine, dass Fußball spannend ist. — *I think that football is exciting.*

Meiner Meinung nach ist diese Mannschaft am besten. — *In my opinion, this team is the best.*

What do you think of — Was denkst du über

I believe that — Ich glaube, dass

As far as skills are concerned — Von der Fähigkeiten her

## Magst du...? — *Do you like...?*

**Vocabulary**

| | | | | |
|---|---|---|---|---|
| mögen | *to like* | sich freuen auf | | *to look forward to* |
| genießen | *to enjoy* | es ist mir egal | | *I don't care* |
| lieben | *to love* | es kommt darauf an, ob... | | *it depends whether...* |
| hassen | *to hate* | halten ... für | | *to think of ... as* |

*Elena's enjoyment of bungee jumping depends on whether she's properly clipped in.*

**Grammar — ...gefällt mir (nicht)**

'Das gefällt mir' means 'I like that'.
'Gefallen' is a dative verb, so you need to use the dative case for articles and pronouns.

Fußball gefällt mir. — *I like football.*
Joggen gefällt mir nicht. — *I don't like jogging.*

Dieses Buch gefällt ihm nicht. — *He doesn't like this book.*

'Ihm' is the dative form of 'er'. See p.108 for all the dative case pronouns.

Ich halte sie für langweilig. — *I think it is boring.*

If you've got a masculine or a neuter noun, you need 'ihn' or 'es' instead.

You might not have an opinion on something, so use one of these phrases to sit on the fence:

Ich bin mir nicht sicher. — *I'm not sure.*

Ich bin weder dafür noch dagegen. — *I'm neither for nor against it.*

## Ich spiele lieber... — *I prefer to play...*

You can add more detail by saying what you prefer. Just put in 'lieber'.

Ulrich spielt gern Schach, aber er treibt lieber Sport. — *Ulrich likes playing chess, but he prefers to do sport.*

he prefers to listen to music — er hört lieber Musik

Wir hassen Hausaufgaben. Wir sehen lieber fern. — *We hate homework. We prefer to watch TV.*

We prefer to go to the cinema — Wir gehen lieber ins Kino

## Use describing words to explain your opinions

**Vocabulary**

| | | | | | | | |
|---|---|---|---|---|---|---|---|
| toll | *great, amazing* | gut | *good, well* | schlimm | *bad, serious* | | |
| interessant | *interesting* | schlecht | *bad, badly* | langweilig | *boring* | | |
| lustig | *funny, enjoyable* | schrecklich | *terrible, awful* | einfach | *easy* | | |
| wichtig | *important* | blöd | *stupid, dumb* | schwierig | *difficult* | | |

## 'Weil' and 'denn' — Because

*You've always got to put a comma before 'weil' and 'denn'.*

'Weil' means '<u>because</u>'. When you use '<u>weil</u>', the <u>verb</u> in that part of the sentence gets shoved to the <u>end</u>.

Der Film gefällt mir. Er ist interessant.
*I like the film. It is interesting.*

Der Film gefällt mir, weil er interessant ist.
*I like the film because it is interesting.*

'Denn' means '<u>because</u>' too, but it <u>doesn't</u> change the word order.

Ich mag ihn. Er ist wirklich nett.
*I like him. He is really nice.*

Ich mag ihn, denn er ist wirklich nett.
*I like him because he is really nice.*

*Don't confuse 'denn' with 'dann', which means 'then'.*

## Putting it all together

Include an <u>opinion phrase</u> and a super <u>adjective</u> or two — then <u>justify</u> your view.

Meiner Meinung nach ist er der beste Künstler, weil er sehr kreativ ist.
*In my opinion, he's the best artist because he is very creative.*

Ich mag Gemüse nicht, denn sie sind nicht lecker. Ich esse lieber Obst.
*I don't like vegetables because they are not tasty. I prefer eating fruit.*

**Question**
Was denkst du über diese Zeitung?
*What do you think about this newspaper?*

**Simple Answer**
Ich mag diese Zeitung.
*I like this newspaper.*

**Extended Answer**
Ich mag diese Zeitung, weil sie sehr interessant ist. Sie handelt über wichtige Themen.
*I like this newspaper because it's very interesting. It deals with important topics.*

### Practice Question

Q1 Listen to Anja and Christian discuss the things they like to do. Decide whether each statement is true or false.

a) Anja hates shopping because it is boring. [1 mark]
b) Christian likes concerts because they are exciting. [1 mark]
c) Anja doesn't like concerts, even when the band plays well. [1 mark]
d) Christian prefers to do sport than watch TV. [1 mark]

---

### BONUS: leaked extract from 'Diary of an Examiner'...

Dear Diary, as I wait for this exam season, my heart yearns for backed-up opinions. Seeing students develop their opinions using 'weil' and 'denn' (plus better adjectives than just 'gut' or 'schlecht') would make my heart skip a beat.

*Find the CGP RevisionHub at cgpbooks.co.uk/Berlin*

# General Stuff — Vocabulary

It's your lucky day — all the general vocab you need to know has been put on these pages for you. You're welcome.

## Numbers

|  |  |
|---|---|
| die Nummer | number |
| die Zahl | number |
| null | zero |
| eins | one |
| zwei | two |
| drei | three |
| vier | four |
| fünf | five |
| sechs | six |
| sieben | seven |
| acht | eight |
| neun | nine |
| zehn | ten |
| elf | eleven |
| zwölf | twelve |
| dreizehn | thirteen |
| vierzehn | fourteen |
| fünfzehn | fifteen |
| sechzehn | sixteen |
| siebzehn | seventeen |
| achtzehn | eighteen |
| neunzehn | nineteen |
| zwanzig | twenty |
| dreißig | thirty |
| vierzig | forty |
| fünfzig | fifty |
| sechzig | sixty |
| siebzig | seventy |
| achtzig | eighty |
| neunzig | ninety |
| hundert | hundred |
| tausend | thousand |
| eine Million, Mio | million |
| erste | first |
| die Menge | quantity, amount |
| die Hälfte | half |
| der Teil | piece |
| zuerst | first (of all) |
| einzig | only, single |
| ein bisschen | a little |
| einige | a few, some |
| viel | a lot |
| viele | a lot, many |
| ungefähr | approximately, about |
| ganz | whole, all the |
| das Meter, m | metre |
| der Zentimeter, cm | centimetre, cm |
| das Prozent | percent |

**Higher:**

|  |  |
|---|---|
| die Anzahl | quantity, number (count, amount) |
| der Rest | rest, remainder |
| zählen | to count |
| übrig | remaining, left, leftover, spare |
| weitere | additional, further, another |
| einzeln | individual, single, separately |
| insgesamt | in all, in total, altogether, overall |

## Times

|  |  |
|---|---|
| die Zeit | time |
| die Stunde | hour |
| die Minute | minute |
| die Sekunde | second |
| Uhr | o'clock |
| Viertel | quarter |
| halb | half |
| vor | before |
| nach | after |
| der Moment | moment, instant |
| der Morgen | morning |
| der Mittag | noon, midday |
| der Nachmittag | afternoon |
| der Abend | evening |
| die Nacht | night |
| dauern | to last, take (time) |

**Higher:**

|  |  |
|---|---|
| der Zeitpunkt | moment, (point in) time |
| geschehen | to happen, occur, take place |

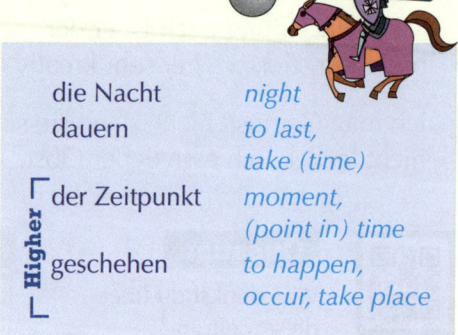

## Dates

|  |  |
|---|---|
| Montag | Monday |
| Dienstag | Tuesday |
| Mittwoch | Wednesday |
| Donnerstag | Thursday |
| Freitag | Friday |
| Samstag | Saturday |
| Sonntag | Sunday |

|  |  |
|---|---|
| der Frühling | spring |
| der Sommer | summer |
| der Herbst | autumn |
| der Winter | winter |

|  |  |
|---|---|
| Januar | January |
| Februar | February |
| März | March |
| April | April |
| Mai | May |
| Juni | June |
| Juli | July |
| August | August |
| September | September |
| Oktober | October |
| November | November |
| Dezember | December |

|  |  |
|---|---|
| der Tag | day |
| die Woche | week |
| das Wochenende | weekend |
| der Monat | month |
| das Jahr | year |
| das Mal | time (occurrence) |
| der Anfang | beginning, start |
| der Beginn | beginning, start |
| das Ende | end, finish |
| die Vergangenheit | past |
| die Zukunft | future |

**H:**

|  |  |
|---|---|
| das Jahrhundert | century |
| die Gegenwart | present |

Section One — General Stuff

## Time Phrases

| | |
|---|---|
| gestern | yesterday |
| neulich | recently, lately, the other day |
| früher | previously, in former times, in the past |
| in letzter Zeit | recently, lately |
| heute | today |
| jetzt | now, currently |
| gleich | straight away, right away, immediately |
| sofort | immediately |
| morgen | tomorrow |

| | |
|---|---|
| endlich | finally, at last, eventually |
| schließlich | finally, at last, eventually |
| danach | afterwards |
| immer | always |
| oft | often, frequently |
| täglich | daily, every day |
| regelmäßig | regular, regularly |
| bald | soon |
| manchmal | sometimes |
| nochmal | again |
| noch | still, yet, else |
| ab und zu | now and again, (every) now and then |
| selten | rare, rarely |

| | |
|---|---|
| einmal | once |
| inzwischen | in the meantime, meanwhile |
| dann | then |
| damals | then, at that time, in those days |
| diesmal | this time |
| gerade *(Higher)* | just now, right now |
| häufig *(Higher)* | frequent, frequently, often |
| ständig *(Higher)* | constant, permanent, constantly, permanently |
| jährlich *(Higher)* | annually |

## Questions

| | |
|---|---|
| die Frage | question, query |
| ja | yes |
| nein, nee, nö | no |
| okay | okay |
| ach | oh |

| | |
|---|---|
| was? | what? |
| wann? | when? |
| wo? | where? |
| warum? | why? |
| wie? | how? |
| wie viele? | how many? |

| | |
|---|---|
| wohin? | where...to? |
| woher? | where...from? |
| wer / wem / wen? | who / whom? |
| welche/r/s? | which (one)? |
| was für? | what sort / type of...? |
| wieso? *(H)* | why? |

## Being Polite

| | |
|---|---|
| hallo | hello, hi |
| guten Morgen | good morning |
| guten Tag | good afternoon |
| guten Abend | good evening |
| willkommen | welcome |
| auf Wiedersehen | goodbye |
| bis bald | bye for now, see you soon |
| tschüss | bye |
| es geht mir... | I am... |
|   gut / schlecht |   fine, well / not well |
| bitte | please, you're welcome |
| danke | thanks |
| das geht | that's fine, that's possible |

*(Contains gluten)*

| | |
|---|---|
| alles klar | all right, that's fine, okay, understood |
| es tut mir leid | I'm sorry |
| die Entschuldigung | apology, excuse |
| Entschuldigung | sorry, excuse me |
| entschuldigen | to excuse |
| sich entschuldigen (bei) | to apologise (to) |
| Herr | Mr. |
| Frau | Mrs. |
| die Dame | lady |
| die Vorstellung *(Higher)* | introduction, idea |
| vorstellen *(Higher)* | to introduce |
| danken *(Higher)* | to thank |
| herzlich *(Higher)* | cordial, warm, warmly |

## Opinions — Giving Your Opinion

| | |
|---|---|
| die Meinung | opinion, view |
| meiner Meinung nach | in my opinion |
| meinen | to think, have an opinion |
| denken (an) | to think (of) |
| finden | to find |
| erzählen (von) | to tell (about) |
| diskutieren (über) | to discuss (+ noun) |
| gern, gerne | gladly, like to (+ verb) |
| mögen | to like |
| genießen | to enjoy |
| lieben | to love |
| hassen | to hate, detest |
| freuen | to please, make happy |

| | |
|---|---|
| sich freuen | to be happy / pleased |
| sich freuen auf | to look forward to |
| sich interessieren (für) | to be interested (in) |
| egal | (it's all) the same, indifferent, doesn't matter |
| es ist mir egal | I don't care |
| es kommt darauf an, ob... | it depends whether... |
| schade | (it's a) pity, (it's a) shame |
| der Grund | reason, basis |
| halten ... für *(Higher)* | to think of ... as |
| von ... her *(Higher)* | as far as... is concerned |
| der Gegensatz *(Higher)* | opposite, contrast |
| das Gegenteil *(Higher)* | opposite |

# General Stuff — Vocabulary

## Opinions — Adjectives and Adverbs

|  |  |
|---|---|
| gut | good, well |
| schlecht | bad, badly |
| perfekt | perfect, perfectly |
| fantastisch | fantastic, super, terrific |
| toll | great, amazing |
| interessant | interesting |
| lustig | funny, enjoyable |
| wichtig | important |
| wunderbar | wonderful |
| klar | clear, obvious |
| ideal | ideal |
| schrecklich | terrible, awful, dreadful, terribly, awfully, dreadfully |
| blöd | stupid, dumb |
| schlimm | bad, serious |
| langweilig | boring |
| einfach | easy, easily, simple, simply |

|  |  |
|---|---|
| schwierig | difficult, hard, tough |
| extrem | extreme, extremely |
| wahr | true, real, genuine |
| falsch | false, wrong |
| schnell | quickly, fast |
| langsam | slow, slowly |
| voll | full, complete |
| leer | empty |
| kurz | short, brief |
| notwendig | necessary |
| super | super |
| wert | worth, worthy of |
| zufrieden | satisfied, happy, content |
| ungewöhnlich | unusual, unusually |
| unglaublich | unbelievable, incredible, unbelievably |
| verrückt | crazy, insane, mad |

(Higher: notwendig, super, wert, zufrieden, ungewöhnlich, unglaublich)

## Opinions — Giving Reasons

|  |  |
|---|---|
| weil | because |
| denn | because |
| auch | also, too, as well |
| also | so, therefore |
| deshalb | therefore |
| deswegen | for this reason, therefore |
| zum Beispiel, z.B. | for example, e.g. |
| und so weiter, usw. | and so on, etc. |
| dagegen | on the other hand |

|  |  |
|---|---|
| auf der einen / anderen Seite | on the one / other hand |
| jedoch | however |
| trotzdem | nevertheless |
| insbesondere | especially, particularly |
| offensichtlich | obvious, obviously |
| selbstverständlich | natural, self-evident, obvious, naturally, obviously |

(H: selbstverständlich)

## Useful Nouns

|  |  |
|---|---|
| das Ding | thing, object |
| die Sache | thing, matter |
| die Art | type, kind, sort |
| das Beispiel | example, instance |
| das Mittel | means, average |
| das Thema | topic, theme |
| die Themen | topics, themes |
| die Idee | idea |
| die Lust | desire |
| der Unterschied | difference |
| der Vergleich | comparison |
| die Sicherheit | certainty |
| der Hintergrund | background |
| der Punkt | dot, point, full stop |
| die Tatsache | fact |
| die Wahrheit | truth |
| der Gedanke | thought, idea |
| das Konzept | concept, idea, plan |
| die Ahnung | suspicion, idea |
| der Eindruck | impression, effect |

(Higher: die Tatsache, die Wahrheit, der Gedanke, das Konzept, die Ahnung, der Eindruck)

|  |  |
|---|---|
| die Weise | way, manner |
| die Alternative | alternative |
| die Änderung | change, modification, alteration |
| der Vorschlag | suggestion, proposal |
| die Entscheidung | decision |
| der Ausdruck | term, expression |
| die Bedeutung | meaning, significance |
| der Sinn | sense, meaning |
| der Wert | value, worth |
| der Zweck | purpose, aim |
| die Beschreibung | description |
| der Schluss | end, conclusion, finish, closure |
| der Titel | title |
| die Liste | list |
| die Reihe | row, line, queue |
| die Hoffnung | hope |
| der Zweifel | doubt |
| das Gute | the good thing |
| etwas Nettes | something nice |

(Higher: der Sinn, der Wert, der Zweck, die Beschreibung, der Schluss, der Titel, die Liste, die Reihe, die Hoffnung, der Zweifel, das Gute, etwas Nettes)

Section One — General Stuff

## Useful Adjectives and Adverbs

|  |  |
|---|---|
| anders | different, differently |
| besonders | particularly, especially |
| bestimmt | certain, definite, certainly, definitely |
| ehemalig | former |
| einmal | once |
| fast | almost, nearly |
| fest | firm, solid, steady |
| ganz | quite |
| gar | at all |
| genau | exact, exactly, precise, precisely |
| genauso | just as |
| genug | enough |
| irgendwann | sometime, someday |
| irgendwie | somehow |
| irgendwo | somewhere |
| los | rid of, going on |
| meist | most, mostly, usually |
| möglich | possible |
| natürlich | of course, certainly |
| nochmal | again |
| normalerweise | normally, usually |
| nur | only, just |
| offenbar | apparent, obvious, apparently, obviously |
| plötzlich | sudden, suddenly |
| sicher | certain, sure, of course |
| total | total, complete, totally, completely |
| typisch | typical, typically |
| vielleicht | perhaps, maybe, possibly |
| wahrscheinlich | likely, probable, probably |
| wieder | again |
| wirklich | real, actual, really, actually, truly |
| wohl | well, probably, arguably |
| ziemlich | quite, fairly, pretty |

E.g. 'Er ist das Problem <u>los</u>.' (He is <u>rid of</u> the problem). 'Etwas ist <u>los</u>.' (Something is <u>going on</u>.)

### Higher

|  |  |
|---|---|
| absolut | absolute, complete, absolutely, completely |
| allgemein | general |
| alles (Andere) | everything (else) |
| bereit | ready |
| deutlich | clear, clearly |
| eigentlich | actual, real, actually, really |
| entfernt | distant, away |
| gerade | straight, just, just now, right now |
| gering | low, small |
| hoffentlich | hopefully |
| individuell | individual, individually |
| künstlich | artificial, artificially |
| niedrig | low |
| relativ | relative, relatively, comparatively |
| sogenannt | so-called |
| tief | deep, low |
| unterschiedlich | different, varied, variable, diverse |
| verschieden | different, various, diverse |
| vollständig | complete, completely, thoroughly |
| völlig | completely, absolutely |

## Useful Verbs

|  |  |
|---|---|
| beginnen | to begin, start |
| enden | to end, finish |
| brauchen | to need, use |
| benutzen | to use |
| sehen | to see, watch |
| holen | to get, fetch |
| bringen | to bring |
| kriegen | to get, receive |
| tun | to do, put |
| stellen | to place, set, put |
| sich stellen | to place oneself, stand |
| ziehen | to pull, move |
| zeigen | to show, point |
| sprechen | to speak, talk |
| bedeuten | to mean |
| verändern | to change |
| versuchen | to try |
| hoffen (auf) | to hope (for) |
| sich erinnern | to remember |
| gehen | to go |
| gehen um | to be about |
| verdienen | to deserve |
| scheinen | to seem, shine, appear |
| vergessen | to forget |
| erinnern (an) | to remind (about) |

When you're talking about remembering something that's a noun, say 'sich erinnern **an**'.

### Higher

|  |  |
|---|---|
| bemerken | to notice |
| merken | to notice |
| sich [dat.] merken | to remember |
| denken (an) | to think (of) |
| sich [dat.] denken | to imagine |
| bestehen (auf [dat.]) | to insist (on) |
| bestehen (aus) | to consist (of) |
| nachdenken | to think about, reflect |
| vergleichen (mit) | to compare |
| legen | to lay, put |
| überlegen | to consider, think about, think of |
| sich handeln um | to be about |
| sich drehen um | to be about |

These phrases can only be used with the subject pronoun 'Es'. E.g. 'Es geht um...', 'Es handelt sich um...', 'Es dreht sich um...'.

|  |  |
|---|---|
| entstehen | to originate, develop |
| entwickeln | to develop |
| schaffen | to create, manage, accomplish |
| ändern | to change, alter |
| überzeugen | to convince, persuade |
| annehmen | to accept, assume |

### Higher

|  |  |
|---|---|
| verlangen | to request, demand |
| bitten um | to request, ask for |
| rufen | to call, shout |
| beschließen | to decide |
| erfahren | to experience, find out |
| reichen | to reach, be enough |
| gehören | to belong |
| erwarten | to expect |
| aufmachen | to open |
| setzen | to set, place, put |

Find the CGP RevisionHub at cgpbooks.co.uk/Berlin

# Revision Summary Test for Section One

Willkommen to the first summary test — it's time to see whether you've mastered this section.
- These questions are **hard**, but they'll really help you see **how well you know your stuff**.
- Tackle the **revision summary test** below, or scan the QR code to do it **online**. You can **track your progress** online and see **which areas need more work**.
- There are **sample answers** for the test here: www.cgpbooks.co.uk/BerlinExtras

## Numbers and Time

1) In words, write the numbers 1-20 in German.
2) Write down the German for these numbers:
   a) thirty-three   b) sixty-one   c) seventy-five   d) two hundred and ninety   e) eight thousand
3) Translate the following sentence into English:
   'Der erste Tag war sonnig, aber am zweiten Tag und am dritten Tag hat es geregnet.'
4) 'Es gibt eine große Menge von Fragen. Ich habe ungefähr eine Hälfte beantwortet. Es gibt noch einige Fragen, die ich ganz schwierig finde.' What does this mean in English?
5) Say the current time in German. Then write the German for each of these times:
   a) 03:00   b) 06:30   c) 18:22   d) 12:45   e) 09:15
6) Write the German for: a) to count   b) additional   c) in total   d) remaining   e) individual

## Times and Dates

7) How do you say the following in German?
   a) today   b) tomorrow   c) yesterday   d) morning   e) midday   f) afternoon   g) evening
8) List the days of the week in German. Then list them again in reverse order.
9) Write the months of the year in German, then list the four seasons.
10) Leonie tells you: 'Abends spiele ich Tennis und manchmal gehe ich wandern. Ich lese täglich und regelmäßig gehe ich schwimmen.' When or how often does she:
    a) play tennis   b) go hiking   c) read   d) go swimming?

## Questions

11) a) Make a list of German question words. There are 11 you need to know (plus 1 for Higher tier).
    b) Write five questions of your own. Start each question with a different question word.
12) Give the English for: a) Wer bist du?   b) Was für einen Beruf hast du?   c) Wohin gehst du?
13) Write questions to go with these answers. Each question should use 'wo' with a preposition.
    a) Ich habe von ihm geträumt.   b) Ich liege auf meinem Bett.   c) Ich schreibe über meinen Urlaub.

## Being Polite

14) Write down a short conversation in German between two people who don't know each other very well. Have them say hello to each other, ask each other how they are and then say goodbye.
15) What do the following mean in English? a) danke   b) alles klar   c) es tut mir leid   d) das geht
16) Anselm says: 'Ich möchte mich bei dir entschuldigen.' What has he said?
17) Xiaoyan asks, 'Kann ich das nehmen, bitte?' Rephrase this question so it is more polite.
18) Without using 'Ich möchte', say in German: a) I would like to play.   b) I would like new shoes.

## Opinions

19) List 5 adjectives for expressing a positive opinion and 5 adjectives for expressing a negative opinion.
20) Translate these phrases into English:
    a) es ist mir egal   b) meiner Meinung nach   c) es kommt darauf an, ob...   d) Was meinst du?
21) Wie findest du Actionfilme? Answer the question in German.

# Section Two — Identity and Relationships with Others

## About Yourself

You only get one chance at a first impression, so when you're introducing yourself in German, make sure you get it right. And that the other person speaks German, obviously...

*Remember there's also lots of online content here: www.cgpbooks.co.uk/Berlin*

### Über dich — About yourself

*Ich bin sluggisch.*

**Vocabulary**

| | | | | | | |
|---|---|---|---|---|---|---|
| der Name | name | englisch | English | | britisch | British |
| heißen | to be called | deutsch | German | | österreichisch | Austrian |
| das Alter | age | europäisch | European | **Higher** | Schweizer | Swiss |
| der Geburtstag | birthday | hetero(sexuell) | straight | | vorstellen | to introduce |
| geboren | born | bi(sexuell) | bisexual | | sich nennen | to be called |
| wohnen | to live | gay | gay | | stammen aus | to come from |

Ich heiße Annaliese, aber meine Familie nennt mich Lili.

I am called Annaliese, but my family calls me Lili.

*My name is — Mein Name ist*

Ich bin fünfzehn Jahre alt und ich habe am ersten Mai Geburtstag.

I am fifteen years old and my birthday is on the 1st of May.

*Check p.6 for a reminder of how to say dates.*

Ich bin in Deutschland geboren. Jedoch ist meine Familie französisch. Meine Eltern stammen aus Paris.

I was born in Germany. However, my family is French. My parents come from Paris.

*Scottish — schottisch*
*Irish — irisch*
*Welsh — walisisch*

Ich komme aus einer kleinen Stadt in England.

I come from a small town in England.

*on the coast — an der Küste*

Als Kind habe ich in Leeds gewohnt, aber jetzt wohne ich in London.

As a child, I lived in Leeds, but now I live in London.

### Practice Question

Q1 Read the following text out loud. [5 marks]

*SPEAKING*

Ich heiße Karl. Ich bin sechzehn Jahre alt und ich habe am zweiten Februar Geburtstag. Ich bin deutsch, aber ich bin in Cardiff geboren. Jetzt wohne ich in Bristol. Ich möchte in Deutschland wohnen.

Answer the questions below in German.
a) Wie heißt du?
b) Wie alt bist du?
c) Wann hast du Geburtstag?
d) Wo wohnst du? [10 marks]

Finn had a foolproof way of making sure he got all the birthday cake.

**Top Tip for Higher Students**
✓ Develop your answers by using different tenses, e.g. talking about where you used to live.

## Don't be geboring when you say where you were geboren...

If you want to give more than a basic introduction of yourself, you could add extra details about perfectly normal things, like where you live, what your parents do and why your favourite hobby is extreme unicycling.

# My Family and Friends

Examiners are a nosy bunch, which means they don't only want to hear about you — they're interested in your family and friends, too. Luckily, these pages will help you talk all about them.

## Meine Familie — *My family*

### Vocabulary

| | | | | | |
|---|---|---|---|---|---|
| die Familie | *family* | die Mutter | *mother* | der Onkel | *uncle* |
| das Mitglied | *member* | der Sohn | *son* | die Tante | *aunt* |
| die Person | *person* | die Tochter | *daughter* | der Cousin | *male cousin* |
| der Mensch | *person* | der Bruder | *brother* | die Cousine | *female cousin* |
| die Eltern (pl) | *parents* | die Brüder (pl) | *brothers* | das Tier | *animal* |
| die Geschwister (pl) | *siblings* | die Schwester | *sister* | der Hund | *dog* |
| das Kind | *child* | die Großeltern (pl) | *grandparents* | die Katze | *cat* |
| das Einzelkind | *only child* | der Opa | *grandad* | der Vogel | *bird* |
| der Vater | *father* | die Oma | *grandma* | die Generation | *generation* |

## Wie ist deine Familie? — *What's your family like?*

Ich habe einen Bruder und eine Schwester.
*I have a brother and a sister.* → stepsister — Stiefschwester

Mein Vater hätte gern zwei Tiere: einen Hund und eine Katze.
*My father would like to have two animals: a dog and a cat.* → pets — Haustiere

Meine Familie ist groß, weil mein Opa und meine Oma viele Kinder haben.
*My family is big because my grandad and grandma have lots of children.* → around the corner — um die Ecke

Meine Großeltern wohnen im Ausland. Ich sehe sie nicht oft, aber manchmal rufe ich sie an.
*My grandparents live abroad. I don't see them often, but sometimes I call them.* → nearby — in der Nähe

Wenn ich älter bin, möchte ich einen Sohn und eine Tochter haben.
*When I am older, I would like to have a son and a daughter.* → am an adult — erwachsen bin

have my own family — meine eigene Familie habe

**Q&A Audio**

### Question
Kannst du deine Familie beschreiben?
*Can you describe your family?*

### Simple Answer
Ich wohne mit meiner Mutter und meiner Halbschwester.
*I live with my mother and my half-sister.*

### Grammar — compound words
In German, you can put words together to make new ones — these are called compound words. The gender of the new word is determined by the gender of the last noun.
'Halb' + 'Bruder' = 'Halbbruder'  *half-brother*
'Bruder' is masculine, so it's 'der Halbbruder'.

### Extended Answer
Ich bin ein Einzelkind, aber meine Tanten und Onkel haben viele Kinder, also habe ich viele Cousins. Meine Eltern sind seit fünf Jahren geschieden. Neulich hat mein Vater wieder geheiratet, also habe ich jetzt eine Stiefmutter.
*I am an only child, but my aunts and uncles have lots of children, so I have many cousins. My parents have been divorced for five years. Recently, my father got married again, so now I have a stepmother.*

With Yasmin and Safa's help, Dad always looked his best.

Section Two — Identity and Relationships with Others

# Meine Freunde — My friends

> The German words for 'boyfriend' and 'girlfriend' are the same as for 'friend': 'Freund' and 'Freundin'. See p.24 for how to differentiate them.

## Vocabulary

| | | | | | |
|---|---|---|---|---|---|
| der Freund | *male friend* | kennen | *to know* | sich treffen | *to meet up* |
| die Freundin | *female friend* | kennenlernen | *to get to know* | verbringen | *to spend (time)* |
| beste | *best* | anrufen | *to ring, phone* | gemeinsam | *mutual* |
| sprechen | *to speak* | treffen | *to meet* | **H** sich unterhalten | *to chat* |

Meine beste Freundin heißt Anina.
Wir sind uns sehr ähnlich.

*My best friend is called Anina.
We are very similar to each other.*

close — enge

Ich habe meine Freundin Manuela
in der Grundschule getroffen.

*I met my friend Manuela
at primary school.*

Ich habe eine große Freundesgruppe.
Wir verbringen gern Zeit miteinander.

*I have a big friendship group.
We like spending time together.*

> Use 'verbringen' to talk about spending time and 'ausgeben' to talk about spending money.

Meine Freunde und ich treffen
uns jedes Wochenende.

*My friends and I meet up
every weekend.*

Meine Freunde machen mich glücklich,
wenn ich schlechte Laune habe.

*My friends make me happy
when I'm in a bad mood.*

difficult — schwierig

Es ist normalerweise für mich einfach,
Freunde zu finden.

*It is normally easy for me
to make friends.*

to talk to people — mit Menschen zu sprechen

## Practice Questions

**Q1** Write a description of your family and friends.
You should write about 50 words in German. Describe:

- the size of your family
- the members of your family
- who you are friends with. [10 marks]

> **Top Tip for Higher Students**
> ✓ Use subordinate clauses containing two verbs, e.g. 'Ich mag Lewis, weil er mich immer unterstützt hat.'

**Q2** Joachim has written about his family and friends.
Read his comments and then answer the questions below in English.

*Higher*

> Ich wohne mit meinem Vater, meiner Mutter, meiner Schwester und meinen zwei Brüdern. Bald bekommen wir eine Katze. Meine Geschwister und ich haben versprochen, uns um sie zu kümmern. Am Wochenende verbringe ich Zeit mit meinen Freunden. Wir unterhalten uns viel und wir spielen Videospiele zusammen. Ich habe in letzter Zeit jemanden kennengelernt, die Petra heißt. Ich habe sie durch gemeinsame Freunde getroffen.

a) How many siblings does Joachim have? [1 mark]
b) What have Joachim and his siblings promised to do? [1 mark]
c) What does Joachim do with his friends? Give **two** details. [2 marks]
d) How did Joachim meet Petra? [1 mark]

## Time to get familiar with the vocab for your Familie...

One nice thing about the German words for family members is that lots of them look really similar to how they do in English. Just like how I look really similar to my dog — everyone says we're practically twins.

# Describing People

It's time to describe people in all their glory. You can be honest — but maybe not too honest...

## Das Aussehen — *Appearance*

**Vocabulary**

| | | | | | |
|---|---|---|---|---|---|
| beschreiben | *to describe* | jung | *young* | schwarz | *black* |
| aussehen | *to appear, look* | alt | *old* | weiß | *white* |
| das Gesicht | *face* | die Farbe | *colour* | hell | *light, bright* |
| das Haar | *hair* | rot | *red* | dunkel | *dark* |
| das Auge | *eye* | gelb | *yellow* | dünn | *thin* |
| groß | *big, tall* | grün | *green* | hässlich | *ugly, hideous* (Higher) |
| klein | *little* | blau | *blue* | hübsch | *pretty, cute* |
| dick | *fat* | braun | *brown* | der Ausdruck | *expression* |
| schlank | *slim, thin* | grau | *grey* | erkennen | *to recognise* |

Meine Eltern haben braune Haare.
*My parents have brown hair.*

- blonde — blonde
- long — lange
- short — kurze
- straight — glatte
- curly — lockige

Mein Bruder war sehr klein, aber seit seinem zwölften Geburtstag ist er viel gewachsen.
*My brother was very small, but since his twelfth birthday he has grown a lot.*

Sein bester Freund Garo hat eine Tätowierung.
*His best friend Garo has a tattoo.*

- a beard — einen Bart
- a moustache — einen Schnurrbart

Ich sehe wie meinen Vater aus, weil wir beide ziemlich schlank sind und wir haben ähnliche Gesichter.
*I look like my father because we are both quite slim and we have similar faces.*

- the same eye colour — dieselbe Augenfarbe

Meine jüngere Schwester denkt, dass sie hässlich aussieht, wenn sie ihre Brille trägt, aber ich denke, sie sieht hübsch aus.
*My younger sister thinks that she looks ugly when she wears her glasses, but I think she looks pretty.*

- older — ältere
- lovely — schön

## Dich beschreiben — *To describe yourself*

Q&A Audio

**Question**
Wie siehst du aus?
*What do you look like?*

**Simple Answer**
Ich bin klein und schlank. Ich habe braune Haare.
*I am small and thin. I have brown hair.*

**Grammar — plurals**

Some words that are plural in English are singular in German...

　　Sie trägt eine Brille.　*She wears glasses.*
　　Meine Hose ist rot.　*My trousers are red.*

...and some are singular in English but plural in German.

　　Seine Haare sind braun.　*His hair is brown.*

**Extended Answer**
Ich bin dünn und so groß wie meine Mutter. Ich habe lange Haare und meine Augen sind hellblau. Ich trage auch eine Brille. Viele in meiner Familie denken, dass ich wie meine Cousine aussehe.
*I am thin and as tall as my mother. I have long hair and my eyes are light blue. I also wear glasses. A lot of my family think that I look like my cousin.*

*Adjectives have to agree if they come before a noun, but they don't have to if they're after one. See p.123 for more.*

# Die Persönlichkeit — Personality

## Vocabulary

| | | | |
|---|---|---|---|
| freundlich | *friendly* | komisch | *comical, odd* |
| glücklich | *happy* | ernst | *serious* |
| nett | *nice* | faul | *lazy, idle* |
| ehrlich | *honest* | großzügig | *generous* |
| geduldig | *patient* | hilfreich | *helpful* |
| positiv | *positive* | stolz | *proud* |
| negativ | *negative* | eifersüchtig | *jealous* |
| böse | *angry, naughty* | sich verhalten | *to behave, act* |

(Higher: großzügig, hilfreich, stolz, eifersüchtig, sich verhalten)

### Grammar — adverbs

Using adverbs is a good way to make your sentences more interesting. They're words like '<u>sehr</u>' *(very)* and '<u>ziemlich</u>' *(quite)*. See p.126 for how to <u>use</u> them.

---

Meine Mutter ist freundlich und kreativ.
*My mother is friendly and creative.*

Einer meiner Brüder ist ruhig, aber mein anderer Bruder ist laut. Beide sind sehr nett.
*One of my brothers is quiet, but my other brother is loud. Both are very nice.*

Meiner Meinung nach bin ich sehr witzig. Mein Bruder meint jedoch, dass ich ärgerlich bin.
*In my opinion, I'm very funny. However, my brother thinks that I'm annoying.*

Meine Schwester ist großzügig. Sie denkt immer an ihre Familie.
*My sister is generous. She always thinks of her family.*

- helpful — hilfsbereit
- polite — höflich

Ich bin Ben. / ICH BIN LAUT!

- mean — gemein
- embarrassing — peinlich
- selfish — egoistisch

## Practice Questions

**Q1** Your German friend Jamal is talking about his family. Answer the questions in English. *(LISTENING)*

  a) What does Jamal think of his brother and sisters? **[1 mark]**
  b) What difference between his mum and sister does Jamal describe? **[1 mark]**
  c) What does Jamal's half-sister look like? Give **two** details. **[2 marks]**
  d) Why does Jamal think it is funny that his brother is taller than him? **[1 mark]**

*Listening Track 4*

**Q2** Read this extract from an email in which Dagmar describes her best friend. *(WRITING)*

> Sie hat lange, dunkle Haare und ist ziemlich groß. Sie trägt meistens blaue Hemden, weil das ihre Lieblingsfarbe ist. Als sie ein Kind war, war sie ein bisschen faul, aber jetzt ist sie wirklich aktiv. Sie ist auch freundlich und sie redet gern mit anderen Menschen.

Write a description about your best friend to your exchange partner. You should write about 90 words in German. Describe:

- the appearance and personality of your best friend
- why this person is your best friend
- an activity that you and your best friend will do together. **[15 marks]**

**Top Tip for Higher Students**
✓ Use a range of superlatives to talk about your friend's best qualities.

---

## I've got my father's genes — sadly, they don't quite fit me...

...but one thing that does have to fit is the spelling of adjectives before a noun. An adjective's spelling will depend on the case, gender and number of the noun, so make sure you've grasped those spelling rules.

*Find the CGP RevisionHub at cgpbooks.co.uk/Berlin*

Section Two — Identity and Relationships with Others

Quick Quiz

# Relationships and Partnerships

For your exams, you'll need to build a strong relationship with the words on these pages. My advice? Spend time with them, take them out to dinner... You know, standard stuff.

## Sich verstehen — *To get on well*

**Vocabulary**

| | | | |
|---|---|---|---|
| die Beziehung | *relation, relationship* | unterstützen | *to support* |
| sich verstehen mit | *to get on well with* | versprechen | *to promise* |
| auskommen mit | *to get on with* | vertrauen | *to trust* |
| der Streit | *argument* | halten ... für | *to think of ... as* |
| streiten | *to argue* | der Konflikt | *conflict* |
| helfen | *to help* | gegenseitig | *mutual, each other* |
| hören auf | *to listen to* | | |

(vertrauen, halten ... für, der Konflikt, gegenseitig — Higher)

Sie verstehen sich ganz gut mit ihren Geschwistern.
*They get on quite well with their siblings.*

Obwohl ich normalerweise gut mit meinen Eltern auskomme, ärgere ich mich manchmal über ihre strengen Regeln.
*Although I usually get on well with my parents, I sometimes get annoyed about their strict rules.*

Ich mag meinen Freund, selbst wenn er mir ab und zu auf die Nerven geht.
*I like my boyfriend, even if he gets on my nerves now and then.*

Ich habe eine gute Beziehung zu meinen Freunden. Wir unterstützen uns gegenseitig.
*I have a good relationship with my friends. We support each other.*

**Grammar — reflexives (sich + verb)**

Reflexives use 'sich'.
'Sich' changes for different people.

| | |
|---|---|
| ich — mich | wir — uns |
| du — dich | ihr — euch |
| er / sie / es — sich | Sie — sich |

**Ich verstehe mich gut mit Finn.**
*I get on well with Finn.*

See p.111 and p.132 for more on reflexive verbs.

## Die Partnerschaft — *Partnership*

**Vocabulary**

| | | | |
|---|---|---|---|
| das Paar | *couple* | ledig | *single, unmarried* |
| der Partner | *partner* | zusammen | *together* |
| das Gefühl | *feeling* | allein | *alone* |
| die Liebe | *love* | getrennt | *separated* |
| lieben | *to love* | sich trennen (H) | *to separate* |

**Grammar — Freund / Freundin**

'Freund/in' can mean 'friend' or 'boyfriend / girlfriend'. It's usually obvious which, but if you want to make it clear:

- say 'mein Freund / meine Freundin' for boyfriend / girlfriend
- use 'ein Freund / eine Freundin von mir' for a friend

Ich bin seit sechs Monaten mit meinem Freund zusammen. Ich liebe ihn sehr.
*I have been together with my boyfriend for six months. I love him a lot.*

→ We are in love — Wir sind verliebt

Ich bin gerne ledig, aber in der Zukunft hätte ich gerne einen Partner.
*I like being single, but in the future I would like to have a partner.*

→ I would like to meet someone — möchte ich jemanden treffen

Meine Schwester und ihr Partner haben sich neulich getrennt.
*My sister and her partner have recently separated.*

Section Two — Identity and Relationships with Others

## Die Ehe — Marriage

### Vocabulary

| | | | |
|---|---|---|---|
| heiraten | to marry | die Frau | wife |
| verheiratet | married | geschieden | divorced |
| die Hochzeit | wedding, marriage | die zivile Partnerschaft | civil partnership |
| der Mann | husband | | |

### Grammar — future

The future tense can be made with a present tense form of 'werden' and an infinitive verb.

**Ich werde ihn heiraten.**
*I will marry him.*
**Wir werden ledig bleiben.**
*We will stay single.*

See p.136 for more.

### Question
Möchtest du heiraten?
*Would you like to get married?*

### Simple Answer
Ich glaube, dass ich heiraten werde. Aber ich bin noch jung, also könnte ich meine Meinung ändern.
*I think that I will get married. But I'm still young, so I could change my mind.*

### Extended Answer
Ich bin nicht sicher, ob ich heiraten will. Meiner Meinung nach kann man eine lebenslange Beziehung haben, ohne verheiratet zu sein. Das Wichtigste ist, dass man seinem Partner vertrauen kann.
*I'm not sure if I want to get married. In my opinion, you can have a lifelong relationship without being married. The most important thing is that you can trust your partner.*

## Practice Questions

**Q1** Look at the photo, then answer the following questions in German.

a) Sag mir etwas über das Foto.
b) Verstehst du dich immer gut mit deinen Freunden? Warum / warum nicht?
c) Warum ist es wichtig, dass man gute Beziehungen hat?

[6 marks]

**Q2** Read this extract from Zehra's diary, where she talks about her love life. Answer the following questions in English.

> Ich traf\* meinen Partner vor fünf Jahren. Nach drei Jahren entschieden wir, uns zu trennen, weil wir nicht mehr gut auskamen. Seitdem bin ich ledig, und ich habe gelernt, unabhängiger zu sein. Ich verbringe auch mehr Zeit mit meinen Freunden, die mir sehr wichtig sind. Im Moment bin ich glücklich, ledig zu sein, aber in der Zukunft hoffe ich noch, dass ich heiraten und Kinder haben werde.

\*traf — met

a) When did Zehra meet her ex-partner? [1 mark]
b) Why did Zehra and her ex-partner separate? [1 mark]
c) What does Zehra say she has learnt to be? [1 mark]
d) What does Zehra say about her friends? Give **one** detail. [1 mark]
e) What does Zehra hope to do in the future? Give **two** details. [2 marks]

---

### "Ich, you may now kiss ~~the bride~~ your reflexive pronoun..."

\*wipes tear\* ich and mich are such a beautiful pair. As are du and dich, and sie and sich... I just love when reflexive pronouns match their subject. (As do examiners, by the way, so make sure to get these learnt.)

# Identity and Relationships with Others — Vocabulary

You know what they say — keep your friends close, but keep your GCSE German vocab closer...

## About Yourself

|  |  |
|---|---|
| der Name | name |
| heißen | to be called |
| das Alter | age |
| der Geburtstag | birthday |
| geboren | born |
| -jährig | years old |
| wohnen | to live |
| englisch | English |
| deutsch | German |
| europäisch | European |
| französisch | French |
| spanisch | Spanish |
| hetero(sexuell) | straight |
| bi(sexuell) | bi, bisexual |
| gay | gay |
| trans(gender) | transgender |
| nicht binär, nichtbinär | non-binary |
| die Religion | religion |
| der / die Christ(in) | Christian |
| der Muslim | Muslim (male) |
| die Muslime | Muslim (female) |
| der Jude | Jewish (male), Jewish person |
| die Jüdin | Jewish (female) |
| der / die Hindu | Hindu |
| der Deutsche | the German (male) |
| ein Deutscher | a German (male) |
| die Deutsche | the German (female) |
| eine Deutsche | a German (female) |
| Deutsche | Germans |
| die Deutschen | the Germans |

**Higher:**
|  |  |
|---|---|
| die Geburt | birth |
| britisch | British |
| österreichisch | Austrian |
| türkisch | Turkish |
| Schweizer | Swiss |
| berliner | (of) Berlin |
| vorstellen | to introduce |
| nennen | to name, call |
| sich nennen | to be called |
| stammen aus | to come from |

*These words to talk about Germans are adjectival nouns. The spelling of the word changes depending on the article used before it and whether it's singular or plural.*

## My Family and Friends

|  |  |
|---|---|
| die Familie | family |
| das Mitglied | member |
| die Person | person |
| der Mensch | human being, person |
| die Eltern (pl) | parents |
| die Geschwister (pl) | siblings |
| das Kind | child |
| das Einzelkind | only child |
| der Vater | father |
| die Mutter | mother |
| der Sohn | son |
| die Tochter | daughter |
| der Bruder | brother |
| die Brüder (pl) | brothers |
| die Schwester | sister |
| die Großeltern (pl) | grandparents |
| der Opa | grandpa, grandad, grandfather |
| die Oma | grandma, grandmother |
| der Onkel | uncle |
| die Tante | aunt |
| der Cousin | cousin (male) |
| die Cousine | cousin (female) |
| Stief- | step- |
| das Tier | animal |
| der Hund | dog |
| die Katze | cat |
| der Vogel | bird |
| das Pferd | horse |
| der / die Erwachsene | adult, grown-up |
| der Junge | boy |
| das Mädchen | girl |
| der Nachbar | neighbour |
| der Betreuer | carer |
| der / die Jugendliche | young person, adolescent |
| der Typ | bloke, guy |
| der Freund | male friend |
| die Freundin | female friend |
| beste | best |
| eng | close |
| sprechen | to speak, talk |
| sagen | to say, tell |
| kennen | to know |
| kennenlernen, kennen lernen | to meet (for first time), get to know |
| anrufen | to ring, phone |
| treffen | to meet |
| sich treffen | to meet up |
| verbringen | to spend (time) |
| lachen | to laugh |
| lächeln | to smile |
| verstehen | to understand |
| gemeinsam | common, mutual, in common, joint |
| ähnlich | similar, similarly |
| gute / schlechte Laune haben | to be in a good / bad mood |
| das Gespräch | conversation, talk |

**Higher:**
|  |  |
|---|---|
| die Generation | generation |
| die Jugend | youth |
| pflegen | to care for, nurse, cultivate (e.g. a friendship) |
| sich unterhalten | to chat |

After the doorbell had been ringing for ten minutes, Anton finally let his Freundin.

## Appearances

|  |  |
|---|---|
| beschreiben | to describe |
| aussehen | to appear, look |
| das Gesicht | face |
| das Haar | hair |
| das Auge | eye |
| die Größe | size, height |
| groß | big, tall |
| klein | small, little, short |
| dick | fat |
| schlank | slim, thin |
| kurz | short |
| lang | long |
| rund | round |
| jung | young |
| alt | old |
| die Farbe | colour |
| rot | red |
| gelb | yellow |
| grün | green |
| blau | blue |
| braun | brown |
| grau | grey |
| schwarz | black |
| weiß | white |
| hell | light, bright |
| dunkel | dark |
| schön | lovely, beautiful |
| schauen | to look |

**Higher:**

|  |  |
|---|---|
| dünn | thin |
| hässlich | ugly, hideous |
| hübsch | pretty, cute, lovely |
| die Brille | (pair of) glasses |
| die Tätowierung | tattoo, tattooing |
| der Ausdruck | expression |
| erkennen | to recognise, admit, realise |

## Personalities

|  |  |
|---|---|
| die Persönlichkeit | personality |
| freundlich | kind, nice, friendly |
| glücklich | happy, fortunate, happily |
| froh | happy, glad |
| nett | nice |
| ehrlich | honest |
| geduldig | patient |
| positiv | positive |
| lieb | dear, kind |
| süß | sweet, cute |
| hilfsbereit | helpful, cooperative |
| witzig | funny, witty, comical |
| höflich | polite |
| ruhig | quiet, calm |
| kreativ | creative, creatively |
| sportlich | sporty, athletic |
| negativ | negative |
| traurig | sad |
| böse | bad, mad, naughty, angry |
| komisch | funny, comical, strange, odd, weird |
| ernst | serious |
| faul | lazy, idle |
| streng | strict, severe |
| unabhängig | independent |
| gemein | mean, cruel, nasty |
| peinlich | embarrassing, awkward |
| ärgerlich | annoying, irritating |
| sich verlieren | to get lost (in thought) |

**Higher:**

|  |  |
|---|---|
| großzügig | generous |
| hilfreich | helpful |
| stolz | proud |
| frech | cheeky, naughty |
| eifersüchtig | jealous |
| die Eigenschaft | quality, characteristic, trait |
| sich verhalten | to behave, act |

## Relationships and Partnerships

|  |  |
|---|---|
| die Beziehung | relation, relationship |
| sich verstehen mit | to get on well with |
| auskommen mit | to get on with |
| der Streit | argument, fight, dispute |
| streiten | to quarrel, argue, dispute |
| helfen | to help |
| hören auf | to hear, listen, to listen to, obey someone |
| unterstützen | to support |
| die Unterstützung | support |
| versprechen | to promise |
| jemandem auf die Nerven gehen | to get on someone's nerves |
| sorgen | to care, worry |
| sich kümmern um | to take care of, concerned about |
| fehlen | to be missing |
| das Paar | pair, couple |
| der Partner | partner |
| das Gefühl | feeling |
| die Liebe | love |
| lieben | to love |
| ledig | single, unmarried |
| zusammen | together, altogether |
| allein, alleine | alone |
| miteinander | with each other |
| getrennt | separated |
| die Ehe | marriage |
| heiraten | to marry |
| verheiratet | married |
| die Hochzeit | wedding, marriage |
| die zivile Partnerschaft | civil partnership |
| der Mann | husband, man |

To say 'I miss you' in German, you say 'Du fehlst mir', which literally means 'you are missing to me'.

|  |  |
|---|---|
| die Frau | wife, woman |
| geschieden | divorced |

**Higher:**

|  |  |
|---|---|
| vertrauen | to trust |
| halten ... für | to think of ... as |
| kritisieren | to criticise |
| enttäuschen | to disappoint, frustrate |
| stören | to disturb, bother |
| der Konflikt | conflict, dispute |
| gegenseitig | mutual, each other |
| sich trennen | to separate |
| das Verständnis | understanding, sympathy |
| die Erinnerung | memory |

Section Two — Identity and Relationships with Others

# Revision Summary Test for Section Two

Friendship is one of life's greatest gifts — and so is this page of summary questions...
- Yep, these questions are **hard** — they'll really help you see **how well you know your stuff**.
- Tackle the **revision summary test** below, or scan the QR code to do it **online**.
  Use the CGP RevisionHub to **track your progress** and see **which areas need more work**.
- You can find **sample answers** here: www.cgpbooks.co.uk/BerlinExtras

## About Yourself

1) Introduce yourself in German. Mention your name, age, birthday and where you live.
2) How many adjectives can you name in German that describe where someone is from? There are 5 you need to know (plus 5 for Higher tier).
3) Give as many German words related to gender and sexuality as you can. There are at least 5 you need to know.
4) [H] Aafreena says: 'Ich stamme aus Berlin.' How would you say this in English?

## My Family and Friends

5) a) How many family members can you give in German? There are at least 16 you need to know.
   b) Which prefix do you use to talk about: i) step-family   ii) half-siblings?
6) Translate this into English: 'Mein Nachbar hat drei Tiere: einen Hund, eine Katze und einen Vogel.'
7) How would you say each of the following verbs in English?
   a) kennenlernen   b) lachen   c) sprechen   d) anrufen   e) treffen   f) lächeln
8) Your German cousin wants to know about your friends. In German, tell them about your group of friends and what you do when you spend time with them.
9) [H] Worüber unterhältst du dich mit deinen Freunden? Answer in German.

## Describing People

10) How many German words can you think of to describe someone's personality? There are at least 25 you need to know (plus 5 more for Higher tier).
11) Describe two members of your family. Give details about their personality and their appearance.
12) 'Munir ist jünger als seine Schwester, aber nicht so alt wie sein Bruder. Er hat blaue Augen, die sehr schön sind.' What do these sentences mean in English?
13) Translate these sentences into German: 'Yadira is very kind and she is also funny. Although she is annoying sometimes, I am fortunate that she is my friend.'
14) [H] Was sind die besten und schlechtesten Eigenschaften in einem Freund? Answer in German.

## Relationships and Partnerships

15) How would you say these words in German?
    a) civil partnership   b) married   c) single   d) divorced   e) separated   f) wedding
16) Translate these sentences into English: 'Mein Bruder und ich haben eine schwierige Beziehung. Er geht mir immer auf die Nerven. Wir haben keine gemeinsame Interessen und wir streiten oft.'
17) Describe a relationship in your life. Do you get on well with this person? Why / why not? Answer in German. Give as much detail as you can.
18) Estelle says: 'Die Ehe ist heute bedeutungslos und unnötig. Ich will nicht heiraten.' Do you agree with her? Why / why not?
19) In German, name a person that you trust and explain why you trust them.
20) Translate the following sentences into English:
    a) Wir schaffen Erinnerungen.        c) Ich halte dich für großzügig.
    b) Er enttäuscht mich nie.           d) Sie stört mich manchmal.

Section Two — Identity and Relationships with Others

# Section Three — Healthy Living and Lifestyle

## Food

Quick Quiz

~ TODAY'S SPECIALS ~ Starter: vocab mix • Main Course: tender Q&A • Sides: tasty questions

### Was isst du gern? — *What do you like eating?*

*Don't forget you can access your online content here: www.cgpbooks.co.uk/Berlin*

**Vocabulary**

| | | | | | | | |
|---|---|---|---|---|---|---|---|
| das Essen | *food, meal* | der Käse | *cheese* | scharf | *spicy, hot* | | |
| essen | *to eat* | das Ei | *egg* | das Frühstück | *breakfast* | | |
| trinken | *to drink* | das Fleisch | *meat* | das Mittagessen | *lunch* | | |
| der Hunger | *hunger* | das Hähnchen | *chicken* | das Abendessen | *dinner* | | |
| der Durst | *thirst* | die Wurst | *sausage* | der / die Veganer(in) | *vegan* | | |
| kochen | *to cook, boil* | der Fisch | *fish* | der / die Vegetarier(in) | *vegetarian* | | |
| das Gemüse | *vegetables* | das Wasser | *water* | das Getränk | *drink* | (Higher) |
| das Obst | *fruit* | lecker | *tasty, delicious* | das Gericht | *dish* | |
| das Brot | *bread* | süß | *sweet, sugary* | schmecken | *to taste* | |

Ich finde, dass Hähnchen lecker schmeckt. — *I find that chicken tastes delicious.*

Ich mag kein scharfes Essen. — *I don't like spicy food.*

Ich trinke gern Kaffee, aber ich finde Cola zu süß für mich. — *I like drinking coffee, but I find cola too sweet for me.*

Ich habe Hunger und ich habe Durst. — *I'm hungry and I'm thirsty.*

*awful* — schrecklich
*sweet* — süßes

**Q&A Audio**

**Question**
Was isst du gern?
*What do you like eating?*

**Simple Answer**
Ich esse sehr gern Fisch außer Lachs.
*I really like eating fish except salmon.*

**Extended Answer**
Mein Lieblingsgericht ist Nudeln mit Käse und Gemüse.
Ich finde es lecker. Da ich Vegetarier bin, esse ich kein Fleisch.
*My favourite meal is pasta with cheese and vegetables.*
*I find it tasty. Because I'm a vegetarian, I don't eat meat.*

**Grammar** — essen *(to eat)*

'Essen' is irregular. Here are its forms in the present tense:

| | |
|---|---|
| ich esse | wir essen |
| du isst | ihr esst |
| er / sie / es isst | Sie / sie essen |

See p.145 for how to use 'essen' in the past tense.

### Practice Question

Q1 Elsa, Lina and Moritz are discussing their food preferences. Complete the sentences.  LISTENING

a) Lina prefers to drink...    **A.** milk    **B.** coffee    **C.** water
b) Lina only eats bread...    **A.** at breakfast    **B.** at lunch    **C.** at dinner
c) Moritz enjoys...    **A.** cooking    **B.** eating healthily    **C.** eating out
d) Elsa doesn't eat...    **A.** cheese    **B.** meat and fish    **C.** vegetables    *[4 marks]*

Listening Track 5

---

### Sausage isn't all it's cracked up to be — it's just the Wurst...

To learn this vocab, draw the food items on this page, then write the German word next to each picture.
E.g.  = der Käse. (Drawing that many pictures isn't necessary — I just love cheese.)

# Healthy and Unhealthy Living

Learning five German words a day is really good for you — it's part of a healthy lifestyle...

## Die Gesundheit — *Health*

**Vocabulary**

| | | | |
|---|---|---|---|
| gesund | *healthy, healthily* | abnehmen | *to lose weight* |
| das Leben | *life* | zunehmen | *to put on weight* |
| die Energie | *energy* | die Ernährung | *food, diet, nutrition* (Higher) |
| aufstehen | *to stand up, get up* | erhalten | *to preserve, maintain* (Higher) |
| schlafen | *to sleep* | sich entspannen | *to relax* (Higher) |
| liegen | *to lie, be lying down* | einschlafen | *to fall asleep, doze off* (Higher) |

Tiddles was very aware of the importance of rest for his health.

Es ist nötig, dass man genug schläft. — *It is necessary that you sleep enough.* ← you drink a lot of water — man viel Wasser trinkt

Ich versuche, mich nach der Schule zu entspannen, damit ich nicht müde werde. — *I try to relax after school so that I don't get tired.* ← stressed — gestresst

Ich will gesünder sein, also muss ich mehr Obst essen. — *I want to be healthier so I must eat more fruit.* ← give up chocolate — Schokolade aufgeben

## Sich bewegen — *To exercise*

**Vocabulary**

| | | | | | |
|---|---|---|---|---|---|
| die Bewegung | *exercise, movement* | in Form sein | *to be in form / good shape* | stark | *strong* |
| der Sport | *sport* | joggen | *to jog* | schwach | *weak* |
| die Aktivität | *activity* | laufen | *to run, walk* | die Turnhalle | *gymnasium* (Higher) |
| die Fitness | *fitness* | schwimmen | *to swim* | die Kraft | *strength, power* (Higher) |
| das Fitness-Studio | *gym* | sportlich | *sporty, athletic* | die Übung | *exercise* (Higher) |
| Sport treiben | *to do sport* | aktiv | *active, energetic* | aufbauen | *to build up* (Higher) |
| | | | | führen | *to lead* (Higher) |

Ich möchte in Form sein. — *I would like to be in good shape.* ← a bit healthier — ein bisschen gesünder

Um mich fit zu halten, schwimme ich dreimal pro Woche. — *To keep myself fit, I swim three times a week.* ← jog — jogge

Regelmäßige Bewegung ist wichtig für die Gesundheit. — *Regular exercise is important for your health.* ← A balanced diet — Eine ausgewogene Ernährung

**Q&A Audio**

**Question**
Meinst du, dass Bewegung wichtig ist?
*Do you think that exercise is important?*

**Simple Answer**
Ja. Bewegung ist sehr wichtig. Sie kann die Gesundheit verbessern.
*Yes. Exercise is very important. It can improve your health.*

**Extended Answer**
Es ist wichtig, sich fit zu halten, aber man muss sich auch entspannen und eine gesunde Ernährung erhalten, um völlig gesund zu sein.
*It is important to keep yourself fit, but you also have to relax and maintain a healthy diet in order to be completely healthy.*

# Ein ungesundes Leben — *An unhealthy life*

## Vocabulary

| | | | | | | |
|---|---|---|---|---|---|---|
| die Gefahr | *danger, risk, threat* | die Zigarette | *cigarette* | drohen | *to threaten* | |
| gefährlich | *dangerous, risky* | rauchen | *to smoke* | aufgeben | *to give up, quit* | |
| der Alkohol | *alcohol* | vermeiden | *to avoid* | aufhören | *to stop* | Higher |
| die Droge | *drug* | abhängen | *to depend* | übergewichtig | *overweight* | |
| das Fastfood | *fast food* | betrunken | *drunk* | abhängig | *dependent, addicted* | |
| | | faul | *lazy, idle* | süchtig (nach) | *addicted (to)* | |

## Grammar — modal verbs

Modal verbs are useful for discussing healthy and unhealthy living. P.140 has more info.

| | | | | | |
|---|---|---|---|---|---|
| müssen | *to have to, must* | mögen | *to like to* | sollen | *to be supposed to, should, ought to* |
| können | *to be able to, can* | wollen | *to want to* | dürfen | *to be allowed to, may* |

These verbs are usually followed by a second verb in the infinitive, which goes to the end of the clause.

**Du musst mehr Sport treiben.**   *You must do more sport.*

Ich will kein ungesundes Leben führen.   *I don't want to lead an unhealthy life.*  ← *to eat any fast food — kein Fastfood essen*

Ich habe nie geraucht. Rauchen ist für die Gesundheit sehr gefährlich.   *I have never smoked. Smoking is very dangerous for your health.*   *taken drugs — Drogen genommen*

Man soll Drogen immer vermeiden.   *You should always avoid drugs.* ← *cigarettes — Zigaretten*

Es ist schwierig auf Partys, wenn man keinen Alkohol trinkt.   *It's difficult at parties if you don't drink alcohol.* ← *you're teetotal — man abstinent ist*

## Practice Questions

Q1  Write a short article about healthy living. You should write about 90 words in German. Describe:
- some benefits of healthy living
- some dangers of unhealthy living
- what you've done recently to keep fit.   [15 marks]

**Top Tip for Higher Students**
✓ Use conditional phrases to say what you should do, e.g. 'man sollte'.

Q2  Read Mia's article about her lifestyle. Answer the following questions in English.

> Früher war ich wirklich ungesund. Häufig aß ich Fastfood und ich rauchte viele Zigaretten. Meine Gesundheit war in Gefahr und ich wusste, dass ich mich ändern musste. Ich begann, regelmäßig ins Fitness-Studio zu gehen. Ich rauche auch nicht mehr. Jetzt fühle ich mich gesünder und ich bin zufrieden mit meinem Fortschritt.

a) What was unhealthy about Mia's lifestyle? Give **two** details.   [2 marks]
b) What **two** things has Mia done to be healthier?   [2 marks]
c) How does Mia describe herself now? Give **two** details.   [2 marks]

## I know all my model verbs — strut, pose, pout...

The examiner was wowed but quite confused too. They were more interested in *modal* verbs, which are really handy for talking about what you should and shouldn't do (like forgetting to learn your modal verbs).

# Illnesses and Treatments

Here are *ACHOO* two pages on *ACHOO* illnesses for *ACHOO* you. Sorry about the snot...

## Ich fühle mich krank — I feel ill

### Vocabulary

|  |  |
|---|---|
| die Krankheit | illness, disease |
| krank | sick, ill |
| die Schmerzen | pains, aches |
| die Angst | fear, anxiety |
| die Sorge | care, worry |
| müde | tired |
| sich fühlen | to feel |
| sich sorgen (um) | to worry (about) |
| verletzen | to injure, hurt |
| leiden (an [dat.]) | to suffer (from) |
| der Schmerz | pain, ache |
| der Unfall | accident, crash |
| körperlich | physical, physically |
| sich brechen | to break |

(Higher: der Schmerz, der Unfall, körperlich, sich brechen)

Als ich Kind war, war ich häufig krank. Oft musste ich zum Arzt gehen. — When I was a child, I was frequently ill. I had to go to the doctor often.

*I couldn't see my friends — konnte ich meine Freunde nicht sehen*

Wegen dieser Krankheit bin ich immer müde. Ich finde alles anstrengend. — Because of this illness, I'm always tired. I find everything tiring.

*I fall asleep quickly — Ich schlafe schnell ein*

Letztes Jahr habe ich mir den Arm gebrochen. Die Ärztin hat ihn verbunden. — Last year I broke my arm. The doctor bandaged it.

*You need to use dative reflexive pronouns with 'sich brechen'. See p.111 for more.*

## Schmerzen haben — To be in pain

### Vocabulary

|  |  |
|---|---|
| der Körper | body |
| der Kopf | head |
| der Arm | arm |
| die Hand | hand |
| das Bein | leg |
| der Fuß | foot |
| der Rücken | back |
| das Ohr | ear |
| das Auge | eye |
| die Schulter | shoulder |
| der Bauch | belly |
| das Knie | knee |
| die Knie | knees |
| der Zahn | tooth |

(Higher: die Schulter, der Bauch, das Knie, die Knie, der Zahn)

### Grammar — compound words

In German, if you want to say a part of the body is in pain or aches, you usually attach the name of the body part to the front of 'schmerzen' to make a compound word.

**Bein**schmerzen — Leg **pain**
**Kopf**schmerzen — Head**ache**

There's more about compound words on p.103.

Ich habe Kopfschmerzen. Ich brauche Ruhe. — I have a headache. I need rest.

*medication — Medikamente*
*a glass of water — ein Glas Wasser*

Seit seinem Unfall hat er ständige Rückenschmerzen. — Since his accident he has constant back pain.

*neck pain — Nackenschmerzen*

Sie leidet seit drei Tagen an Ohrenschmerzen. — She's been suffering from earache for three days.

### Question
Wie fühlst du dich heute?
*How do you feel today?*

### Simple Answer
Ich fühle mich nicht gut. Ich habe Bauchschmerzen.
*I don't feel well. I have a stomach ache.*

### Extended Answer
Heute fühle ich mich schrecklich. Neulich habe ich mir den Fuß verletzt und der Schmerz ist noch nicht verschwunden.
*Today I feel awful. Recently I injured my foot and the pain still hasn't disappeared.*

Section Three — Healthy Living and Lifestyle

## Zum Arzt gehen — *To go to the doctor*

### Vocabulary

| | | | | |
|---|---|---|---|---|
| der Arzt / die Ärztin | *doctor* | | das Medikament | *medicine* |
| das Krankenhaus | *hospital* | | der / die Patient(in) | *patient* |
| helfen | *to help* | **Higher** | die Ursache | *reason, cause* |
| sich kümmern um | *to take care of* | | der Termin | *appointment* |
| verbessern | *to improve* | | medizinisch | *medical* |
| empfehlen | *to recommend* | | behandeln | *to treat* |

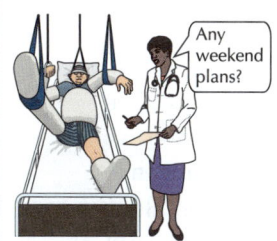

Laut vieler Studien wirkt dieses Medikament wirklich gut. — *According to many studies this medicine works really well.* ← specialists — Spezialisten

Der Arzt hat meine körperliche Gesundheit mit mir diskutiert. — *The doctor discussed my physical health with me.* ← my mental health — meine psychische Gesundheit

Die Ärztin behandelt die Frau, während sie im Krankenhaus bleibt. — *The doctor treats the woman while she stays in hospital.* ← takes care of — kümmert sich um

Wenn man immer Sorgen hat, ist es wichtig, um Hilfe zu bitten. — *If you always have worries, it is important to ask for help.* ← advice — Rat

Ich muss jeden Monat ins Krankenhaus gehen, weil ich langfristige Gesundheitsprobleme habe. — *I have to go to the hospital every month, because I have long-term health problems.* ← serious — ernste

### Practice Questions

**Q1** Read the following text out loud. [5 marks]

> Gestern hatte ich Kopfschmerzen und Muskelschmerzen. Heute bin ich noch krank und müde. Deswegen will ich den Arzt besuchen. Später werde ich ihn anrufen.

**Top Tip for Higher Students**
✓ Use superlative structures like 'am wichtigsten' and 'am liebsten' in your responses.

Answer the questions below in German.

a) Warum ist es wichtig, dass man den Arzt besucht?
b) Möchtest du in der Zukunft Arzt / Ärztin sein? Warum / warum nicht? [4 marks]

**Q2** Listen to this conversation between Asaf and Ingeborg, then write down whether the following statements are true or false.

a) Ingeborg was suffering from back pain.
b) It was easy for Ingeborg to book an appointment.
c) The doctor couldn't find the cause of Ingeborg's problem at first.
d) Ingeborg hasn't had any pains since the incident. [4 marks]

Listening Track 6

### Did you see the video about the common cold? It went viral...

Forget how long I spent sneezing — have you seen the length of some German compound words? But don't panic — just split them into their parts. E.g. Gesundheitsvorteile = Gesundheit + Vorteile ('health benefits').

*Find the CGP RevisionHub at cgpbooks.co.uk/Berlin*  Section Three — Healthy Living and Lifestyle

# Healthy Living and Lifestyle — Vocabulary

Sick of not knowing all the Section Three spec vocab? Don't worry, this page will help you get better...

## Food

| | | | |
|---|---|---|---|
| das Essen | food, meal | lecker | tasty, delicious |
| essen | to eat | süß | sweet, sugary |
| trinken | to drink | scharf | spicy, hot |
| der Hunger | hunger | frisch | fresh, freshly |
| der Durst | thirst | das Frühstück | breakfast |
| kochen | to cook, boil | das Mittagessen | lunch |
| das Gemüse | vegetables | das Abendessen | dinner |
| das Obst | fruit | nehmen | to have something to eat or drink |
| das Brot | bread | | |
| der Käse | cheese | der Imbiss | snack, refreshment |
| das Ei | egg | der / die Veganer(in) | vegan |
| die Pommes (frites) | chips, fries | der / die Vegetarier(in) | vegetarian |
| das Fleisch | meat | das Restaurant | restaurant |
| das Hähnchen | chicken | die Speisekarte, die Karte | menu |
| die Wurst | sausage | | |
| der Fisch | fish | das Stück | piece |
| der Zucker | sugar | die Flasche | bottle |
| der Kuchen | cake | das Glas | glass |
| das Eis | ice, ice cream | das Kilo(gramm), kg | kilo, kilogram |
| das Wasser | water | bestellen | to order |
| die Cola | cola | das Getränk *(Higher)* | drink |
| die Milch | milk | das Gericht *(Higher)* | dish |
| der Kaffee | coffee | das Produkt *(Higher)* | product |
| der Wein | wine | das Protein *(Higher)* | protein |
| das Bier | beer | schmecken *(Higher)* | to taste |

## Healthy Living

| | | | |
|---|---|---|---|
| die Gesundheit | health | laufen | to run, walk |
| gesund | healthy, healthily | schwimmen | to swim |
| das Leben | life | spazieren | to (go for a) walk, stroll |
| die Energie | energy | wandern | to (go on a) walk / hike, ramble (in the countryside) |
| bewusst | conscious, aware | | |
| aufstehen | to stand up, get up | sportlich | sporty, athletic |
| stehen | to stand | aktiv | active, energetic |
| schlafen | to sleep | stark | strong |
| liegen | to lie, be lying down | schwach | weak |
| abnehmen | to lose weight | schnell | quickly, fast |
| zunehmen | to put on weight | die Ernährung *(Higher)* | food, diet, nutrition |
| die Bewegung | exercise, movement | erhalten *(Higher)* | to preserve, maintain |
| der Sport | sport | sich entspannen *(Higher)* | to relax |
| die Aktivität | activity | einschlafen *(Higher)* | to fall asleep, doze off |
| die Fitness | fitness | die Turnhalle *(Higher)* | gymnasium |
| das Fitness-Studio | gym | die Kraft *(Higher)* | strength, power |
| bewegen | to move | die Übung *(Higher)* | exercise |
| sich bewegen | to exercise | halten *(Higher)* | to stop, hold, keep |
| Sport treiben | to do sport | aufbauen *(Higher)* | to build up |
| in Form sein | to be in form / good shape | führen *(Higher)* | to lead |
| joggen | to jog | | |

Section Three — Healthy Living and Lifestyle

## Unhealthy Living

| | |
|---|---|
| die Gefahr | danger, risk, threat |
| gefährlich | dangerous, risky |
| der Alkohol | alcohol |
| die Droge | drug |
| das Fastfood | fast food |
| die Zigarette | cigarette |
| rauchen | to smoke |
| vermeiden | to avoid |
| abhängen | to depend |
| betrunken | drunk |
| faul | lazy, idle |

**Higher**

| | |
|---|---|
| die Krise | crisis |
| drohen | to threaten |
| aufgeben | to give up, quit |
| aufhören | to stop |
| übergewichtig | overweight |
| abhängig | dependent, addicted |
| süchtig (nach) | addicted (to), hooked (on) |
| verzichten auf | to do without |
| enthalten | to contain |

## Illnesses and Treatments

| | |
|---|---|
| die Krankheit | illness, disease |
| krank | sick, ill |
| die Schmerzen | pains, aches |
| die Angst | fear, anxiety |
| die Sorge | care, worry |
| sorgen | to care |
| sich sorgen (um) | to worry (about) |
| müde | tired |
| das Gefühl | feeling |
| fühlen | to feel (+ noun) |
| sich fühlen | to feel (+ adjective) |
| sitzen | to sit |
| verletzen | to injure, hurt |
| leiden (an [dat.]) | to suffer (from) |
| leiden (unter [dat.]) | to suffer (as a result of) |
| weinen | to cry |
| sterben (an [dat.]) | to die (from) |
| tot | dead |
| der Körper | body |
| der Kopf | head |
| der Arm | arm |
| die Hand | hand |
| das Bein | leg |
| der Fuß | foot |
| der Rücken | back |
| das Ohr | ear |
| das Auge | eye |
| der Mund | mouth |
| der Muskel | muscle |
| das Herz | heart |
| der Arzt / die Ärztin | doctor |
| das Krankenhaus | hospital |
| retten | to save, rescue |
| sich kümmern um | to take care of, be concerned about |
| verbessern | to improve |
| empfehlen | to recommend |

**Higher**

| | |
|---|---|
| der Schmerz | pain, ache |
| der Unfall | accident, crash |
| körperlich | physical, physically |
| der Tod | death |
| töten | to kill |
| anstrengend | exhausting, strenuous, tiring |
| spüren | to sense, notice, feel |
| sich legen | to lie down |
| sich setzen | to sit down |
| sich [dat.] brechen | to break (a bone) |
| die Schulter | shoulder |
| der Bauch | belly |
| das Knie | knee |
| die Knie | knees |
| die Haut | skin |
| die Nase | nose |
| der Zahn | tooth |
| der Finger | finger |
| das Blut | blood |
| der / die Doktor(in), Dr. | doctor |
| der / die Patient(in) | patient |
| die Ursache | reason, cause |
| der Termin | appointment |
| das Medikament | medicine |
| medizinisch | medical |
| untersuchen | to examine |
| behandeln | to treat |
| pflegen | to care, nurse |
| verbinden | to bandage |
| verhindern | to prevent |
| warnen (vor [dat.]) | to warn (of / about) |

to break (a dance)

# Revision Summary Test for Section Three

Feast your eyes on this mouth-watering page of summary questions, prepared by yours truly. Yum.
- These questions are **really tricky**, but they'll help you see **how well you know your stuff**.
- Tackle the **revision summary test** below, or scan the QR code to do it **online**.
  You can **keep track of your progress** online and see **which areas need more work**.
- There are **sample answers** here: www.cgpbooks.co.uk/BerlinExtras

## Food ☐

1) List all the different types of food you can remember in German. There are 13 in this section.
2) In German, how many different types of drinks can you name? There are 6 you need to know.
3) Was isst du gern zum Frühstuck, zum Mittagessen und zum Abendessen? Answer in German.
4) In German, explain to a relative that you're vegetarian and your brother is vegan.
5) Write down the German for these words:
   a) to order   b) glass   c) menu   d) tasty   e) snack   f) bottle
6) Yusuf says: 'Ich hasse süßes Essen. Ich esse lieber scharfes Essen.' What is he saying?
7) In German, how would you tell someone that you're hungry and thirsty?

## Healthy and Unhealthy Living ☐

8) Warum ist es wichtig, dass man in Form bleibt? Answer in German.
9) Translate into German: 'I avoid alcohol and drugs because they can be dangerous.'
10) Write down the opposites of these words:  a) zunehmen   b) schwach   c) faul   d) aufstehen
11) Translate into English: 'Täglich trinke ich genug Wasser und jede Nacht schlafe ich mindestens acht Stunden.'
12) List as many German nouns as you can that are to do with sport and exercise.
    There are 6 in this section (plus 3 more for Higher tier).
13) Was denkst du über Zigaretten? Answer this question in German.
14) Give the German for these words:  a) health   b) energy   c) to run   d) danger   e) to avoid
15) Gibt es eine Drogenkrise unter Jugendlichen? Answer this question in German. ⌐H
16) Give the English for these words:  a) sich entspannen   b) aufbauen   c) führen   d) drohen

## Illnesses and Treatments ☐

17) Translate into English: 'Leider muss ich zum Arzt gehen, weil ich Ohrenschmerzen habe.'
18) Was kann man machen, wenn man Angst hat? Answer in German.
19) Name as many parts of the body as you can. There are
    11 you need to know (plus 8 more for Higher tier).
20) Imagine you have a medical problem. In German, explain
    what's wrong, then say what a doctor might do or advise.
21) In German, say: 'He is often tired because he suffers from a serious illness.'
22) Give the English for these words:  a) die Sorge    c) das Gefühl       e) sterben an    g) retten
                                       b) bewusst     d) das Krankenhaus  f) verletzen     h) empfehlen
23) 'Meine Oma hatte einen Unfall, also hat die Ärztin ihr Bein verbunden.' Translate this into English.
24) Was kann man machen, um die Krankheit zu verhindern? Answer this question in German.
25) Give the German for these words:  a) to kill       c) exhausting    e) medical    g) to examine
                                      b) to lie down   d) appointment   f) physical   h) to care

Section Three — Healthy Living and Lifestyle

# Section Four — Education

## School Subjects

Quick Quiz

If I had it my way, you'd have German all the time — but you need to learn other subjects too.

### Fächer — *Subjects*

Head to the CGP RevisionHub for all your online content: www.cgpbooks.co.uk/Berlin

**Vocabulary**

| | | | | | |
|---|---|---|---|---|---|
| das Fach | *subject* | das Englisch | *English* | die Musik | *music* |
| die Mathematik, die Mathe | *mathematics, maths* | das Deutsch | *German* | das Theater | *drama* |
| die Biologie | *biology* | das Französisch | *French* | der Sport | *sport, PE* |
| die Chemie | *chemistry* | das Spanisch | *Spanish* | das Kochen | *cookery* |
| die Physik | *physics* | die Geschichte | *history* | einfach | *simple, easy* |
| die Wissenschaft | *science* | die Erdkunde | *geography* | schwierig | *difficult, tough* |
| die Technik | *technology* | die Religion | *religion* | interessant | *interesting* |
| | | die Kunst | *art* | langweilig | *boring* |

Sport gefällt mir immer, **obwohl es sehr anstrengend ist**.
*I always enjoy PE, although it is very strenuous.*
← *because I prefer being outdoors —* weil ich lieber an der freien Luft bin

Kunst mag ich nicht, weil **ich nicht sehr kreativ bin**.
*I don't like art because I'm not very creative.*
← *I find it boring —* ich es langweilig finde

Ich mag Physik, da **ich verstehen will, wie alles funktioniert**.
*I like physics because I want to understand how everything works.*
← *the experiments are fun —* die Experimente Spaß machen

Ich lerne gern Fremdsprachen, denn **sie sind nützlich**.
*I like learning foreign languages because they are useful.*
← *I would like to work abroad —* ich möchte im Ausland arbeiten

### Mein Lieblingsfach ist... — *My favourite subject is...*

Q&A Audio

**Question**
Was ist dein Lieblingsfach?
*What is your favourite subject?*

**Simple Answer**
Mein Lieblingsfach ist Geschichte, weil ich die Vergangenheit interessant finde.
*My favourite subject is history because I find the past interesting.*

**Extended Answer**
Ich lerne sehr gern Geschichte. Trotzdem studiere ich am liebsten Biologie, da die Wissenschaften einfach für mich sind.
*I really like studying history. Nevertheless, I like studying biology the most, as the sciences are easy for me.*

You've got to stop living in the past.

### Practice Question

Q1 You are writing an email about your school subjects. Aim to write about 90 words in German. Mention:
- the subjects you enjoy and why
- the subjects you find more difficult and why
- the subjects you liked to study last year.

WRITING

[15 marks]

**Top Tip for Higher Students**
✓ Use superlatives to talk about what you like the most or what is the most difficult, e.g. 'ich studiere am liebsten...', 'das schwerste Fach ist...'.

### German: ein Fach — German grammar: not so einfach...

Whenever you're talking about liking or not liking a particular subject, try to say just *why* you think that. You can use 'weil', 'da' and 'denn' to say 'because' — 'weil' and 'da' send verbs to the end of the clause.

# School Life

Every day's a school day, they say. Great, that's my weekend plans in the bin.

## Der Schulalltag — *School routine*

### Vocabulary

| | |
|---|---|
| die Schule | *school* |
| der Alltag | *daily routine* |
| anfangen | *to start* |
| enden | *to end, finish* |
| die Stunde | *lesson, period* |
| die Ferien | *holidays* |
| die Grundschule [H] | *primary school* |
| das Gymnasium [H] | *grammar school* |

### Grammar — verb is the second idea

In German statements, the verb is always the second idea. It isn't necessarily the second word though. See p.112 for more.

**Jede Woche habe ich Sport.**
1st idea — 2nd idea
*Every week, I have PE.*

**Um 11 Uhr gibt es eine Pause.**
1st idea — 2nd idea
*At 11 o'clock there is a break.*

**Question**
Kannst du mir deinen Schulalltag beschreiben?
*Can you describe your school routine to me?*

**Simple Answer**
Jeden Tag haben wir sechs Stunden. Die Schule endet um 16 Uhr.
*Each day we have six lessons. School ends at 4 pm.*

**Extended Answer**
Die Schule fängt um Viertel vor neun an. Wir haben Mathe und Englisch jeden Tag. Zweimal in der Woche lernen wir Erdkunde.
*School starts at quarter to nine. We have maths and English every day. Twice a week we study geography.*

Der Schultag fängt um 9 Uhr an.
*The school day starts at 9 o'clock.*

Montags in der ersten Stunde habe ich Deutsch.
*On Mondays, I have German in the first period.*

*in the second period —* in der zweiten Stunde

Am Ende des Tages habe ich Geschichte.
*At the end of the day, I have history.*

*Before the lunch break —* Vor der Mittagspause

## Der Unterricht — *Lessons*

### Vocabulary

| | | | | | |
|---|---|---|---|---|---|
| der / die Schüler(in) | *pupil, school student* | die Klasse | *class* | die Hausaufgaben | *homework* |
| | | lernen | *to learn, study* | die Aufgabe | *task, exercise* |
| der / die Student(in) | *student* | erklären | *to explain* | die Aktivität | *activity* |
| der / die Lehrer(in) | *teacher* | lesen | *to read* | das Papier | *paper* |
| das Klassenzimmer | *classroom* | schreiben | *to write* | das Blatt | *sheet* |

Für mich war die Aufgabe sehr schwierig, aber die Lehrerin hat sie deutlich erklärt.
*For me, the task was really difficult, but the teacher explained it clearly.*

*the activity —* die Aktivität

Er bittet um ein weiteres Blatt Papier, weil er viel geschrieben hat.
*He asks for another sheet of paper because he has written a lot.*

Gestern habe ich zusammen mit einem anderen Schüler die Hausaufgaben gemacht.
*Yesterday I did the homework together with another student.*

*calculations —* Berechnungen

Section Four — Education

# In der Pause — *During break*

## Vocabulary

| | | | | | |
|---|---|---|---|---|---|
| der Club | *club* | die Kantine | *canteen, cafeteria* | dauern | *to last* |
| die Mannschaft | *team* | reden | *to talk* | die Turnhalle | *gymnasium* |
| der Sportplatz | *sports pitch* | spielen | *to play* | die Sportanlage | *sports facility* |

Ich rede mit meinen Freunden in der Pause und ich esse meinen Snack.
*I talk with my friends during break and I eat my snack.*
*I meet up* — Ich treffe mich

Es gibt eine große Turnhalle in unserer Schule.
*There is a big gymnasium in our school.*
*a modern sports facility* — eine moderne Sportanlage

Ich habe die Hausaufgaben vergessen, also muss ich in der Pause arbeiten, statt Fußball zu spielen.
*I forgot my homework, so I have to work during break instead of playing football.*
*I have a detention during lunch break* — muss ich in der Mittagspause nachsitzen

In der Mittagspause esse ich in der Kantine. Danach lese ich in der Bibliothek.
*During lunch break I eat in the cafeteria. Afterwards I read in the library.*
*I go to the new sports pitch* — gehe ich zum neuen Sportplatz

## Practice Questions

**Q1** Your Swiss pen pal writes to you about their school routine. Read their letter and answer the questions.

> Der Schultag fängt um 8 Uhr an und für mich ist das sehr früh. Ich bin den ganzen Tag sehr müde. Mittwochs freue ich mich auf den Schultag, weil wir in der letzten Stunde Erdkunde haben und das ist mein Lieblingsfach. Die Mittagspause dauert eine Stunde. Für mich ist das toll, da ich langsam essen kann und danach an einem Club teilnehmen.

What do they think of different aspects of their school?
Write **P** for a positive opinion and **N** for a negative opinion.

a) The time their school day starts.
b) Their lessons on Wednesdays.
c) The length of their lunch break.

[3 marks]

Dear Swiss pen pal, please send me lots and lots of chocolate.

**Q2** Anna is being interviewed about her life at school.
There are two true statements in each list below. Choose the correct statements from each list.

a) Anna...
   A. goes to a grammar school.
   B. finds physics easy.
   C. finishes school at 1 pm.

b) Anna thinks...
   A. the school buildings look modern.
   B. the cafeteria is too small.
   C. the sports facility is great.

[4 marks]

---

## Don't forget to take regular Pausen while you're revising...

Phew, there's a whole lot to take away from these pages. It's important to give yourself regular breaks to let all that revision sink in — so kick your feet up, grab a cup of tea and think about how much you've learnt.

# School Pressures and Difficulties

sORRy, I sEem tO bE hAVIng sOmE TeChnICAl diFFICulTiEs... wHILe I wOrK oUt wHaT iS gOiNg oN hERe, wHY nOt hAvE a LOok aT sOMe sCHooL vOcAb...

## Es gibt strenge Regeln — *There are strict rules*

### Vocabulary

| | | | | | |
|---|---|---|---|---|---|
| die Regel | *rule* | müssen | *to have to, must* | verboten | *forbidden, banned* |
| streng | *strict, severe* | dürfen | *to be allowed to, may* | die Uniform | *uniform* |
| sollen | *to ought to, should* | nötig | *necessary, required* | verbieten [H] | *to forbid, prohibit, ban* |
| | | erlauben | *to allow, permit* | | |

Man darf das Handy in den Stunden nicht benutzen. Man soll auf die Lehrer hören.

*You are not allowed to use your mobile phone in lessons. You should listen to the teachers.*

Der Lehrer erlaubt uns, Wasser in der Klasse zu trinken, aber das Essen ist streng verboten.

*The teacher allows us to drink water in class, but food is strictly forbidden.*

Man muss jeden Tag pünktlich sein.

*You must be on time every day.*

### Grammar — modal verbs

Using 'man' with a modal verb is a handy way to describe rules. You'll also need a second verb that's in the infinitive — this goes at the end of the clause. See p.140 for more.

**Man darf nicht** rauchen.
**You're not allowed** to smoke.

*put on the correct uniform — die richtige Uniform anziehen*

## Schwierigkeiten in der Schule — *Difficulties at school*

### Vocabulary

| | | | | |
|---|---|---|---|---|
| das Mobbing | *bullying* | der Fehler | *mistake, error* | |
| erfolgreich | *successful* | verbessern | *to improve, correct* | |
| der Erfolg | *success* | die Herausforderung | *challenge* | [Higher] |
| sich vorbereiten (auf) | *to prepare oneself (for)* | die Fähigkeit | *ability, capability, skill* | |
| die Prüfung | *exam, test* | die Kenntnis | *knowledge* | |
| das Schulzeugnis | *report* | der Druck | *pressure, stress* | |
| die Note | *mark, grade* | bestehen | *to pass (an exam)* | |
| die Leistung | *performance, achievement* | leisten | *to perform, achieve, do* | |
| erreichen | *to achieve, reach* | sich konzentrieren (auf) | *to concentrate (on)* | |

Wir stehen unter Druck, weil wir gute Noten erreichen wollen.

*We are under pressure because we want to achieve good grades.*

*We pay attention* — Wir passen auf
*We work hard* — Wir arbeiten fleißig

Ich meine, das Mobbing ist ein großes Problem in den Schulen.

*I think bullying is a big problem in schools.*

*damages a pupil's development — schadet der Entwicklung eines Schülers*

**Question**
Was denkst du über Prüfungen?
*What do you think about exams?*

**Simple Answer**
Ich mache viele Fehler, wenn ich gestresst bin. Meiner Meinung nach sind Prüfungen unnötig.
*I make a lot of mistakes when I'm stressed. In my opinion, exams are unnecessary.*

**Extended Answer**
Ich konzentriere mich auf die Prüfungen, da ich sie bestehen will. Es ist eine Herausforderung, aber ich bin sicher, dass ich die Fähigkeit habe.
*I concentrate on my exams because I want to pass them. It's a challenge, but I'm sure that I have the ability.*

Section Four — Education

# Ich brauche Unterstützung — I need support

### Vocabulary

| | | | |
|---|---|---|---|
| die Unterstützung | support | die Erfahrung | experience |
| unterstützen | to support | das Interesse | interest |
| hilfsbereit | helpful | die Entwicklung | development |
| fragen (nach) | to ask (about) | die Verantwortung | responsibility |
| arbeiten (an [dat.]) | to work (on) | erfahren | to experience |

[Higher] applies to die Entwicklung, die Verantwortung, erfahren

Wir haben alle die Verantwortung, eine freundliche Stimmung zu schaffen. — We all have the responsibility to create a friendly atmosphere.

to be helpful and patient — hilfsbereit und geduldig zu sein

Ihre Schule bietet Unterstützung für Studenten, die Schwierigkeiten haben. — Her school provides support for students who have difficulties.

ask for help — nach Hilfe fragen

Meine Lehrer hören mir zu, wenn ich Sorgen habe. — My teachers listen to me if I have worries.

support my interests — unterstützen meine Interessen

Wenn ich die Schule schwierig finde, spreche ich mit meinen Freunden. — When I find school tough, I speak with my friends.

experience problems — Probleme erfahre

## Practice Questions

**Q1** Look at these two photos related to the topic of school pressures and difficulties. In German, say something about each of the photos. Try to talk for around one minute.

[5 marks]

Now answer the following questions in German.
- a) Wie fühlst du dich, wenn du dich auf eine Klassenarbeit vorbereitest?
- b) Wie findest du die Regeln in deiner Schule? Warum?
- c) Gibt es genug Unterstützung in deiner Schule?
- d) Was können Schüler und Lehrer tun, wenn es Mobbing in der Schule gibt?

[8 marks]

**Q2** [Higher] Translate the following sentences into German.
- a) She will get her school report in the summer.
- b) I work hard in order to be successful.
- c) We don't know whether we will achieve good grades.
- d) I am preparing for my exams.

[8 marks]

---

### This section's almost over — one less thing to stress about...

One way to put less pressure on learning German vocab is to follow the motto 'little and often'. That's ten minutes each day learning ten words — much better than cramming it all in the night before the exam.

# Education — Vocabulary

I'm not one to say what you should and shouldn't do — but you really should learn the words on these pages...

## School Subjects

|  |  |
|---|---|
| das Fach | subject |
| das Lieblingsfach | favourite subject |
| die Mathematik, die Mathe | mathematics, maths |
| die Biologie | biology |
| die Chemie | chemistry |
| die Physik | physics |
| die Wissenschaft | science |
| die Technik | technology |
| die Sprache | language |
| das Englisch | English |
| das Deutsch | German |
| das Französisch | French |
| das Spanisch | Spanish |
| die Literatur | literature |
| die Geschichte | history |
| die Erdkunde | geography |
| die Religion | religion |
| die Kunst | art |
| die Musik | music |
| das Theater | drama |
| der Sport | sport, PE |
| das Kochen | cookery |
| leicht | easy, simple |
| einfach | simple, easy simply, easily |
| schwer | difficult, hard |
| schwierig | difficult, hard, tough |
| hart | hard |
| stark | strong |
| schwach | weak |
| wichtig | important |
| praktisch | practical, useful |
| nützlich | useful |
| interessant | interesting |
| langweilig | boring |
| kreativ | creative, creatively |
| musikalisch | musical |
| wissenschaftlich | scientific |
| **H** anstrengend | exhausting, strenuous, tiring |

## School Life — School Routine and Lessons

|  |  |
|---|---|
| die Schule | school |
| der Alltag | daily routine, everyday life |
| spät | late |
| früh | early |
| pünktlich | punctual, in / on time, prompt |
| anfangen | to start |
| enden | to end, finish |
| die Stunde | lesson, period (school timetable) |
| die Ferien | holidays, school break |
| der / die Schüler(in) | pupil, school student |
| der / die Student(in) | student |
| der / die Lehrer(in) | teacher |
| der / die Direktor(in) | headteacher, principal |
| der Unterricht | lessons, classes, teaching, tuition |
| die Klasse | class |
| das Klassenzimmer | classroom |
| lernen | to learn, study |

### Vocab Test

|  |  | |
|---|---|---|
| erklären | to explain | 21 |
| lesen | to read | 21 |
| schreiben | to write | |
| wiederholen | to repeat | |
| übersetzen | to translate | |
| teilen | to divide | |
| die Hausaufgaben | homework | |
| die Aufgabe | task, exercise, assignment | |
| die Aktivität | activity | |
| die Tätigkeit | activity | |
| die Rechnung | calculation | |
| der Kurs | course | |
| das Papier | paper | |
| das Blatt | sheet | |
| die Grundschule | primary school | |
| das Gymnasium | grammar school | |
| die Übung | practice, exercise | |
| unterrichten | to teach, tutor | |
| die Erklärung | explanation | |
| der Satz | sentence, phrase | |
| bitten um | to request (+ noun), ask for (+ noun) | |

(Higher)

## School Life — During Break

| | |
|---|---|
| die Pause | break, pause |
| der Club | club |
| die Mannschaft | team |
| der Sportplatz | sports pitch |
| die Kantine | canteen, cafeteria |
| die Information | information |
| der / die Trainer(in) | coach |
| reden | to talk |
| spielen | to play |
| dauern | to last, take (time) |
| die Turnhalle | gymnasium |
| die Sportanlage [H] | sports facility |
| die Anlage | facility, complex |

## School Pressures and Difficulties

| | |
|---|---|
| die Ausbildung | training, education, development |
| die Regel | rule |
| streng | strict, severe |
| sollen | to ought to, be supposed to, should |
| müssen | to have to, must |
| dürfen | to be allowed to, may |
| nötig | necessary, required |
| erlauben | to allow, permit |
| verboten | forbidden, banned |
| die Uniform | uniform |
| das Mobbing | bullying |
| erfolgreich | successful |
| der Erfolg | success |
| das Studium | study, studies |
| sich vorbereiten (auf) | to prepare oneself (for) |
| die Prüfung | exam(ination), test |
| die Klassenarbeit | school test |
| die Antwort | answer, reply, response |
| antworten (auf) | to answer, respond, reply |
| beantworten | to answer |
| das Zeugnis | report |
| das Schulzeugnis | school report |
| die Note | mark, grade |
| die Leistung | performance, achievement |
| erreichen | to achieve, reach |
| sitzen bleiben / sitzenbleiben | to repeat a school year |
| richtig | right, correct |
| falsch | false, wrong |
| der Fehler | mistake, error |
| stimmen | to be correct |
| verbessern | to improve, correct |
| verstehen | to understand |
| üben | to practise |
| die Unterstützung | support |
| unterstützen | to support |
| hilfsbereit | helpful, co-operative |
| die Hilfe | help, assistance |
| fragen (nach) | to ask (about) |
| sich fragen | to wonder |
| die Arbeit | work |
| arbeiten (an [dat.]) | to work (on) |

*The noun 'Jugendliche' acts like an adjective, so the ending changes depending on gender and the article you use. See more on p.123.*

| | |
|---|---|
| der / die Jugendliche | (the) young person, adolescent |
| ein Jugendlicher / eine Jugendliche | (a) young person, adolescent |
| Jugendliche | young people |
| die Jugendlichen | (the) young people |
| jung | young |
| die Erfahrung | experience |
| das Interesse | interest |
| die Bildung | education, learning |
| bilden | to educate |
| verbieten | to forbid, prohibit, ban |
| die Herausforderung | challenge |
| das Abitur | school leaving exams, A levels |
| untersuchen | to examine, research |
| prüfen | to examine, check |
| der Versuch | attempt, experiment |
| abgeben | to give in, hand in, submit |
| das Ergebnis | result, outcome |
| erhalten | to receive |
| die Fähigkeit | ability, capability, skill |
| die Kenntnis | knowledge |
| der Druck | pressure, stress |
| bestehen | to pass (an exam) |
| leisten | to perform, achieve, do |
| aufpassen | to pay attention, take care |
| konzentrieren (auf) | to concentrate (on) |
| sich konzentrieren (auf) | to concentrate (on) |
| die Entwicklung | development |
| die Verantwortung | responsibility |
| die Diskussion | discussion, debate |
| der Austausch | exchange, replacement |
| erfahren | to experience, find out |

[Higher]

Nick is concentrating on his Biscuit Criticism exam.

*You'll mostly use the reflexive verb 'sich konzentrieren', e.g. when you want to say that you're focusing on something: 'Ich konzentriere mich auf meine Arbeit.'*

# Revision Summary Test for Section Four

I've just checked your timetable and it looks like you're scheduled for a Revision Summary Test...
- These questions are **hard**, but they'll really help you see **how well you know your stuff**.
- Tackle the **revision summary test** below, or scan the QR code to do it **online**.
  You can **track your progress** online and see **which areas need more work**.
- There are **sample answers** for the test here: www.cgpbooks.co.uk/BerlinExtras

## School Subjects
1) List all the school subjects you can remember. There are 20 in this section.
2) Jahi asks: 'Was ist dein Lieblingsfach? Warum?' What has he asked you? Answer him in German.
3) Give one synonym for each of these words: a) einfach  b) schwer  c) nützlich
4) Say these words in German: a) boring  b) strong  c) weak  d) hard  e) creative  f) musical
5) Write about a school subject that you studied in the past and what you thought of it.
6) [H] List these words in English: a) wissenschaftlich  b) anstrengend

## School Life
7) Choose a school day and describe your routine for that day in German.
8) What does 'Wir machen die Rechnungen für die Aufgabe auf einem Blatt Papier.' mean in English?
9) How would you say 'I am always late' in German? How about early? And on time?
10) Give two words for 'student' in German. Write the masculine and feminine versions of each one.
11) In class, Lena asks: 'Ich verstehe das nicht. Können Sie das wiederholen?' What does this mean?
12) Say these words in English: a) erklären  b) lernen  c) schreiben  d) übersetzen  e) teilen
13) 'Der Unterricht' has four meanings in English. What are they?
14) Was machst du in der Mittagspause? Answer this question in German.
15) Name the two types of school you can find in this section.
16) [H] Beschreib die Anlage in deiner Schule.

## School Pressures and Difficulties
17) 'Gibt es strenge Regeln in deiner Schule?' Say this in English, then in German list three
    school rules, each starting with one of these phrases: a) Man darf  b) Man soll  c) Man muss
18) Translate this into English: 'Ich habe in der Klassenarbeit viele Fehler gemacht.
    Ich glaube, dass ich Unterstützung brauche.'
19) What are the opposites of these words in German?  a) richtig  b) fragen nach
20) Was denkst du über Prüfungen? Answer in German.
21) What are these words in English?
    a) sitzen bleiben  b) der Erfolg  c) die Leistung  d) erlauben  e) stimmen  f) die Erfahrung
22) Translate 'I improved my work and I achieved good grades in my school report.' into German.
23) In German, write about problems in your school, giving at least two examples.
24) What are these words in German?
    a) to concentrate on  b) ability  c) knowledge  d) to receive  e) attempt  f) exchange
25) [Higher] You want to tell your friend you passed a school test. What would be the correct thing to say?
    a) Ich untersuche das Thema für die Diskussion.
    b) Ich habe die Klassenarbeit bestanden.
    c) Ich gebe die Prüfung ab.
26) In German, describe two pressures young people experience in school.

# Section Five — Future Study and Work

## Education Post-16

Quick Quiz

There's loads you can do once school is over. Just take a look below — your future awaits...

### Nach der Schule — *After school*

Remember there's also lots of online content here: www.cgpbooks.co.uk/Berlin

**Vocabulary**

| | | | |
|---|---|---|---|
| die Ausbildung | *training, education* | die Note | *mark, grade* |
| die Universität, die Uni | *university* | verlassen | *to leave* |
| das Studium | *study, studies* | entscheiden | *to decide* |
| der / die Student(in) | *student* | die Möglichkeit | *opportunity* |
| der Kurs | *course* | die Oberstufe | *sixth form* (Higher) |
| studieren | *to study (at university)* | das Abitur | *A levels* |
| lernen | *to learn, study* | die Lehre | *apprenticeship* |

Ich werde die Schule verlassen, denn ich möchte praktische Erfahrung bekommen.
*I am going to leave school because I want to gain practical experience.*

Ich möchte in der Ausbildung bleiben, um meine Berufsmöglichkeiten zu erhöhen.
*I would like to stay in education to increase my job opportunities.*

Nach dem Abitur werde ich auf die Uni gehen, um Biologie zu studieren.
*After my A levels, I will go to uni to study biology.*

*to work voluntarily* — ehrenamtlich arbeiten

*to attend a course* — einen Kurs besuchen

*study abroad* — im Ausland studieren

Q&A Audio

**Question**
Was wirst du nach den Prüfungen machen?
*What will you do after your exams?*

**Simple Answer**
Ich möchte Erdkunde an der Universität studieren.
*I would like to study geography at university.*

**Extended Answer**
Zuerst habe ich vor, ein Jahr im Ausland zu verbringen, weil ich unbedingt reisen will. Danach werde ich wahrscheinlich eine Lehre machen.
*Firstly, I'm planning to spend a year abroad because I really want to travel. After that, I will probably do an apprenticeship.*

### Practice Question

Q1 Look at the two photos below. Talk in German about what is in the photos. You should talk for about a minute and say something about both photos.

SPEAKING

**Top Tip for Higher Students**
✓ Use Higher-tier vocab to talk about what you see, e.g. 'die Lehre' and 'die Gelegenheit'.

[5 marks]

---

### My plans for after school? Watch telly with a brew, probably...

When describing photos, you'll get marks for using any relevant vocab, not just the vocab in this section. Luckily, this book is packed with vocab you could use for all sorts of photos — don't say I don't spoil you.

**Quick Quiz**

# Career Choices and Ambitions

What do I want to be when I grow up? No idea. But I do want a briefcase — ideally full of cake.

## Die Berufe — *Professions*

**Vocabulary**

| | | | |
|---|---|---|---|
| arbeiten | *to work* | der / die Betreuer(in) | *carer, care worker* |
| die Arbeit | *work, employment* | der / die Polizist(in) | *police officer* |
| der Job | *job* | der / die Journalist(in) | *journalist* |
| der Beruf | *occupation, profession* | der / die Direktor(in) | *director (of a company)* |
| die Stelle | *job, position* | | |
| die Karriere | *career* | der / die Sänger(in) | *singer* |
| arbeitslos | *unemployed* | der / die Schauspieler(in) | *actor* |
| der / die Verkäufer(in) | *shop assistant, salesperson* | der / die Künstler(in) | *artist, performer* |
| | | [Higher] der Bauer / die Bäuerin | *farmer* |
| der Arzt / die Ärztin | *doctor* | der / die Wissenschaftler(in) | *scientist* |
| der / die Trainer(in) | *coach* | der Anwalt / die Anwältin | *lawyer, solicitor* |

**Grammar — jobs and genders**

With German job titles, you have to show whether the person is a <u>man</u> or a <u>woman</u>. You often add '<u>-in</u>' to the masculine form to show you're talking about a woman.

<u>der</u> Verkäufer    <u>die</u> Verkäufer<u>in</u>
*shop assistant (m)*    *shop assistant (f)*

Meine Mutter ist Direktorin von einer großen Firma.
*My mother is the director of a big company.*

Meine Eltern arbeiten beide im Rathaus.
*My parents both work in the town hall.*

## Was ist dein Traumjob? — *What is your dream job?*

Ich suche eine Stelle als Bauer, weil ich draußen arbeiten will.
*I'm looking for a position as a farmer because I want to work outside.*

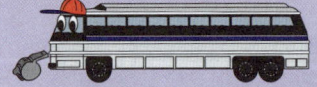
with animals — mit Tieren
in the fresh air — im Frischen

Ich möchte Trainer werden, weil ich Bewegung liebe.
*I would like to become a coach because I love exercise.*

In der Zukunft möchte ich Ärztin werden, obwohl der Beruf viele Herausforderungen hat.
*In the future, I'd like to become a doctor, although the profession has lots of challenges.*

You don't usually use an article like 'ein' or 'der' when you talk about jobs in German.

**Q&A Audio**

**Question**

Was willst du als Beruf machen?
*What do you want to do for a living?*

**Simple Answer**

In der Zukunft will ich Sängerin sein.
*In the future, I want to be a singer.*

**Extended Answer**

Im Moment habe ich einen Teilzeitjob bei einer Fabrik, aber nach dem Studium will ich Anwalt werden, um einen besseren Lohn zu verdienen.
*At the moment, I have a part-time job in a factory, but after my studies I want to become a lawyer in order to earn a better wage.*

**Grammar — 'in der Zukunft'**

Use the phrase '<u>in der Zukunft</u>' to say what you want to do '<u>in the future</u>'. You often use it with verbs like '<u>werde</u>', '<u>will</u>' and '<u>möchte</u>'. Remember to send the second verb in the clause to the end.

<u>In der Zukunft werde ich</u> in einem Büro arbeiten.
*<u>In the future, I will</u> work in an office.*

# Bei der Arbeit — At work

## Vocabulary

|  |  |
|---|---|
| der / die Chef(in) | boss |
| der Kollege / die Kollegin | colleague |
| der Arbeitsplatz | workplace |
| das Büro | office |
| das Geschäft | business, shop |
| die Firma | firm, company |
| die Erfahrung | experience |
| die Aufgabe | job, duty, task |
| verdienen | to earn |
| der / die Arbeitgeber(in) | employer *(Higher)* |
| der / die Arbeitnehmer(in) | employee *(Higher)* |
| die Fabrik | factory *(Higher)* |
| das Vorstellungsgespräch | job interview *(Higher)* |
| die Zusammenarbeit | cooperation, teamwork *(Higher)* |
| der Lohn | wage, pay, salary *(Higher)* |
| besitzen | to own *(Higher)* |
| gelingen | to succeed *(Higher)* |

Abends arbeite ich als Kellnerin in einem Hotel. — *In the evening, I work as a waitress in a hotel.*

Ich arbeite Teilzeit in einem Büro. — *I work part-time in an office.*

Ich habe einen Wochenendjob in einer Bäckerei. Ich muss in Schichten arbeiten. — *I have a weekend job in a bakery. I have to work shifts.*

Nächste Woche habe ich ein Vorstellungsgespräch bei einer Fabrik, um Arbeitserfahrung zu bekommen. — *Next week, I have a job interview at a factory to get work experience.*

It was only her first day, but Aleyna was already on a roll.

do a work placement — ein Praktikum zu machen

## Practice Questions

**Q1** Write a blog post of 90 words about jobs and careers. Write something about each bullet point. Mention:
- a job someone in your family does
- your experience of work in the past
- what your dream job would be in the future.

**Top Tip for Higher Students**
✓ Use conjunctions like 'weder... noch' (neither... nor) and 'ob' (whether, if) to develop your answers.

*WRITING* [15 marks]

**Q2** Read this passage about Nils's job and answer the questions below. *(Higher)*

> In den Sommerferien habe ich einen Teilzeitjob als Verkäufer bekommen, damit ich Geld für mein Jahr im Ausland verdienen konnte. Ich hatte viel zu tun und ich habe es geliebt, viel mit meinen Kunden zu sprechen. Da ich viele Aufgaben hatte, bin ich oft unter Druck gewesen und ich habe mich am Ende des Tages sehr müde gefühlt. Die Erfahrung war sehr gut, aber jetzt weiß ich, dass ich keinen Vollzeitjob haben will. Es wäre aber toll, für mich selbst zu arbeiten.

a) Why did Nils get a job? [1 mark]
b) Why did Nils feel tired? Give **one** detail. [1 mark]
c) What does Nils say about work in the future? Give **two** details. [2 marks]

## Professional napper — a real dream job...

When talking about careers, don't worry if you don't have plans yet — just make something up. You could tell your examiner you want to be an aardvark tamer — if your German is correct, you'll get the marks.

# Future Study and Work — Vocabulary

I'm actually a time traveller, here to pass on a message from your future self — you said you should learn this vocab.

## Education Post-16

| | |
|---|---|
| die Ausbildung | training, education, development |
| die Universität, die Uni | university |
| das Studium | study, studies |
| der / die Student(in) | student |
| der Kurs | course |
| studieren | to study (at university) |
| lernen | to learn, study |
| die Note | mark, grade |
| verlassen | to leave |
| entscheiden | to decide |
| sich entscheiden (für) | to decide (on) |

| | |
|---|---|
| wählen | to choose, select |
| die Wahl | choice, selection |
| die Chance | chance, opportunity |
| die Möglichkeit | possibility, chance, opportunity |
| praktisch | practical, useful |
| träumen | to dream |
| **Higher**: die Oberstufe | sixth form |
| das Abitur | school leaving exam, A levels |
| der Abschluss | school leaving certificate, degree, diploma |
| die Lehre | apprenticeship |
| die Gelegenheit | opportunity, chance |

## Career Choices and Ambitions

| | |
|---|---|
| arbeiten | to work |
| die Arbeit | work, job, employment |
| der Job | job |
| der Beruf | occupation, job, profession |
| die Stelle | job, position |
| die Rolle | role |
| die Karriere | career |
| arbeitslos | unemployed |
| der / die Verkäufer(in) | shop assistant, sales person |
| der Arzt / die Ärztin | doctor |
| der / die Trainer(in) | coach |
| der / die Betreuer(in) | carer, care worker |
| der / die Polizist(in) | police officer |
| der / die Journalist(in) | journalist |
| der / die Direktor(in) | director (of a company) |
| der / die Sänger(in) | singer |
| der / die Schauspieler(in) | actor |
| der / die Künstler(in) | artist, performer |
| der Traum | dream |
| die Zukunft | future |
| das Ziel | goal, aim, target |
| suchen | to look for |
| der / die Chef(in) | boss |
| der Kollege / die Kollegin | colleague |
| der / die Mitarbeiter(in) | employee, co-worker, colleague |
| der Kunde / die Kundin | customer, client |
| der Arbeitsplatz | workplace, job, employment |
| das Büro | office |

| | |
|---|---|
| das Geschäft | business, shop |
| die Firma | firm, company, business |
| die Firmen | firms, companies, businesses |
| die Erfahrung | experience |
| die Aufgabe | job, duty, task |
| verdienen | to earn |
| die Arbeitslosigkeit | unemployment |
| der Bauer / die Bäuerin | farmer |
| der / die Wissenschaftler(in) | scientist |
| der Anwalt / die Anwältin | lawyer, solicitor |
| der / die Arbeitgeber(in) | employer |
| der / die Arbeitnehmer(in) | employee, worker |
| beschäftigen | to employ |
| die Industrie | industry |
| das Unternehmen | company, firm |
| die Organisation | organisation |
| die Gesellschaft | company |
| die Fabrik | factory |
| **Higher**: das Werk | work, plant, factory |
| die Maschine | machine |
| das Vorstellungsgespräch | job interview |
| die Zusammenarbeit | cooperation, teamwork |
| die Entwicklung | development |
| die Tätigkeit | work, occupation |
| der Lohn | wage, pay, salary |
| das Gehalt | salary, pay, wages, earnings |
| sich beschäftigen (mit) | to be busy (with) |
| besitzen | to own |
| gelingen | to succeed |
| handeln | to deal, trade |
| vorhaben | to be planning, have in mind, intend |

# Revision Summary Test for Section Five

Your work for this section is almost done — just a few summary questions and then you're off-duty.
- Yep, these questions are **hard** — they'll really help you see **how well you know your stuff**.
- Tackle the **revision summary test** below, or scan the QR code to do it **online**. Use the CGP RevisionHub to **track your progress** and see **which areas need more work**.
- You can find **sample answers** here: www.cgpbooks.co.uk/BerlinExtras

## Education Post-16

1) What do these words mean in English?  a) die Note   b) entscheiden   c) das Studium
2) Answer the following question in German.  Was für eine Ausbildung möchtest du nach deinen Prüfungen machen?  Warum?
3) Translate these words into German:  a) practical   b) choice   c) to dream   d) to choose
4) Translate the following sentence into English.  'Wenn ich die Schule verlasse, möchte ich einen Universitätskurs anfangen, zum Beispiel Biologie.'
5) Answer the following question in German. Was sind die Vorteile und Nachteile von der Universität?
6) List the German words that mean 'opportunity'. There are 2 you need to know (plus 1 for Higher tier).
7) Translate these words into German:  a) A levels   b) diploma   c) apprenticeship

## Career Choices and Ambitions

8) Translate these words into English:  a) die Aufgabe   b) der Traum   c) das Ziel
9) Was möchtest du gern als Beruf machen?  Answer in German, including two reasons.
10) There are 11 job titles you need to know in German (plus 3 for Higher tier). How many can you name?  Give the masculine and feminine forms for each one.
11) Translate this into English, then answer it in German: 'Was ist dir für eine Karriere wichtig?'
12) 'In meiner neuen Rolle werde ich mit vielen Kunden arbeiten.'  How would you say this in English?
13) 'I earn nothing because I'm unemployed.  I'm looking for work, but it's difficult because I have no experience.'  Translate this into German.
14) 'Where do you work?'  Say this in German and then list as many German words for places you might work as you can remember.  There are 5 you need to know (plus 5 for Higher tier).
15) In German, write down at least one synonym for each of these words. a) der Kollege   b) die Stelle
16) Translate these sentences into English.  'In der Zukunft habe ich vor, ein Unternehmen zu besitzen.  Ich möchte Arbeitgeber werden, und ich will viele Leute beschäftigen.  Dazu möchte ich unabhängig sein und ein höheres Gehalt verdienen.'
17) What is the German for these words?  a) industry   b) to deal   c) machine   d) interview
18) Würdest du lieber in einem Büro arbeiten, oder etwas Praktisches machen?  Warum?  Answer this question in German.

# Section Six — Free-time Activities

## Cinema and TV

Quick Quiz

Binge-watching a show might be fun, but binge-revising German is better.

*Don't forget you can access your online content here: www.cgpbooks.co.uk/Berlin*

### Die Filme — Films

**Vocabulary**

| | | | |
|---|---|---|---|
| der Film | *film, movie* | streamen | *to stream* |
| das Kino | *cinema, movies, pictures* | sehen | *to watch, see* |
| das Ticket | *ticket* | ansehen | *to watch, look at* |
| der Krimi | *thriller, detective film* | der Inhalt (Higher) | *content, plot* |
| die Komödie | *comedy* | die Werbung (Higher) | *advert* |
| der Liebesfilm | *romantic film* | die Spannung (Higher) | *suspense, tension* |
| spannend | *exciting, thrilling* | anschauen (Higher) | *to watch, look at* |

Sie haben den Krimi spannend gefunden, aber ich habe gedacht, dass er langweilig war. Komödien gefallen mir besser.

*They found the detective film thrilling but I thought it was boring. I like comedies better.*

- action films — Actionfilme
- dramas — Dramen

Der Film handelt von einer Frau, die die Welt vor einer großen Gefahr rettet.

*The film is about a woman who saves the world from a great danger.*

- a family that goes on holiday — einer Familie, die in den Urlaub fährt

**Q&A Audio**

**Question**
Was für Filme siehst du gern an?
*What kind of films do you like to watch?*

**Simple Answer**
Ich sehe gern Krimis an, weil die Geschichte immer spannend ist.
*I like to watch crime films because the story is always exciting.*

**Extended Answer**
Fantasyfilme gefallen mir, weil die Filmmusik immer beeindruckend ist. Ich würde dagegen keine romantische Komödie sehen, da der Inhalt blöd ist.
*I like fantasy films because the soundtrack is always impressive. On the other hand, I wouldn't watch a romantic comedy because the plot is stupid.*

### Gehst du gern ins Kino? — Do you like going to the cinema?

Jetzt gehe ich nie ins Kino, weil ich viele Filme online streame.

*Now I never go to the cinema because I stream lots of films online.*

- only watch TV — nur fernsehe

Obwohl ich die Werbungen ärgerlich finde, gehe ich gern ins Kino. Es gibt immer eine spannende Stimmung.

*Although I find the adverts annoying, I like going to the cinema. There's always an exciting atmosphere.*

- the snacks expensive — die Snacks teuer

Ich gehe häufig mit meiner Familie ins Kino. Es gibt Tickets im Angebot für große Gruppen.

*I often go to the cinema with my family. There are tickets on offer for big groups.*

- with my friends — mit meinen Freunden

**Grammar — ins / im Kino**

'In' is a preposition. It can take the accusative or the dative case.
If there's movement, use the accusative. 'Ins' is short for 'in das'.
    Wir gehen ins Kino.   *We're going to the cinema.*
If there's no movement, use the dative. 'Im' is short for 'in dem'.
    Wir sind im Kino.   *We're in the cinema.*
See p.116-118 for more on cases and prepositions.

*Samantha hates films. She only watches them for the popcorn.*

# Das Fernsehen — *Television*

## Vocabulary

| | | | |
|---|---|---|---|
| das Fernsehen | *television* | die Seifenoper | *soap opera / series* |
| fernsehen | *to watch television* | die Serie | *series* |
| die Sendung | *programme* | die Folge | *(TV) episode* |
| das Programm | *(TV) channel* | darstellen | *to depict, portray, show, represent* |
| die Nachrichten | *the news* | | |

(die Serie, die Folge, darstellen — Higher)

Mein Bruder sieht gern die Nachrichten, aber ich würde lieber einen Krimi sehen.

*My brother likes watching the news, but I would rather watch a crime show.*

Ich sehe dreimal in der Woche mit meiner Familie eine bekannte Seifenoper.

*I watch a well-known soap opera with my family three times in the week.*

Diese Serie stellt alle Arten von Menschen dar. Ich finde das echt wichtig.

*This series depicts all kinds of people. I find that really important.*

Ich schaue lieber Programme an, die keine Werbungen zeigen.

*I prefer to watch channels that don't show adverts.*

a quiz show — eine Quizsendung
a reality show — eine Reality-Show

### Grammar — fernsehen

'Fernsehen' *(to watch TV)* is a separable verb. It splits into two parts — 'fern' and 'sehen'.

**Ich sehe fern.**
*I watch TV.*

If it's used in the infinitive form, it's not separated.

**Ich will fernsehen.**
*I want to watch TV.*

See p.139 for more.

## Practice Questions

**Q1** Write an article about the TV shows and films you watch. You should write around 90 words in German. Describe:
- your favourite film
- something you recently watched on TV
- when you will next go to the cinema.   [15 marks]

*WRITING*

**Top Tip for Higher Students**
✓ Use the simple past tense when talking about what you watched on TV.

**Q2** Read Marlene's opinions about TV, then answer the questions below in English. *(Higher)*

> Ich sehe regelmäßig fern, meistens abends oder am Wochenende. Am liebsten sehe ich Quizsendungen, weil sie mich unterhalten. Leider gibt es auch viele langweilige Sendungen im Fernsehen, zum Beispiel die Nachrichten oder Sportsendungen, die mich überhaupt nicht interessieren. Die Werbungen gehen mir auf die Nerven. Ich verlasse das Wohnzimmer, wenn es eine Werbepause* gibt. Meine Schwester sitzt stundenlang vor dem Fernseher, deswegen sorgt sich meine Mutter, dass sie fernsehsüchtig ist.

*Werbepause — ad break

a) Why does Marlene like to watch quiz shows the most?   [1 mark]
b) Which **two** types of TV programme don't interest Marlene at all?   [2 marks]
c) What does Marlene do when adverts come on the TV?   [1 mark]
d) Why does Marlene's mum think her sister is addicted to the TV?   [1 mark]

## Soap operas — not the good, clean entertainment I hoped for...

Lots of film and TV genres in German are super similar to the English — 'Fantasyfilm', 'Dokumentarfilm' and 'Komödie' mean exactly what they say on the tin, which is pretty handy when you're learning all this vocab.

# Music

I should warn you that this page might get stuck in your head like ein Ohrwurm*.  Sounds painful.

 **Die Musik** — *Music*

## Vocabulary

|  |  |
|---|---|
| singen | *to sing* |
| das Lied | *song* |
| hören | *to listen* |
| herunterladen | *to download* |
| der Rock | *rock music* |
| klassisch | *classical* |
| musikalisch | *musical* |
| die Band | *band, group* |
| die Gruppe | *group, band* |
| spielen | *to play* |
| lernen | *to learn, study* |
| das Instrument | *instrument* |
| das Konzert | *concert* |
| klingen | *to sound* |

### Grammar — 'used to...'

You can use the perfect tense and 'früher' *(before, earlier)* to say what you used to do regularly.

**Früher habe** ich Klavier **gespielt.**
*I used to play the piano.*

See p.133 for more on the perfect tense.

 **Q&A Audio**

**Question**
Spielst du ein Instrument?
*Do you play an instrument?*

**Simple Answer**
Ich spiele kein Instrument. Früher habe ich Gitarre gespielt.
*I don't play an instrument. I used to play the guitar.*

**Extended Answer**
Ich spiele seit vier Jahren Querflöte. Als ich jünger war, habe ich Klarinette gespielt. Früher habe ich auch in einem Chor gesungen.
*I've been playing the flute for four years. When I was younger, I played the clarinet. I also used to sing in a choir.*

## Ich höre gern... — *I like listening to...*

Jeden Tag höre ich Musik **auf meinem Handy**.
*Every day I listen to music **on my mobile phone**.*
- on the radio — im Radio

Ich höre klassische Musik, wenn ich **nicht einschlafen kann**.
*I listen to classical music, when I **can't fall asleep**.*
- want to relax — mich entspannen will

Ich mag **sowohl Jazzmusik als auch Techno**. Mein Bruder liebt nur **Rockmusik**.
*I like **both jazz and techno**. My brother only loves **rock music**.*
- rap — Rapmusik
- indie music — Indie

Meine Schwester meint, dass Opernmusik **schön klingt**.
*My sister thinks that opera music **sounds lovely**.*
- is the worst music genre — das schlechteste Musikgenre ist

### Practice Question

Q1 A group of friends are talking about the role of music in their lives. Match each of them with **one** of the statements from the list.

a) Preethi...  A. ...prefers classical music.  D. ...plays in a band.
b) Jürgen...   B. ...played an instrument as a child.  E. ...will start music lessons.
c) Frieda...   C. ...has never been to a concert.  F. ...went to a rock concert.

[3 marks]

Listening Track 8

---

### Not to blow my own trumpet, but I'm the star of my brass band...

It'd be boring to use 'ich mag' all the time to talk about music you like — 'gern', 'lieber' and 'gefallen' are all great phrases to mix up your German a bit more. So put those 'like' phrases on shuffle and away you go.

*an earworm

# Sport

Quick Quiz

Even if you peaked in your Year 4 egg-and-spoon race, learning this page will make you a winner.

## Sport treiben — *To do sport*

### Vocabulary

| | | | |
|---|---|---|---|
| der Sport | *sport* | der Wettbewerb | *competition, contest* |
| die Mannschaft | *team* | das Spiel | *game, match* |
| der Fußball | *football, soccer* | gewinnen | *to win* |
| der Basketball | *basketball* | verlieren | *to lose* |
| das Tennis | *tennis* | teilnehmen (an [+ dat.]) | *to take part (in)* |
| das Fahrrad | *bicycle* | der / die Gegner(in) | *opponent, competitor* |
| schwimmen | *to swim* | klettern | *to climb* |

Q&A Audio

### Question
Wie oft treibst du Sport?
*How often do you do sport?*

### Simple Answer
Ich treibe ziemlich selten Sport, aber ich wandere gern. Es ist eine wunderbare Aktivität.
*I don't do sport very often, but I like hiking. It is a wonderful activity.*

### Grammar — word order

Word order stays the same with coordinating conjunctions, e.g. 'aber' (but).

**Ich mag Fußball, aber ich finde Tennis langweilig.**
*I like football, but I find tennis boring.*

Word order changes with subordinating conjunctions, e.g. 'weil' (because). The verb moves to the end.

**Ich mag Fußball, weil es spannend ist.**
*I like football because it is exciting.*

For more on word order, see p.112.

### Extended Answer
Ich bin Mitglied einer Fußballmannschaft. Wir machen dreimal in der Woche Training und jeden zweiten Samstag haben wir ein Spiel. Letztes Mal haben wir gewonnen und ich habe ein Tor geschossen.
*I'm a member of a football team. We train three times a week and every other Saturday we have a match. Last time, we won and I scored a goal.*

Bevor ich an einem Wettbewerb teilnehme, habe ich immer Angst.
*Before I take part in a competition, I'm always anxious.*

*I'm usually excited* — bin ich normalerweise begeistert

Ich möchte zu einem Tanzclub gehen.
*I would like to go to a dance club.*

*cycling club* — Fahrradverein

Obwohl ich gern Fußball im Fernsehen sehe, treibe ich keinen Sport.
*Although I like watching football on TV, I don't do any sport.*

*the Olympics* — die Olympischen Spiele

### Practice Question

Q1 Translate the following sentences into English.
 a) Ich genieße Fußball, aber Tennis ist besser.
 b) Die Mannschaft gewinnt fast jedes Spiel.
 c) Nächstes Jahr werde ich an einem Wettbewerb teilnehmen.  [6 marks]

## Competitive queueing — now there's a sport I can get behind...

Watch out for verbs that look separable but aren't, e.g. 'verlieren' and 'gewinnen'. Verbs beginning with be-, er-, ge- or ver- are all inseparable verbs — the prefixes just won't leave the main part of the verb alone.

# Going Out and Other Hobbies

I know how much you love revising German, but it's important to take some time off as well — there's loads more hobbies here, so I'll be impressed if you can't find something you like.

## Ausgehen — *To go out*

### Vocabulary

| | | | | | |
|---|---|---|---|---|---|
| treffen | *to meet* | kosten | *to cost* | das Restaurant | *restaurant* |
| sich treffen | *to meet up, get together* | die Kosten | *costs, expenses* | die Speisekarte | *menu* |
| einkaufen | *to shop* | Lust auf (+ noun) haben | *to feel like (+ noun)* | die Rechnung | *bill* |
| bezahlen | *to pay* | das Geschäft | *business, shop* | das Museum | *museum* |
| ausgeben | *to spend (money)* | besuchen | *to visit* | probieren | *to try, sample* |
| | | | | die Museen | *museums* |

(H) die Museen

Ich treffe mich mit Freunden und wir gehen einkaufen.
*I meet up with friends and we go shopping.*

buy clothes — kaufen Kleidung

Nach unserem Museumsbesuch sind wir zu einem Café gegangen, denn ich hatte Lust auf einen Kaffee.
*After our visit to the museum we went to a café because I felt like a coffee.*

You can use 'Lust auf (+ noun) haben' to say what you feel like having.

### Grammar — Ich gehe einkaufen

In German, instead of saying 'I go shopping', you say 'I go to shop'. You need to put 'gehen' in the right form for the person and 'einkaufen' in the infinitive (the form ending in '-en').

Ich gehe + einkaufen = Ich gehe einkaufen.    *I go shopping.*

## Kunst und Theater — *Art and theatre*

### Vocabulary

| | | | | |
|---|---|---|---|---|
| die Kunst | *art* | sich interessieren für | *to be interested in* | |
| die Kultur | *culture* | die Veranstaltung | *performance* | |
| das Theater | *theatre, drama* | die Bühne | *stage* | (Higher) |
| das Stück | *play* | malen | *to paint* | |
| kreativ | *creative, creatively* | zeichnen | *to draw* | |

**Question**
Spielst du Theater?
*Do you do drama?*

**Simple Answer**
Nein, ich spiele kein Theater. Ich bin kein Schauspieler. Jedoch mag ich Theaterstücke ansehen.
*No, I don't do drama. I'm no actor. However, I like watching plays.*

**Extended Answer**
Ich liebe Theater! Ich gehöre einem Theaterclub an und in der nächsten Veranstaltung habe ich die Hauptrolle, was mich sehr freut. Ich fühle mich auf der Bühne zu Hause.
*I love drama! I belong to a drama club and in the next performance I have the main role, which makes me very happy. I feel at home on the stage.*

Ich interessiere mich sehr für dieses Stück, weil die Schauspieler bekannt sind.
*I am very interested in this play because the actors are famous.*

it has fantastic reviews — es fantastische Kritiken hat

Mein Bruder ist wirklich kreativ. Er zeichnet täglich, um seine Fähigkeiten zu verbessern.
*My brother is really creative. He draws daily in order to improve his skills.*

paints — malt

# Andere Aktivitäten — Other activities

## Vocabulary

| | | | |
|---|---|---|---|
| die Freizeit | spare time, free time | der Spaß | fun |
| frei | free, available | die Party | party |
| lesen | to read | kochen | to cook |
| das Buch | book | schreiben (an) | to write (to) |
| der Roman | novel | sich entspannen | to relax, chill out |
| der Krimi | detective story | sich amüsieren | to enjoy oneself, have a good time |
| die Zeitung | newspaper | | |
| das Videospiel | video game | sich unterhalten | to amuse oneself, chat |
| der Computer | computer | sich melden | to volunteer, enlist |

(Higher: sich entspannen, sich amüsieren, sich unterhalten, sich melden)

In meiner Freizeit lese ich gern, denn es ist entspannend. Im Moment lese ich einen Liebesroman.

*In my free time I like to read because it is relaxing. At the moment I'm reading a romance novel.*

- a murder mystery — eine Kriminalgeschichte
- an adventure story — eine Abenteuergeschichte

Ich liebe Gartenarbeit. Ich habe eine Gruppe gegründet, die sich um die Blumen im Park kümmert.

*I love gardening. I have established a group that looks after the flowers in the park.*

Die Party hat viel Spaß gemacht. Ich habe getanzt und ich habe mich wirklich amüsiert.

*The party was a lot of fun. I danced and I really enjoyed myself.*

To say something is fun in German, you use the phrase 'Spaß machen' ('to make fun').

Videospiele gefallen mir. Beim Spielen kann ich mich entspannen.

*I like video games. While playing I can relax.*

amuse myself for hours — mich stundenlang unterhalten

## Practice Questions

**Q1** Look at the two photos below. Talk in German about what is in the photos. You should talk for about a minute and say something about both photos. [SPEAKING]

Top Tip for Higher Students
✓ Expand your answers with a relative clause beginning with 'wo' or 'was'.

[5 marks]

**Q2** Listen to what these teenagers say they do in their free time and then answer the questions below. [LISTENING] (Higher)

a) What does Michael like to read?
b) Why does Sabriye say that she draws a lot?
c) How does Yannick feel when he's working in the garden?
d) What does Greta find irritating about video games?

[4 marks]

Listening Track 9

---

## Lust auf einen Kaffee? I'll avert my eyes, if you don't mind...

To bag the top marks, don't just talk about the here and now. You could also say what you used to do, or what you'd like to do in the future (maybe after all these exams are done and dusted — ah, sweet freedom).

*Find the CGP RevisionHub at cgpbooks.co.uk/Berlin*

Section Six — Free-time Activities

# Free-time Activities — Vocabulary

Here are a couple of pages full of vocab about hobbies — what could be more fun...

## Cinema and TV

| | |
|---|---|
| der Film | film, movie |
| das Kino | cinema, movies, pictures |
| das Ticket | ticket |
| die Karte | ticket |
| der Krimi | thriller, detective film, crime film |
| die Komödie | comedy |
| der Liebesfilm | romantic film |
| spannend | exciting, thrilling |
| aufregend | exciting, thrilling |
| streamen | to stream |
| sehen | to watch, see |
| ansehen | to watch, look at |
| sich [dat.] ansehen | to watch, look at |
| das Fernsehen | television |

| | |
|---|---|
| fernsehen | to watch television |
| die Sendung | programme |
| das Programm | (TV) channel |
| die Nachrichten | the news |
| die Seifenoper | soap opera / series |

**Higher:**

| | |
|---|---|
| anschauen | to watch, look at |
| gucken, kucken | to watch, look |
| der Inhalt | content, plot |
| die Werbung | advert, advertisement |
| die Spannung | suspense, tension |
| die Serie | series |
| die Folge | (TV) episode |
| darstellen | to depict, portray, show, represent |

## Music

| | |
|---|---|
| die Musik | music |
| die Note | (musical) note |
| singen | to sing |
| das Lied | song |
| hören | to listen |
| herunterladen | to download |

| | |
|---|---|
| der Rock | rock music |
| klassisch | classical |
| musikalisch | musical |
| die Band | band, group |
| die Gruppe | group, band |
| spielen | to play |

| | |
|---|---|
| lernen | to learn, study |
| das Instrument | instrument |
| das Konzert | concert |

**H:**

| | |
|---|---|
| klingen | to sound |
| leise | quiet, soft, quietly |

## Sport

| | |
|---|---|
| der Sport | sport |
| sportlich | sporty, athletic |
| aktiv | active, energetic |
| die Bewegung | movement, motion, exercise |
| die Fitness | fitness |
| das Fitness-Studio | gym |
| die Mannschaft | team |
| das Team | team |
| der Club | club |
| der Verein | association, club, society |
| das Training | training |
| der Platz | (sport) pitch |
| der / die Trainer(in) | trainer |
| der / die Spieler(in) | player |
| die Technik | technique |
| der Ball | ball |
| der Fußball | football, soccer |
| das Tor | goal |
| der Basketball | basketball |
| das Tennis | tennis |
| das Fahrrad | bicycle |
| Sport treiben | to do sport |
| treiben | to drive, pursue |
| üben | to practise |

| | |
|---|---|
| schlagen | to hit, beat |
| werfen | to throw |
| spazieren | to go for a walk, stroll |
| wandern | to go on a walk / hike |
| schwimmen | to swim |
| tauchen | to dive |
| joggen | to jog |
| springen | to jump |
| tanzen | to dance |
| laufen | to run, walk |
| der Lauf | run, race |
| die Runde | round, lap |
| der Wettbewerb | competition, contest |
| das Spiel | game, match |
| gewinnen | to win |
| verlieren | to lose |
| der / die Teilnehmer(in) | participant, entrant |
| teilnehmen (an [+ dat.]) | to take part (in) |

**Higher:**

| | |
|---|---|
| der / die Gegner(in) | opponent, competitor, rival |
| schießen (auf) | to shoot (at), kick (ball) |
| klettern | to climb |

*'Ein Tor schießen' means 'to score a goal'.*

Section Six — Free-time Activities

## Going Out

| | |
|---|---|
| ausgehen | to go out |
| treffen | to meet |
| sich treffen | to meet up, get together |
| einkaufen | to shop |
| kaufen | to buy |
| ausgeben | to spend (money) |
| kosten | to cost |
| die Kosten | costs, expenses |
| Lust auf (+ noun) haben | to feel like (+ noun) |
| das Geschäft | business, shop |
| der Besuch | visit |
| besuchen | to visit |

| | |
|---|---|
| das Restaurant | restaurant |
| die Speisekarte, die Karte | menu |
| die Rechnung | bill |
| das Museum | museum |

**Higher**

| | |
|---|---|
| das Gericht | dish |
| das Getränk | drink |
| schmecken | to taste |
| probieren | to try, sample |
| die Ausstellung | exhibition, show |
| die Museen | museums |

## Art and Theatre

| | |
|---|---|
| die Kunst | art |
| das Bild | picture, photo |
| das Foto | photo, photograph |
| die Kultur | culture |
| das Theater | theatre, drama |
| das Stück | play (theatre) |
| die Rolle | role, part |
| interessieren | to interest |

| | |
|---|---|
| kreativ | creative, creatively |
| sich interessieren für | to be interested in |
| gefallen | to please |

**Higher**

| | |
|---|---|
| die Veranstaltung | event, performance |
| der Charakter | character |
| die Bühne | stage |
| malen | to paint |
| zeichnen | to draw |

## Other Activities

| | |
|---|---|
| die Freizeit | spare time, free time, leisure time |
| die Ferien | holidays, school break |
| frei | free, available |
| lesen | to read |
| die Literatur | literature |
| der Roman | novel |
| das Buch | book |
| der Text | text |
| der Krimi | thriller, detective story, crime story |
| die Geschichte | story |
| der / die Autor(in) | author, writer |
| die Zeitung | newspaper |
| der Artikel | article |
| die Nachricht | news, message |
| das Videospiel | video game |
| der Computer | computer |
| der Spaß | fun, joke |
| die Party | party |
| kochen | to cook |

| | |
|---|---|
| der Brief | letter |
| schreiben (an) | to write (to) |
| die Aktivität | activity |
| freiwillig | voluntary, voluntarily |
| eigen | own, private |

**Higher**

| | |
|---|---|
| sich entspannen | to relax, chill out |
| amüsieren | to enjoy |
| sich amüsieren | to enjoy oneself, have a good time |
| unterhalten | to entertain |
| sich unterhalten | to amuse oneself, chat |
| sich melden | to volunteer, enlist |

Tess can't understand why she still hasn't finished 'Große Erwartungen'.

# Revision Summary Test for Section Six

If time flies when you're having fun, it'll go at the speed of light while you do these questions...
- These questions are **really tricky**, but they'll help you see **how well you know your stuff**.
- Tackle the **revision summary test** below, or scan the QR code to do it **online**. You can **keep track of your progress** online and see **which areas need more work**.
- There are **sample answers** here: www.cgpbooks.co.uk/BerlinExtras

## Cinema and TV ☐

1) Translate into English: 'Ich finde Krimis ein bisschen langweilig, jedoch mag ich Komödien.'
2) Gehst du gern ins Kino? Warum / warum nicht? Answer in German.
3) In German, describe a film you watched recently. Say whether or not you liked it and why.
4) Give the German for these words: a) television   b) to stream   c) (TV) channel   d) romantic film
5) Wie oft siehst du fern? Was für Sendungen gefallen dir? Answer in German.
6) Write 'The adverts before the episode of my favourite series get on my nerves.' in German.
7) Give the English for these words: a) der Inhalt   b) die Spannung   c) anschauen   d) darstellen

## Music ☐

8) How would you say 'I would like to play an instrument in a band.' in German?
9) Welche Arten von Musik hörst du gern? Answer in German.
10) Give the German for these words: a) to sing   b) song   c) to download   d) musical
11) Imagine you went to a concert recently. Write at least two sentences in German about it.

## Sport ☐

12) In German, give one sport you like and one sport you don't like. Give reasons for your answer.
13) List all the verbs to do with exercising that you can remember in German. There are at least 12 in this section (plus 2 more for Higher tier).
14) In German, write 'The participants look forward to the competition.'
15) Was sind die Vorteile, wenn man Sport in der Freizeit treibt? Answer in German.
16) Translate into English: 'Morgen hat meine Mannschaft Training. Bald haben wir ein Spiel.'
17) Give these words in German: a) association   b) goal   c) bicycle   d) race   e) lap   f) sporty
18) What does 'verlieren' mean? What is the opposite of 'verlieren' in German? Now write a German sentence with each one.

## Going Out and Other Hobbies ☐

19) Munir tells you: 'Gestern habe ich in einem Restaurant gegessen. Alles auf der Speisekarte hat so viel gekostet und die Rechnung war sehr teuer.' Translate his sentences into English.
20) Give the German for these words and phrases:
    a) to meet up   b) to shop   c) to spend   d) fun   e) costs   f) culture   g) to visit
21) How do you say 'to feel like (+ noun)' in German? Write a sentence that uses this phrase.
22) Interessierst du dich für kreative Aktivitäten? Warum / warum nicht? Answer in German.
23) Your German friend asks you what you will do during the school break. Reply to them in German.
24) Jana says: 'Videospiele sind schlecht. Die Jugendliche sollen keine Videospiele spielen und sie müssen mehr Bücher lesen.' In German, give your opinion on what she said.
25) How would you say 'Museums often have interesting exhibitions.' in German?
26) Give the English for: a) sich entspannen   b) sich amüsieren   c) sich unterhalten   d) sich melden
    Now write a sentence in German for each verb.

# Section Seven — Customs, Festivals and Celebrations

## Celebrations

Quick Quiz

With all this revising to do, you might not feel like celebrating right now. Unless it happens to be your birthday today, in which case, don't let me stop you.

Head to the CGP RevisionHub for all your online content: www.cgpbooks.co.uk/Berlin

### Zeit zum Feiern — *Time to celebrate*

**Vocabulary**

| | | | |
|---|---|---|---|
| die Feier | *celebration, party* | heiraten | *to marry* |
| feiern | *to celebrate, party* | einladen | *to invite* |
| der Geburtstag | *birthday* | überraschen | *to surprise* |
| die Hochzeit | *wedding, marriage* | wünschen | *to want, wish, desire* |
| Silvester | *New Year's Eve* | schenken | *to give (as a present)* |
| das Geschenk | *gift, present* | das Feuerwerk | *fireworks* |

Wenn ich Geburtstag habe, werde ich meine Freunde zu meiner Feier einladen.

*When I have my birthday, I will invite my friends to my party.*

Zu Silvester gibt es viele Feuerwerke.

*On New Year's Eve, there are lots of fireworks.*

Ich freue mich auf die Hochzeit meines Bruders, die diesen Sommer stattfinden wird.

*I am looking forward to my brother's wedding, which will take place this summer.*

**Grammar** — sich freuen auf

Use 'sich freuen auf' + accusative to say you're looking forward to something. Don't forget to choose the right reflexive pronoun (p.111).

**Ich freue mich auf die Silvesterfeier.**
*I am looking forward to the New Year's Eve party.*

Jeremy was especially surprised since his birthday wasn't for another three months.

Q&A Audio

**Question**
Wie feierst du deinen Geburtstag?
*How do you celebrate your birthday?*

**Simple Answer**
Meine Freunde und ich gehen mit meinem Geburtstagsgeld einkaufen.
*My friends and I go shopping with my birthday money.*

**Extended Answer**
An meinem Geburtstag singt meine Familie für mich. Wir essen auch Kuchen und ich öffne meine Geschenke. Da mein Geburtstag im Sommer ist, gehen meine Freunde und ich am Abend zum Park.
*On my birthday, my family sings to me. We also eat cake and I open my presents. As my birthday is in the summer, my friends and I go to the park in the evening.*

### Practice Question

Q1 Marie and Jan are talking about how they celebrate different occasions.

There are two true statements in each list below. Choose the correct statements from each list.

Listening Track 10

a) A. Marie likes weddings the most.
   B. Marie loves wedding food.
   C. Marie spends New Year's Eve with her friends.

b) A. Jan's family surprised him on his last birthday.
   B. Last year, Jan had a birthday dinner.
   C. Jan gets lots of birthday presents.

[4 marks]

### Learn to celebrate the smaller things in life...

...like prepositions. Why? Well, these little words do a lot of work — they might tell you where someone is going (e.g. 'Ich gehe *zur* Feier'), or pop up in phrases like 'sich freuen *auf*'. Check out p.116-118 for more.

# Customs and Festivals

Quick Quiz

More celebrating? Don't mind if I do — now, where's the buffet table...?

## Frohe Weihnachten — *Merry Christmas*

### Vocabulary

| | | | |
|---|---|---|---|
| Weihnachten | *Christmas* | bekommen | *to get, receive* |
| der Heilige Abend | *Christmas Eve* | hängen (H) | *to hang* |
| der erste Weihnachtstag | *Christmas Day* | der König | *king* |

Am Heiligen Abend gehen viele Familien **in die Kirche**.
On Christmas Eve, lots of families go **to church**.
→ *to the Christmas market — zum Weihnachtsmarkt*

Meine Eltern **hängen die Lichter an** den Weihnachtsbaum.
My parents **hang the lights on** the Christmas tree.
→ *decorate — schmücken*

In Deutschland **bekommt man die Geschenke** am Heiligen Abend.
In Germany, **people receive presents** on Christmas Eve.

Ich singe gern **Weihnachtslieder**.
I like singing **Christmas songs**.

**Am zwölften Weihnachtstag** feiern einige Familien mit einem großen Essen den **Dreikönigstag**.
**On the twelfth day of Christmas**, some families celebrate **Three Kings' Day** with a big meal.

Not quite what Ella was hoping for...

## Ostern — *Easter*

In the German-speaking world, <u>Easter</u> is celebrated much like in the UK. <u>Karneval</u> (or <u>Fasching</u>) is celebrated in <u>Germany, Switzerland and Austria</u> just <u>before Lent</u> with <u>carnival parades</u> and <u>parties</u>.

### Vocabulary

| | | | | | | |
|---|---|---|---|---|---|---|
| Ostern | *Easter* | kulturell | *cultural* | | Karneval | *Carnival* |
| die Kultur | *culture* | historisch | *historical* | | das Ereignis | *event, occurrence* |
| die Küche | *cuisine* | besondere | *special* | Higher | die Stimmung | *mood, atmosphere* |
| die Tradition | *tradition* | bunt | *colourful* | | der Lärm | *noise* |
| traditionell | *traditional* | erleben | *to experience* | | verbinden | *to connect, link, unite* |

Karneval ist ein traditionelles Fest, **das sieben Wochen vor Ostern stattfindet**.
Carnival is a traditional celebration **that takes place seven weeks before Easter**.
→ *participants put on fancy dress — verkleiden sich Teilnehmer*

In der Schweiz, Österreich und Deutschland **nehmen viele Leute an Paraden teil**.
In Switzerland, Austria and Germany, **lots of people take part in parades**.
→ *parades attract lots of tourists — ziehen Umzüge eine Menge Touristen an*

Diese **Feste** haben eine besondere Stimmung. Sie können auch viele Menschen **verbinden**.
These **festivals** have a special atmosphere. They can also **unite** lots of people.
→ *street parties — Straßenfeste*

Am Ostersonntag **suchen** wir im Garten viele bunte Ostereier.
On Easter Sunday, we **look for** lots of colourful Easter eggs in the garden.
→ *hide — verstecken*

Section Seven — Customs, Festivals and Celebrations

# Mehr Religionen und Feste — More religions and festivals

## Vocabulary

| | | | |
|---|---|---|---|
| die Religion | religion | der / die Hindu | Hindu |
| der Muslim | Muslim (male) | glauben (an) | to believe (in) |
| die Muslime | Muslim (female) | das Fest | festival, celebration |
| der Jude | Jewish (male), Jewish person | Eid (-al-Fitr) | Eid |
| | | das Licht | light |
| die Jüdin | Jewish (female) | bekannt | well-known |
| der / die Christ(in) | Christian | stattfinden | to take place, occur |

*In German, you often use a noun instead of an adjective when talking about the religion you belong to.*

Ich bin Jude / Jüdin. — I am Jewish.

Chanukka dauert acht Tage. — Hanukkah lasts for eight days.

Jedes Jahr freue ich mich auf das Lichterfest. — Every year, I look forward to the festival of lights.

Sikh — Sikh
Buddhist — Buddhist(in)
Diwali — Diwali
Passover — Passah

**Question**
Welche Feste feierst du?
*Which festivals do you celebrate?*

**Simple Answer**
Ich feiere Eid mit meiner Familie.
*I celebrate Eid with my family.*

**Extended Answer**
Zu Hause feiern wir Eid. Es findet nach Ramadan, einer Fastenzeit, statt, die einen Monat dauert. Wir laden alle von unserer Familie zu einem Festessen ein.
*At home, we celebrate Eid. It takes place after Ramadan, a period of fasting, which lasts for a month. We invite all of our family to a festive meal.*

## Practice Questions

**Q1** Translate the following sentences into German.
a) Easter is an important time for Christians.
b) Every year, Muslims celebrate Eid with their families.
c) Religions often have interesting and historical festivals. [6 marks]

**Q2** Read this extract from Toni's diary and answer the questions below.

> Jedes Jahr hängen ich und meine Familie die Lichter auf den großen Weihnachtsbaum, den meine Eltern kaufen. Das ist meine Lieblingstradition. Der Baum steht bis zum neuen Jahr in unserem Wohnzimmer und wir stellen ihn am Dreikönigstag wieder weg. Am Heiligen Abend kocht meine Oma das traditionelle Weihnachtsessen mit Fischgerichten und Würstchen. Letztes Jahr gingen wir am ersten Weihnachtstag alle in die Kirche, um Lieder zu singen. Das war eine sehr gute Erfahrung und danach habe ich eine Verbindung mit den anderen Menschen in der Kirche gefühlt.

a) What is Toni's favourite Christmas tradition? [1 mark]
b) When does Toni's family put the tree away? [1 mark]
c) On which day does her grandma cook a Christmas meal? [1 mark]
d) Why did Toni like going to church? [1 mark]

## Whatever you do, don't ask for a Gift in German...

'Gift' means 'poison' — yikes. Instead of a gift, I'll give you a tip: with separable verbs like 'stattfinden', the second half ('finden') acts like other present-tense verbs, and the first half ('statt') goes at the end of the clause.

# Customs, Festivals and Celebrations — Vocabulary

Here's my gift to you — a page of lovely vocab for you to unwrap and enjoy... I mean, learn.

## Celebrations

| | |
|---|---|
| die Feier | celebration, party, ceremony |
| die Party | party |
| feiern | to celebrate, party |
| der Geburtstag | birthday |
| Herzlichen Glückwunsch | congratulations |
| Herzlichen Glückwunsch zum Geburtstag | Happy Birthday |
| die Hochzeit | wedding, marriage |
| Silvester (m / n) | New Year's Eve |

'Silvester' can be either masculine or neuter. You often talk about 'Silvester' and other celebrations like 'Ostern' and 'Eid' without the article (e.g. 'der' or 'das').

| | |
|---|---|
| das Geschenk | gift, present |
| geben | to give |
| die Karte | card |
| heiraten | to marry |
| einladen | to invite |
| überraschen | to surprise |
| wünschen | to want, wish, desire |
| sich freuen auf | to look forward to |

**Higher:**

| | |
|---|---|
| schenken | to give (as a present) |
| das Feuerwerk | fireworks |
| das Feuer | fire, bonfire |
| die Freude | joy, pleasure |
| amüsieren | to amuse |
| sich amüsieren | to have a good time, enjoy (oneself) |

## Customs and Festivals

| | |
|---|---|
| das Weihnachten | Christmas |
| die Weihnachten | Christmases |
| der Heilige Abend | Christmas Eve |
| der erste Weihnachtstag | Christmas Day |
| das Lied | song |
| bekommen | to get, receive |
| Ostern (n) | Easter |
| die Kultur | culture |
| die Küche | cuisine |
| die Tradition | tradition |
| traditionell | traditional, traditionally |
| kulturell | cultural |
| historisch | historical |
| national | national |
| die Region | region, area |
| besondere | special |
| bunt | colourful, colourfully |
| gemeinsam | common, in common, mutual, joint |
| erleben | to experience |
| passieren | to take place, happen, occur |

| | |
|---|---|
| das Glück | luck, good luck, fortune, happiness |
| Deutsche | Germans |
| die Deutschen | the Germans |
| die Religion | religion |
| der Muslim | Muslim (male) |
| die Muslime | Muslim (female) |
| der Jude | Jewish (male), Jewish person |
| die Jüdin | Jewish (female) |
| der / die Christ(in) | Christian |
| der / die Hindu | Hindu |
| glauben (an) | to believe (in), think |
| das Fest | festival, celebration |
| Eid (-al-Fitr) (n) | Eid |
| der Herr | Lord (addressing God) |
| der Himmel | heaven |
| das Licht | light |
| bekannt | well-known, famous |
| stattfinden | to take place, occur |

**Higher:**

| | |
|---|---|
| hängen | to hang |
| der König | king |
| der Karneval | Carnival |
| die Gesellschaft | society |
| das Ereignis | event, occurrence |
| die Stimmung | mood, atmosphere |
| der Lärm | noise |
| das Gericht | dish |
| speziell | special |
| verbinden, sich verbinden | to connect, link, unite |

At the mention of Christmas, Caroline lit up.

Section Seven — Customs, Festivals and Celebrations

# Revision Summary Test for Section Seven

Here's a page of questions to celebrate reaching the end of the section. *Viel Glück*.
- These questions are **hard**, but they'll really help you see **how well you know your stuff**.
- Tackle the **revision summary test** below, or scan the QR code to do it **online**. You can **track your progress** online and see **which areas need more work**.
- There are **sample answers** for the test here: www.cgpbooks.co.uk/BerlinExtras

## Celebrations

1) How do you say the following celebrations in German?
   a) birthday   b) wedding   c) New Year's Eve
2) Auf welche Feier freust du dich dieses Jahr? Answer this question in German.
3) Your German friend, Mila, tells you: 'Meine Familie hat mich dieses Jahr überrascht. Sie haben für mich eine schöne Geburtstagsparty organisiert und meine Freunde eingeladen. Ich habe viele Geburtstagskarten und Geschenke bekommen.' Translate what she said into English.
4) What would you say to wish somebody...? a) congratulations   b) happy birthday
5) Verbringst du Silvester lieber mit Freunden oder mit deiner Familie? Answer the question in German.
6) Give the German for the these words: a) to marry   b) to wish   c) to celebrate
7) Translate these words into German:
   a) to have a good time   b) to give (as a present)   c) to amuse
8) 'Im November gehen wir zum Feuer im Park. Es macht mir viele Freude, weil ich das Feuerwerk gern anschaue.' What does this mean in English?

## Customs and Festivals

9) Give the German for these words: a) Christmas Day   b) Easter   c) fortune   d) region
10) There are 4 religious identities you need to know in German. How many can you name? Give the masculine and feminine forms for each one.
11) In German, give three things people might do to celebrate Christmas.
12) Translate these words into German: a) religion   b) to believe (in)   c) Lord   d) heaven
13) Which of the following isn't a fact about Easter?
    a) Leute singen Lieder in der Kirche.      c) Christen feiern dieses Fest.
    b) Es gibt viele Lichter um die Stadt.     d) Es findet im Frühling statt.
14) Translate these words into English: a) historisch   b) kulturell   c) national   d) gemeinsam
15) Yasmin tells you: 'Dieses Jahr habe ich Eid mit meinen Nachbarn gefeiert. Bei diesem Fest geniessen wir Essen von unserer Kultur.' Translate what she said into English.
16) Elias tells you: 'On Christmas Eve, my family and I go to church and we sing traditional Christmas songs.' Translate what he has said into German.
17) Translate these questions into English, then answer them in German. 'Was für Feste feierst du mit deiner Familie? Welche Traditionen habt ihr?'
18) Give the English for these words: a) der König   b) die Gesellschaft   c) das Gericht
19) Your friend, Mika, tells you: 'In jeder Region gibt es verschiedene Ereignisse, um Karneval zu feiern, aber überall gibt es eine fantastische Stimmung, die alle verbindet.' Translate what he said into English.
20) Translate this question into English and answer it in German: 'Willst du Karneval erleben? Warum (nicht)?'

# Section Eight — Celebrity Culture

## Favourite Celebrities

Quick Quiz

My favourite celebrity is Günther Graf. He's on the other page over there — dreamy, isn't he? After reading these pages, you'll be able to talk about *your* favourite celebrity.

*Remember there's also lots of online content here: www.cgpbooks.co.uk/Berlin*

### Mein Lieblingsstar ist... — My favourite celebrity is...

**Vocabulary**

| | | | |
|---|---|---|---|
| der Star | celebrity, headliner | der / die Künstler(in) | artist, performer |
| die Persönlichkeit | personality, celebrity | die Band | band, group (music) |
| der / die Sänger(in) | singer | das Vorbild | role model, example |
| der / die Schauspieler(in) | actor | die Vorstellung | performance |
| der / die Spieler(in) | player | der Eindruck | impression, effect |
| der / die Autor(in) | author, writer | unterhalten | to entertain |

(Higher: das Vorbild, die Vorstellung, der Eindruck, unterhalten)

Ich liebe diese Sängerin, weil sie eine schöne und einzigartige Stimme hat.
*I love that singer because she has a beautiful and unique voice.*

Mein Lieblingsstar ist ein englischer Schauspieler. Ich habe alle seine Filme gesehen.
*My favourite celebrity is an English actor. I have seen all of his films.*

Ich mag eine deutsche Band. Ich würde gern zu ihrem Konzert gehen.
*I like a German band. I would like to go to their concert.*

- series — Serien
- group — Gruppe
- get tickets for their next show — Tickets für ihre nächste Show bekommen

### Er / Sie ist berühmt, weil... — He / She is famous because...

**Vocabulary**

| | | | | | |
|---|---|---|---|---|---|
| berühmt | famous | das Stück | play (theatre) | der Einfluss | influence |
| bekannt | well-known, famous | die Rolle | role, part | die Bühne | stage |
| folgen | to follow | der Roman | novel | darstellen | to depict, portray |

(Higher: der Einfluss, die Bühne, darstellen)

Die Autorin hat einen wichtigen Roman geschrieben und sie ist jetzt berühmt. Ich empfehle dir, dass du ihn liest.
*The author wrote an important novel and now she is famous. I recommend that you read it.*

- award-winning — preisgekrönten
- buy it — ihn kaufst

Der bekannte Sänger schreibt Lieder, die kreativ und spannend sind.
*The famous singer writes songs that are creative and exciting.*

Ich folge dieser Vloggerin in den sozialen Medien. Sie macht lustige Videos.
*I follow this vlogger on social media. She makes funny videos.*

- has lots of time for her fans — hat viel Zeit für ihre Fans

Dieser Schauspieler hat für ein Theaterstück vorgesprochen und er hat die Hauptrolle bekommen.
*This actor auditioned for a play and he got the main role.*

Das Modell weiß viel über Mode. Ich liebe seinen Stil und ich möchte ähnliche Kleidung tragen.
*The model knows a lot about fashion. I love his style and I want to wear similar clothes.*

# Andere Arten von Stars — *Other types of celebrities*

Die Influencerin ist ein positives Vorbild. Sie hat eine nette Persönlichkeit.

The influencer is a positive role model. She has a nice personality.

polite — höfliche

Der Fußballspieler spielt für meine Lieblingsmannschaft. Er gibt viel von seinem Geld an Leute, die Hilfe brauchen.

The football player plays for my favourite team. He gives a lot of his money to people who need help.

Ich sehe gern Komödiesendungen. Die Schauspieler sind im wirklichen Leben genauso lustig.

I like watching comedy series. The actors are just as funny in real life.

The vlogger had the perfect plan to blast himself to stardom.

Die berühmte Moderatorin arbeitet an vielen Dokumentarfilmen über die Natur mit.

The famous presenter works on many documentaries about nature.

politician — Politikerin

Die Wissenschaftlerin schreibt Bücher über wunderbare Themen.

The scientist writes books about wonderful topics.

### Question
Wer ist dein Lieblingsstar? Warum?

*Who is your favourite celebrity? Why?*

### Grammar — 'Lieblings-' and 'Haupt-'
You can add 'Lieblings-' to the start of a noun to mean 'favourite'.
    der Lieblingsautor    favourite author

To say something is the 'main' one of something, add 'Haupt-'.
    die Hauptrolle    main role

### Simple Answer
Mein Lieblingsstar ist die Sängerin Agata Krüger. Ich finde sie fantastisch.

*My favourite celebrity is the singer Agata Krüger. I think she is fantastic.*

### Extended Answer
Die Persönlichkeit, die ich am liebsten mag, heißt Günther Graf. Ich mag ihn, weil er interessante und witzige Podcasts macht. Er ist sehr talentiert und ich liebe alles, was er macht.

*The celebrity that I like the most is called Günther Graf. I like him because he makes interesting and funny podcasts. He is very talented and I love everything he does.*

## Practice Questions

Q1   You are listening to two of your friends talk about their favourite celebrities. Answer the questions in English.

    a)   What does Elsa's favourite celebrity do?    [1 mark]
    b)   How many times has Johann seen his favourite celebrity?    [1 mark]
    c)   Where did Elsa meet her favourite celebrity?    [1 mark]
    d)   Why does Elsa like her favourite celebrity?    [1 mark]
    e)   What does Johann hope he will become?    [1 mark]

Q2   Write a blog post about your favourite celebrity. You should write about 50-90 words in German. Describe:

- who they are and what they do
- why they are your favourite celebrity.    [10 marks]

**Top Tip for Higher Students**
✓ Use 'seit' with the present tense to talk about how long your favourite celebrity has been doing something.

## I love Marie Antoinette — fame never went to her head...

In the exam, you might have to talk about your favourite celebrity. To practise, pick a few celebrities and list some adjectives to describe them. E.g. If I were your favourite celebrity, you'd use 'schön' and 'witzig'.

# Celebrity Life

*It's hard being a star, you know — it's tiring hearing people say how much they love me all the time.*

## Das Leben von einem Star — *The life of a star*

**Vocabulary**

| | | | |
|---|---|---|---|
| die Karriere | *career* | das Bild | *picture, image, photo* |
| die Medien (pl) | *media* | sich anziehen | *to get dressed* |
| die Zeitung | *newspaper* | die Rede | *speech, talk* |
| das Interview | *interview* | H wert | *worth, worthy of* |

How are the kids?

Stars gehen oft zu wichtigen Veranstaltungen, zum Beispiel Filmpremieren.
*Celebrities often go to important events, for example film premieres.*
— *often get exciting opportunities* — bekommen oft aufregende Möglichkeiten

Stars erscheinen oft in Zeitungen und in sozialen Medien. Man sieht sie auch im Reality-TV.
*Famous people often appear in newspapers and on social media. People also see them on reality TV.*
*online* — online
*in magazines* — in Zeitschriften
*on the television* — im Fernsehen

Das Publikum erkennt Stars und bittet um Fotos mit ihnen.
*The public recognises celebrities and asks for photos with them.*
*their autographs* — ihre Autogramme

Firmen verwenden Stars in ihrer Werbung, um Produkte zu verkaufen.
*Companies use celebrities in their advertisements in order to sell products.*

## Die guten Aspekte von Berühmtheit — *The good aspects of fame*

**Vocabulary**

| | | | |
|---|---|---|---|
| positiv | *positive* | das Publikum | *audience, public* |
| das Geld | *money* | beliebt | *popular* |
| der Erfolg | *success* | reich | *rich, wealthy* |
| der Preis | *prize, award* | verdienen | *to earn, deserve* |
| der Fan | *fan, supporter* | das Gute | *the good thing* |
| der / die Zuschauer(in) | *viewer, spectator* | H die Reichen | *the rich (ones)* |

Wenn man erfolgreich ist, kann man viel Geld verdienen und reich werden.
*If you are successful, you can earn a lot of money and become rich.*

Stars können einen positiven Einfluss haben. Zum Beispiel machen Sänger Leute durch ihre Musik glücklich.
*Celebrities can have a positive influence. For example, singers make people happy through their music.*
*inspire people* — Menschen inspirieren

Stars bekommen die Möglichkeit, um die Welt zu reisen. Sie können viele tolle Orte besuchen und ihre Fans treffen.
*Celebrities get the opportunity to travel the world. They get to visit a lot of amazing places and meet their fans.*

Samara was disappointed that her fans weren't letting off a cool, refreshing stream of air.

Section Eight — Celebrity Culture

# Die schlechten Aspekte von Berühmtheit — *The bad aspects of fame*

## Vocabulary

| | | | | | |
|---|---|---|---|---|---|
| negativ | *negative* | öffentlich | *public* | die Öffentlichkeit | *public* |
| scharfe Worte | *sharp words* | [H] kritisieren | *to criticise* | [Higher] das Opfer | *victim* |
| sich verhalten | *to behave, act* | die Kritik | *criticism, review* | sinnvoll | *sensible, wise* |

Stars stehen unter viel Druck, weil die Presse und die Leute ihr Verhalten beobachten.

*Celebrities are under a lot of pressure because the press and people observe their behaviour.*

Für viele Stars ist es unmöglich, ihr Privatleben zu schützen.

*It is impossible for many celebrities to protect their private life.*

Berühmte Menschen sind oft Opfer von Online-Mobbing.

*Famous people are often victims of online bullying.*

**Grammar — the prefix 'un-'**

You can add the prefix '<u>un-</u>' to the start of many German adjectives to give it the <u>opposite</u> meaning, e.g.

| <u>un</u>glücklich | <u>un</u>happy |
|---|---|
| <u>un</u>möglich | <u>im</u>possible |

**Q&A Audio**

**Question**
Möchtest du gerne berühmt sein?
Warum / warum nicht?
*Would you like to be famous?
Why / why not?*

**Simple Answer**
Ja, ich will Sänger werden. Ich möchte meine Lieder mit der Welt teilen.
*Yes, I want to be a singer. I would like to share my songs with the world.*

**Extended Answer**
Ich möchte kein Star sein. Leute sind gemein, wenn man einen Fehler macht. Ich hätte das Gefühl, dass ich perfekt sein muss.
*I don't want to be a celebrity. People are cruel when you make a mistake. I would feel like I must be perfect.*

## Practice Questions

Q1 Read this extract from an interview with a famous singer out loud.

> Ich gebe oft Interviews für Zeitungen. Auch arbeite ich mit jungen Sängern. Ich will ihnen mit ihrer Karriere helfen.

**SPEAKING**

**Top Tip for Higher Students**
✓ Use 'die beste Sache' und 'die schlechteste Sache' to talk about the best and worst things about being famous.

Now imagine you're a celebrity. Talk about what you're famous for and what you do. Aim to talk for **two** minutes. [8 marks]

Q2 [Higher] Read this extract from an article by a famous actress, Liesl Nadler. Then answer the questions below in English.

> Ich liebe es, Schauspielerin zu sein. Ich mag es am liebsten, wenn ich vor einem Publikum auftrete. Ich habe auch mit einem sehr bekannten Regisseur* gearbeitet, der für mich ein wichtiges Vorbild ist. Aber die Berühmtheit ist manchmal schwierig. Ich muss lange Stunden arbeiten und ich bekomme auch Kritik. Ich muss mich daran erinnern, dass ich trotz Kritik wert bin.

*Regisseur — *director*

a) What does Liesl like most about being an actress? [1 mark]
b) What does Liesl describe the director as? Give **one** detail. [1 mark]
c) Why does Liesl say being famous can be difficult? Give **two** details. [2 marks]
d) What does Liesl have to remind herself of? [1 mark]

## Become Rich? I'd like to keep my own name, thank you...

In German, write a pros and cons list of what being a celebrity is like. That way, you'll have some nice phrases up your sleeve for the exam (though don't *literally* keep the list up your sleeve — that's cheating).

# Celebrity Culture — Vocabulary

Learn this A-list vocabulary and you'll have the 'it' factor when you step into that exam hall...

## Favourite Celebrities

| | |
|---|---|
| der Star | celebrity, headliner |
| die Persönlichkeit | personality, celebrity |
| Lieblings- (+ noun) | favourite (+ noun) |
| der / die Sänger(in) | singer |
| die Gruppe | group, band |
| der / die Schauspieler(in) | actor |
| der / die Spieler(in) | player |
| der / die Autor(in) | author, writer |
| der / die Künstler(in) | artist, performer |
| die Band | band, group (music) |
| berühmt | famous |
| bekannt | well-known, famous |
| folgen | to follow |
| das Stück | play (theatre) |
| Haupt- (+ noun) | main (+ noun) |
| die Rolle | role, part |
| der Roman | novel |
| das Konzert | concert |
| die Musik | music |
| die Stimme | voice |
| das Video | video |
| das Foto | photo, photograph |
| das Fernsehen | television |
| die Sendung | programme |
| die Mannschaft | team |

| | |
|---|---|
| der Sport | sport |
| der Wunsch | wish, desire |
| aufregend | exciting, thrilling |
| kreativ | creative, creatively |
| wichtig | important |
| schön | lovely, beautiful |
| empfehlen | to recommend |
| singen | to sing |
| hören | to hear, listen |
| ansehen | to look at, watch |

*Higher:*
| | |
|---|---|
| das Vorbild | role model, example |
| die Vorstellung | performance, imagination |
| die Veranstaltung | event, performance |
| der Eindruck | impression, effect |
| der Einfluss | influence |
| der Charakter | character |
| die Szene | scene |
| die Bühne | stage |
| die Serie | series |
| die Mode | fashion |
| unterhalten | to entertain |
| darstellen | to depict, portray, show, represent |
| auftreten | to appear, occur, perform |

## Celebrity Life

| | |
|---|---|
| die Karriere | career |
| die Medien (pl) | media |
| die Zeitung | newspaper |
| das Interview | interview |
| das Bild | picture, image, photo |
| tragen | to wear |
| positiv | positive |
| negativ | negative |
| der Vorteil | advantage, benefit |
| der Nachteil | disadvantage |
| das Geld | money, cash |
| der Erfolg | success |
| der Preis | prize, award |
| der Fan | fan, supporter |
| der / die Zuschauer(in) | viewer, spectator |
| das Publikum | audience, public |
| beliebt | popular |
| reich | rich, wealthy, abundant |

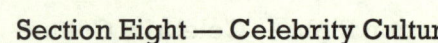

der Bathroomteil

| | |
|---|---|
| verdienen | to earn, deserve |
| scharfe Worte | sharp words |
| sich verhalten | to behave, act |
| öffentlich | public |
| normal | normal |

*Higher:*
| | |
|---|---|
| die Wirklichkeit | reality, truth |
| die Rede | speech, talk |
| berichten | to report |
| das Gute | the good thing |
| die Reichen | the rich (ones) |
| wert | worth, worthy of |
| die Kritik | criticism, review |
| kritisieren | to criticise |
| die Öffentlichkeit | public |
| das Opfer | sacrifice, victim, casualty |
| anschauen | to look at, watch |
| beobachten | to observe, watch |
| sinnvoll | sensible, wise |

# Revision Summary Test for Section Eight

Aaaand now for the grand finale... *drum roll* — a whole page of questions on Celebrity Culture.
- Yep, these questions are **hard** — they'll really help you see **how well you know your stuff**.
- Tackle the **revision summary test** below, or scan the QR code to do it **online**.
  Use the CGP RevisionHub to **track your progress** and see **which areas need more work**.
- You can find **sample answers** here: www.cgpbooks.co.uk/BerlinExtras

## Favourite Celebrities

1) How do you say 'celebrity' in German? There are two words you need to know.
2) Translate the following sentences into English:
   'Sie ist sehr berühmt. Viele Menschen folgen ihr auf den sozialen Medien.'
3) How many different types of celebrity can you name in German?
   There are 4 you need to know. Give the masculine and feminine forms for each.
4) In German, say what your favourite celebrity does. Give at least two details.
5) 'Die Schauspielerin hat in dem Stück eine wichtige Rolle.' What does this mean in English?
6) Write down the English for these words:
   a) die Sendung   b) die Mannschaft   c) das Konzert   d) der Roman   e) das Fernsehen   f) die Stimme
7) Translate the following sentences into German:
   'The well-known band sings lovely songs. I recommend that you listen to their music.'
8) Was für ein Star möchtest du sein? Warum? Answer the question in German.
9) 'Ich habe die Vorstellung des Stars auf der Bühne gesehen.
   Sie hat ihre Rolle sehr gut gespielt.' Say this in English.
10) What is the German for: a) fashion   b) series   c) impression   d) to entertain   e) to depict
11) In German, talk about how celebrities can be good role models and have a positive influence.

## Celebrity Life

12) What is the German for: a) career   b) interview   c) success   d) audience   e) viewer
13) Matteo, a famous artist, is a very private person. Which of the following is he most likely to do?
    a) Er macht Fotos mit seinen Fans.        c) Er benutzt regelmäßig soziale Medien.
    b) Er spricht selten mit Zeitungen.        d) Er nimmt an Reality-TV teil.
14) How do you say the following words and phrases in German?
    a) popular   b) rich   c) public   d) normal   e) sharp words   f) to behave
15) Laura, a retired actress, was asked how she felt about her career.
    She replied: 'Ich bin glücklich, denn ich habe viele Preisen gewonnen.' What has she said?
16) 'Das Leben von einem Star hat Vorteile und Nachteile.'
    In German, explain why this sentence is true. Give as many details as possible.
17) 'The public often criticise celebrities. This criticism is difficult to receive.
    Celebrities sometimes become victims of bullying.' Translate these sentences into German.
18) Give the German for the following words and phrases:
    a) speech   b) reality   c) to report   d) to perform   e) the rich   f) the good thing   g) worthy
19) Stell dir vor, dass du eine berühmte Star bist.
    Was für einen Effekt hätte es auf dein Leben? Answer in German.

# Section Nine — Travel and Tourism

Quick Quiz

## Where to Go

Pack your bags and grab your passport — you're off to Talking-about-holidays-in-German-land.

### Die Länder — *The countries*

Don't forget you can access your online content here: www.cgpbooks.co.uk/Berlin

**Vocabulary**

|  |  |
|---|---|
| das Land | *country, land* |
| die Welt | *world* |
| die Region | *region, area* |
| Deutschland | *Germany* |
| Österreich | *Austria* |
| die Schweiz | *Switzerland* |
| die Türkei | *Turkey* |
| Großbritannien | *Great Britain* |
| England | *England* |
| Frankreich | *France* |
| Italien | *Italy* |
| Spanien | *Spain* |
| Griechenland | *Greece* |
| Europa | *Europe* |
| Amerika (Higher) | *America* |
| die USA (Vereinigte Staaten von Amerika) | *USA (United States of America)* |

Bald fahren wir nach Belgien und Polen.
*Soon we are going to Belgium and Poland.*

Ich fahre nach München, eine Stadt in Deutschland.
*I am going to Munich, a city in Germany.*

Der Rhein ist ein Fluss, der durch sechs Länder in Europa fließt.
*The Rhine is a river that flows through six countries in Europe.*

Als ich jünger war, habe ich Italien besucht. Ich möchte wieder hinfahren, weil es ein schönes Land ist.
*When I was younger, I visited Italy. I want to go there again because it is a beautiful country.*

- Africa — Afrika
- Asia — Asien
- South America — Südamerika
- Australia — Australien
- Cologne — Köln

**Grammar — 'in' / 'nach' + country**

To say you're going somewhere, use 'in' for countries with an article...
**Ich fahre in die Türkei.** *I'm going to Turkey.*
...and nach for countries without an article.
**Ich fahre nach Spanien.** *I'm going to Spain.*

### Das Klima im Ausland — *The climate abroad*

**Vocabulary**

|  |  |  |  |  |  |  |  |
|---|---|---|---|---|---|---|---|
| das Ausland | *abroad* | die Temperatur | *temperature* | sonnig | *sunny* | warm | *warm* |
| das Klima | *climate* | die Sonne | *sun* | heiß | *hot* | kalt | *cold* |

In der Schweiz ist es im Sommer sehr heiß. Im Winter gibt es viel Schnee.
*In Switzerland, it is very hot in the summer. In the winter, there is a lot of snow.*

- spring — Frühling
- autumn — Herbst

Ich liebe es, in sonnige Länder zu reisen. Ich möchte nicht in einem Land Urlaub machen, wo es oft regnet und kalt ist.
*I love travelling to sunny countries. I don't want to go on holiday in a country where it rains often and is cold.*

- cloudy — wolkig
- windy — windig

# Wohin fährst du? — *Where are you going?*

## Vocabulary

| | | | |
|---|---|---|---|
| der Urlaub | *holiday* | reisen | *to travel* |
| der Besuch | *visit* | besuchen | *to visit* |
| fremd | *foreign* | planen | *to plan* |
| fahren | *to go (by transport)* | **H** international | *international* |

Anna's friends had asked for some holiday snaps.

Ich bin noch nie in ein fremdes Land gereist. Ich hoffe, in der Zukunft nach Amerika zu fahren.

*I have never travelled to a foreign country. I hope to travel to America in the future.*

Wir planen einen Besuch im Schwarzwald. Wir fahren im März.

*We are planning a visit to the Black Forest. We are going in March.*

Ich reise lieber in Europa, besonders in Länder mit großen Bergen, wo die Landschaft so schön ist.

*I prefer to travel in Europe, especially to countries with big mountains, where the landscape is so beautiful.*

a trip — eine Reise

booking our tickets for — buchen unsere Tickets für

Q&A Audio

**Question**
Wohin fährst du diesen Sommer?
*Where are you going this summer?*

**Simple Answer**
Ich reise mit meiner Familie nach Frankreich und Italien.
*I'm going to France and Italy with my family.*

**Extended Answer**
Im Juli fliegen meine Eltern und ich nach Griechenland, weil es letzten Sommer jede Menge Spaß gemacht hat.
*In July, my parents and I are flying to Greece because it was so much fun last summer.*

## Practice Questions

**Q1** Read this extract from Deniz's blog post, in which he talks about his holiday. Answer the following questions in English.

> Ich war vierzehn Jahre alt, als ich zum ersten Mal ins Ausland gefahren bin. Mein Vater, meine Stiefmutter und ich sind nach Österreich und in die Schweiz gereist. Wir sind nur drei Tage in jedem Land geblieben aber der Urlaub war fantastisch. Das Klima war super, denn es war sonnig und warm. Ich möchte in der Zukunft wieder ins Ausland reisen, zum Beispiel in die Türkei.

*READING*

a) Where did Deniz travel to on holiday? Name **two** places. [2 marks]
b) How long did Deniz stay in each place for? [1 mark]
c) What was the climate like on Deniz's holiday? Give **two** details. [2 marks]
d) What would Deniz like to do in the future? [1 mark]

**Q2** Beate is talking to her friend about her holiday.

*SPEAKING*

> Letztes Jahr bin ich nach England gereist. Es war ein bisschen kalt. Nächstes Jahr will ich nach Spanien reisen, weil es warm ist.

**Top Tip for Higher Students**
✓ Use infinitive constructions like 'Ich hoffe... zu...' to say where you hope to go.

Now it's your turn. Talk about a previous holiday and what the climate was like. Then talk about where you would like to visit. Aim to talk for about two minutes. [10 marks]

## I collect verbs about travelling — I'm a real go-getter...

'Gehen', 'fahren' and 'reisen' all mean 'to go', but they're used for different things — 'gehen' is for travelling on foot, 'fahren' for travelling in a vehicle, and 'reisen' more generally if you're travelling to a destination.

Quick Quiz

# Accommodation and Travel

Right, you've got your destination, but you need to decide where you're staying and how you're getting there. Well, the next two pages are about exactly that. Want to get stuck in? Be my guest...

## Wo bleibst du? — *Where are you staying?*

### Vocabulary

| | | | | | |
|---|---|---|---|---|---|
| das Hotel | *hotel* | teuer | *expensive* | der Blick | *view* |
| die Wohnung | *apartment, flat* | günstig | *cheap* | der Aufenthalt | *stay, residence* |
| das Zimmer | *room* | sauber | *clean* | das Zelt | *tent* |
| das Bett | *bed* | schmutzig | *dirty* | | |
| der Gast | *guest (male)* | bequem | *comfortable* | | |
| die Gästin | *guest (female)* | die Insel | *island* | | |
| bleiben | *to stay, remain* | die Küste | *coast, shore* | | |
| wohnen | *to stay* | der Berg | *mountain, hill* | | |
| schlafen | *to sleep* | der Wald | *forest, wood* | | |

(der Aufenthalt and das Zelt marked H — Higher)

### Grammar — dative case

You use the <u>dative case</u> when saying <u>where</u> you stayed.

**Wir wohnen in einem Hotel.**
*We are staying in a hotel.*

---

In den Sommerferien wird meine Familie in einem Hotel in Wales wohnen.
*In the summer holidays, my family will stay at a hotel in Wales.*

Die Wohnung ist teuer, denn sie hat einen schönen Blick auf die Bergen.
*The flat is expensive because it has a beautiful view of the mountains.*

Ich würde lieber in einem Hotel bleiben, weil es unbequem ist, in einem Zelt zu schlafen.
*I would prefer to stay in a hotel because it is uncomfortable to sleep in a tent.*

Das Zimmer ist ziemlich günstig. Es kostet nur vierzig Euro pro Nacht.
*The room is quite cheap. It only costs forty euros per night.*

*in the countryside — auf dem Land*

*it is near the forest — liegt in der Nähe des Waldes*

*The inn — Das Gasthaus*
*The youth hostel — Die Jugendherberge*
*The campsite — Der Campingplatz*

## Das Verkehrsmittel — *Means of transport*

### Vocabulary

| | | | | | |
|---|---|---|---|---|---|
| der Verkehr | *transport* | der Bahnhof | *(railway) station* | die Karte | *ticket* |
| nehmen | *to take* | das Schiff | *ship* | die Straßenbahn | *tram* |
| das Auto | *car* | das Flugzeug | *aeroplane* | die U-Bahn | *metro* |
| der Bus | *bus* | der Flughafen | *airport* | das Boot | *boat* |
| der Zug | *train* | fliegen | *to fly* | der Flug | *flight* |

(die Straßenbahn, die U-Bahn, das Boot, der Flug marked Higher)

Ich fahre mit dem Bus nach Wien.
*I'm travelling by bus to Vienna.*

Er hat Flugangst, also fährt er normalerweise mit dem Zug.
*He is scared of flying, so he usually travels by train.*

Im Urlaub fahre ich gern mit der Straßenbahn durch die Stadt, weil es billig und einfach ist.
*On holiday, I like to travel by tram through the city because it's cheap and easy.*

When Hilda messaged to say she was 'on the plane', this wasn't what her friends had pictured.

Section Nine — Travel and Tourism

# Deine Reise — *Your journey*

### Vocabulary

| | | | | | |
|---|---|---|---|---|---|
| die Reise | *journey* | ankommen | *to arrive* | pünktlich | *on time* |
| die Fahrt | *drive* | (in [+dat.]) | *(at)* | spät | *late* |
| das Ziel | *destination* | verlassen | *to leave* | unterwegs | *on the way* |
| die Linie | *line, route (e.g. bus)* | zurückkommen | *to return* | die Verbindung [H] | *connection, link* |
| | | warten (auf) | *to wait (for)* | | |

Es war nur eine kurze Fahrt zum Hotel.  
It was only a short drive to the hotel.

Der Zug nach Köln kommt auf Gleis drei an.  
The train to Cologne arrives at platform three.

Ich werde mein Hotel um halb vier verlassen, damit ich pünktlich im Flughafen ankommen kann.  
I will leave my hotel at half three so that I can get to the airport on time.

Wir werden mit dem Schiff hinreisen, aber mit dem Zug nach Hause zurückkommen.  
We will travel there by ship but we will return home by train.

**Question**  
Wie war die Reise?  
*How was the journey?*

**Simple Answer**  
Die Reise war sehr lang und langweilig. Sie hat vier Stunden gedauert.  
*The journey was very long and boring. It took four hours.*

**Extended Answer**  
Wir hatten unterwegs ein Problem. Der erste Zug hatte eine Verspätung und wir haben unsere Verbindung verpasst. Wir mussten dann zwei Stunden auf das nächste Boot warten.  
*We had a problem on the way. The first train was delayed and we missed our connection. Then we had to wait two hours for the next boat.*

## Practice Questions

Q1 Translate the following sentences into German.

a) Our room was very clean. [2 marks]  
b) We stayed in a cheap apartment. [2 marks]  
c) They went by bus to France. [2 marks]  
d) My bed was comfortable and warm. [2 marks]  
e) I arrived at the hotel. [2 marks]

The guests were buzzing to stay at Klaus's B&B.

Q2 Your Austrian friend Viola is talking about her holiday. Answer the questions in English. 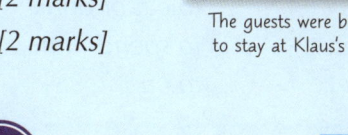 [Higher]

a) How does Viola describe her journey to Greece? [1 mark]  
b) Why did Viola arrive late to the airport? [1 mark]  
c) What was the problem with Viola's new ticket? [1 mark]  
d) How long did Viola's journey to Greece take in total? [1 mark]  
e) What did Viola see on her way to the hotel? Give **two** details. [2 marks]

---

### Campingplatz — a great hairstyle for staying in a tent…

They say that life is about the journey and not the destination. It's a nice idea, but for the purposes of your exam, holidays are about both — so feel free to rant about the delayed flight out *and* the dodgy hotel.

Quick Quiz

# What to Do

So much to do, so little time — these pages will guide you through the major tourist attractions.

## Wohin bist du gegangen? — *Where did you go to?*

**Vocabulary**

| | | | |
|---|---|---|---|
| der Ort | *place, town* | der See | *lake* |
| das Gebäude | *building* | das Restaurant | *restaurant* |
| das Museum | *museum* | das Café | *café, coffee shop* |
| das Schloss | *castle* | historisch | *historical* |
| der Markt | *market* | bekannt | *well-known, famous* |
| der Strand | *beach, shore* | **H** die Hauptstadt | *capital city* |

Ich bin zu einem bekannten Schloss gegangen. Es war sehenswert.

*I went to a famous castle. It was worth seeing.*

Wir haben eine historische Stadt neben einem großen See besucht.

*We visited a historical town next to a big lake.*

Wir sind zum Markt gegangen, um leckeres Essen zu kaufen.

*We went to the market to buy delicious food.*

It's good to get away from it all.

## Was hast du gemacht? — *What did you do?*

**Vocabulary**

| | | | |
|---|---|---|---|
| der Plan | *plan* | bestellen | *to reserve* |
| die Kultur | *culture* | entspannend | *relaxing* |
| kulturell | *cultural* | ruhig | *quiet, calm* |
| die Küche | *cuisine* | der Ausflug | *trip, outing* |
| der / die Tourist(in) | *tourist* | sich entspannen | *to relax* |
| nehmen | *to have something to eat or drink* | entdecken | *to discover* |
| | | führen | *to lead, guide* |
| verbringen | *to spend (time)* | unterhalten | *to entertain* |
| finden | *to find* | anbieten | *to offer* |

(entdecken, führen, unterhalten, anbieten marked **Higher**)

Abends gehe ich gern in eine lokale Stadt und gebe mein Geld für Eis aus.

*In the evenings, I like to go to a local town and spend my money on ice cream.*

Ich habe mit meiner Kamera viele Fotos gemacht. Ich werde ein Fotobuch über meinen Urlaub machen.

*I took lots of photos with my camera. I am going to make a photo book about my holiday.*

Meine Familie hat viel Zeit am Strand verbracht. Dort war es entspannender als in der Stadt, wo es viele Besucher gab.

*My family spent a lot of time at the beach. It was more relaxing there than in the city, where there were lots of tourists.*

*souvenirs* — Andenken

**Grammar** — making person nouns

You can often remove the '-en' and add '-er' to a verb stem to change the verb into a noun which describes someone doing the same action:

**besuchen** → **der Besucher**
*to visit* → *visitor*

Add '-in' to the noun if you want to talk about a female person.

**die Besucherin** *(female) visitor*

Section Nine — Travel and Tourism

# Im Urlaub... — On holiday...

|  |  |
|---|---|
| Im Urlaub sonne ich mich gern am Strand, während meine Schwester im Sand spielt. | On holiday, I like to sunbathe on the beach while my sister plays in the sand. |
| Ich möchte etwas Neues erleben. Vielleicht werde ich eine Galerie besuchen. | I would like to experience something new. Maybe I will visit a gallery. |
| Die Museen in Wien waren interessanter als die Museen zu Hause. | The museums in Vienna were more interesting than the museums at home. |

- swims in the sea — im Meer schwimmt
- go on a guided tour — eine Führung machen

**Q&A Audio**

### Question
Was machst du gern im Urlaub?
*What do you like to do on holiday?*

### Simple Answer
Ich gehe gern wandern und fotografiere die Landschaft.
*I like to go hiking and take photos of the landscape.*

### Extended Answer
Im Urlaub mag ich die lokale Küche probieren. Ich entdecke gern neue Gerichte, die ich dann zu Hause kochen kann.
*When I'm on holiday, I like to try the local cuisine. I like discovering new dishes that I can then cook at home.*

### Grammar — comparatives

*See p.125 for more on comparisons.*

To <u>compare</u> one thing to another in German, you usually just add '**er**' to the end of the <u>adjective</u>:

klein ➞ klein**er**    small ➞ small**er**

München ist <u>ruhiger</u> als Berlin.
Munich is <u>quieter</u> than Berlin.

If the adjective is one syllable and its vowel is 'a', 'o' or 'u', you normally add an <u>umlaut</u> as well:

lang ➞ l**ä**ng**er**    long ➞ long**er**

Der Strand ist <u>näher</u> als das Schloss.
The beach is <u>closer</u> than the castle.

A really common exception is '<u>gut</u>' (good):

gut ➞ <u>besser</u>    good ➞ <u>better</u>

## Practice Questions

**Q1** Look at the photo, then answer the following questions in German. **[SPEAKING]**

a) Sag mir etwas über das Foto.
b) Machst du lieber Urlaub am Strand oder in der Stadt? Warum?
c) Was hast du neulich im Urlaub gemacht?    [6 marks]

**Top Tip for Higher Students**
✓ Use plural reflexive verbs to say what you and others do on holiday, e.g. 'Wir entspannen uns am Strand.'

**Q2** Read Nida's description of her holiday. Answer the following questions in English. **[READING]**

*Higher*

> Im Urlaub war ich viel am Strand. Er war echt ruhig, also konnte ich mich entspannen. Im Hotel haben wir günstige Getränke gekauft und dann sind wir schwimmen gegangen. Laut meinen Eltern muss ein Urlaub auch kulturell sein und das finde ich auch. Deshalb haben wir Museen und die Hauptstadt besucht, um mehr über das Land zu lernen. Ich hoffe, nächstes Jahr zurückzugehen, weil ich einen Ausflug zu einem berühmten Schloss machen möchte.

a) What did Nida do at the beach?    [1 mark]
b) What did Nida do at her hotel? Give **one** detail.    [1 mark]
c) Give **two** places that Nida visited to learn about the country.    [2 marks]
d) Why does Nida want to go back?    [1 mark]

## Note to self: write joke when back from beach...

You might not have fun all the time on holiday — luckily, comparatives let you say what you liked more than something else. Make sure to learn the common odd ones out, like 'gut / besser' and 'viel / mehr'.

# Travel and Tourism — Vocabulary

Make sure these words aren't foreign to you — they'll be your ticket to success...

## Where to Go

|  |  |
|---|---|
| das Land | country, land, state, countryside |
| die Welt | world |
| die Region | region, area |
| Deutschland (n) | Germany |
| die Bundesrepublik, BRD | Federal Republic (of Germany) |
| Österreich (n) | Austria |
| das Bundesland | state, province (Germany, Austria) |
| die Schweiz | Switzerland |
| die Türkei | Turkey |
| Großbritannien (n) | Great Britain |
| England (n) | England |
| Frankreich (n) | France |
| Italien (n) | Italy |
| Spanien (n) | Spain |
| Griechenland (n) | Greece |
| München | Munich |
| Köln | Cologne |
| Wien | Vienna |
| der Rhein | the Rhine |
| die Ostsee | the Baltic Sea |
| Europa (n) | Europe |
| die EU (Europäische Union) | EU (European Union) |

|  |  |
|---|---|
| das Ausland | abroad, foreign countries |
| das Klima | climate |
| die Temperatur | temperature |
| die Sonne | sun |
| sonnig | sunny |
| heiß | hot |
| warm | warm |
| kalt | cold |
| der Urlaub | holiday |
| der Besuch | visit |
| fremd | foreign |
| fahren | to go (by transport), drive |
| reisen | to travel |
| besuchen | to visit |
| planen | to plan |
| Amerika (n) | America |
| die USA (Vereinigte Staaten von Amerika) | USA (United States of America) |
| international | international |
| gelten | to be valid |

(Higher: Amerika, die USA, international, gelten)

Thermometer: sehr warm — aahhhh / warm / kalt / e-e-extrem k-k-kalt — sehr kalt

Countries and continents that have (n) after them are neuter, but you don't need to use the article 'das' when you're talking about them in German.

## Accommodation

|  |  |
|---|---|
| das Hotel | hotel |
| die Wohnung | apartment, flat |
| das Zimmer | room |
| der Raum | room, space |
| der Platz | place, room, square, seat |
| das Bett | bed |
| der Gast | guest, visitor (male) |
| die Gästin | guest, visitor (female) |
| der / die Besucher(in) | visitor, guest |
| die Nähe | vicinity, proximity |
| bleiben | to stay, remain |
| wohnen | to stay (holidays) |
| schlafen | to sleep |
| organisieren | to organise |
| teuer | expensive, dear, costly |
| günstig | cheap, favourable, good, cheaply |
| billig | cheap, cheaply |
| sauber | clean |
| schmutzig | dirty, filthy |

|  |  |
|---|---|
| bequem | comfortable |
| voll | full |
| frei | free, available |
| die Landschaft | landscape, countryside |
| die Insel | island |
| die Küste | coast, shore |
| das Meer | sea, ocean |
| der Berg | mountain, hill |
| der Wald | forest, wood |
| der Blick | view, look, glance |
| willkommen | welcome |
| der Aufenthalt | stay, residence |
| das Zelt | tent |

(H: der Aufenthalt, das Zelt)

The holiday on the coast had been Lucky's choice.

Section Nine — Travel and Tourism

## Travel

| | |
|---|---|
| der Verkehr | transport, traffic |
| das Mittel | means |
| nehmen | to take |
| das Auto | car |
| das Fahrrad | bicycle |
| der Bus | bus |
| die Busse (pl) | buses |
| der Zug | train |
| die Bahn | train, railway |
| der Bahnhof | (railway) station |
| das Schiff | ship |
| das Flugzeug | aeroplane, plane, aircraft |
| der Flughafen | airport |
| fliegen | to fly |
| die Karte | ticket, card |
| das Ticket | ticket |
| die Reise | journey, trip, voyage |
| die Fahrt | drive, trip |
| der / die Fahrer(in) | driver |
| das Ziel | destination |
| der Kilometer | kilometre |
| die Linie | line, route (e.g. bus) |
| kommen | to come |
| mitnehmen | to take along |
| ankommen (in [dat.]) | to arrive (at) |
| verlassen | to leave |
| zurückkommen | to return |
| warten (auf) | to wait (for) |
| pünktlich | in/on time, punctual, prompt |
| spät | late |
| weg | gone, vanished, away |
| unterwegs | on the way |
| direkt | direct, straight, directly, immediately |
| vorne, vorn | at/to the front, ahead |
| weiter | further |
| zurück | back |

**Higher**

| | |
|---|---|
| die Straßenbahn | tram |
| die U-Bahn | metro, underground railway |
| das Boot | boat |
| der Flug | flight |
| die Verbindung | connection, link |
| die Geschwindigkeit | speed |
| ziehen | to move |

## What to Do

| | |
|---|---|
| der Ort | place, town, location |
| das Gebäude | building |
| die Gebäude | buildings |
| das Museum | museum |
| das Schloss | castle |
| der Markt | market |
| der Strand | beach, shore |
| der See | lake |
| die See | sea |
| die Quelle | spring |
| das Restaurant | restaurant |
| das Café | café, coffee shop |
| historisch | historical |
| bekannt | well-known, famous |
| berühmt | famous |
| der Plan | plan |
| die Kultur | culture |
| kulturell | cultural |
| die Küche | cuisine |
| der / die Tourist(in) | tourist |
| nehmen | to have something to eat or drink |
| verbringen | to spend (time) |
| erleben | to experience |
| die Erfahrung | experience |
| finden | to find |
| sich finden | to be found, find oneself |

'See' has two meanings, but you can tell which meaning it is by the gender. 'Der See' means 'lake', and 'die See' means 'sea'.

| | |
|---|---|
| bestellen | to reserve, order |
| entspannend | relaxing |
| ruhig | quiet, calm |
| das Geld | money, cash |
| der Euro | euro (unit of currency) |
| kosten | to cost |
| ausgeben | to spend (money) |
| zahlen | to pay |
| die Kamera | camera |
| das Foto | photo, photograph |
| die Sprache | language, speech |

**Higher**

| | |
|---|---|
| die Hauptstadt | capital city |
| sich entspannen | to relax, chill out |
| entdecken | to discover |
| erfahren | to experience, find out |
| führen | to lead, guide |
| unterhalten | to entertain |
| anbieten | to offer, serve something (with sth.) |
| der Ausflug | excursion, trip, outing |

# Revision Summary Test for Section Nine

You'll be jetting off on holiday before you know it, but pack in these summary questions first.
- These questions are **really tricky**, but they'll help you see **how well you know your stuff**.
- Tackle the **revision summary test** below, or scan the QR code to do it **online**.
  You can **keep track of your progress** online and see **which areas need more work**.
- There are **sample answers** here: www.cgpbooks.co.uk/BerlinExtras

## Where to Go

1) List the countries you know in German. There are 10 you need to know (plus 1 for Higher tier).
2) How would you say the following places in English?
   a) der Rhein   b) Wien   c) Köln   d) München   e) die Bundesrepublik
3) Translate the following into German:   a) province   b) world   c) abroad   d) region
4) Wo bist du neulich in Urlaub gefahren? Mit wem bist du da gereist? Answer in German.
5) Translate these sentences into English: 'Mein Besuch war toll, weil das Klima echt gut war. Die Temperaturen waren perfekt. Jeden Tag war es sonnig, aber nicht so heiß.'
6) Translate these sentences into German: 'Last summer, my family and I travelled to Europe. We planned the holiday well and visited lots of foreign countries.'
7) Lea asks you: 'Welches Land willst du in der Zukunft besuchen? Warum?' Reply in German.

## Accommodation and Travel

8) Jan tells you: 'Ich suche ein Hotel. Es muss ein ruhiges Hotel mit einer kleinen Zahl von Gästen sein. Ich will auch in einem großen Zimmer mit einem bequemen Bett schlafen.' What did he say?
9) Give an antonym of the following words in German: a) sauber   b) teuer   c) ankommen
10) Translate this into German: 'I want to stay in an apartment in the countryside.'
11) a) Name all the landscapes you can remember in German. There are 5 you need to know.
    b) Choose one of the landscapes you listed above. In German, explain why you'd like to stay there.
12) In German, list the 7 types of transport (plus 3 for Higher tier) that you need to know.
13) Kelechi says: 'Die Fahrt zum Bahnhof war lang, weil es viel Verkehr gab.' What did he say?
14) What is the German for: a) to wait   b) to fly   c) to return   d) to organise
15) Sven tells you: 'Auf meiner Reise ist der Bus spät angekommen. Dann habe ich meine Karte verloren.' What two things went wrong on his journey?
16) Wie reist du lieber, wenn du in Urlaub fährst? Warum? Answer in German.
17) Sophie wants to know: 'Bleibst du gern im Zelt? Warum oder warum nicht?' Respond in German.

## What to Do

18) a) A tourist leaflet says: 'Bei dem berühmten Schloss kannst du Fotos von historischen Dingen machen und etwas in unserem Café nehmen.' What does the leaflet say?
    b) In German, write a few sentences for a tourist leaflet for where you live.
19) Translate these nouns into German: a) place   b) market   c) lake   d) building   e) camera
20) Mona is talking about holidays: 'Ich finde Museen wirklich langweilig. Ich verbringe viel Zeit am Strand, weil ich gern im See schwimme.' What does she like and dislike doing on holiday?
21) Your friend Giang is telling you about her holiday: 'The traditional cuisine was great. I also learned a little about the culture and language.' How would you say this in German?
22) Give these adjectives in English: a) bekannt   b) ruhig   c) kulturell   d) entspannend
23) Was machst du gern im Urlaub? Answer in German using as much detail as possible.
24) How would you say the following in German? 'I am planning a trip in the capital city in order to discover the interesting buildings. In the evenings, I will relax at the hotel.'

Section Nine — Travel and Tourism

# Section Ten — Media and Technology

## Technology

Quick Quiz

Whether you can't get enough of gadgets, or the thought of robots taking over the world keeps you up at night, you need to be able to talk about technology in German.

### Die digitale Welt — *The digital world*

*Head to the CGP RevisionHub for all your online content: www.cgpbooks.co.uk/Berlin*

**Vocabulary**

| | | | | | |
|---|---|---|---|---|---|
| die Technologie | *technology* | die App | *app* | kompliziert | *complicated* |
| der Computer | *computer* | anrufen | *to phone* | nützlich | *useful* |
| der Laptop | *laptop* | simsen | *to text* | das Gerät | *appliance* |
| das Handy | *mobile phone* | digital | *digital* | aufladen | *to charge* |
| die SMS | *text message* | modern | *modern* | technisch | *technical* |

(Higher: das Gerät, aufladen, technisch)

Ich mache meine Hausaufgaben auf meinem Laptop.
*I do my homework on my laptop.*

I play video games — Ich spiele Videospiele

Ich simse meinen Freunden, um mit ihnen in Kontakt zu bleiben.
*I text my friends in order to stay in contact with them.*

call my grandparents — rufe meine Großeltern an

Meiner Meinung nach ist Technologie fantastisch, aber einige Leute finden digitale Geräte sehr kompliziert.
*In my opinion, technology is fantastic, but some people find digital appliances very complicated.*

you often need to charge electrical appliances — man muss Elektrogeräte oft aufladen

Q&A Audio

**Question**
Benutzt du oft Technologie?
*Do you often use technology?*

**Simple Answer**
Ja, ich benutze täglich meinen Laptop. Technologie ist in meinem Alltag sehr wichtig.
*Yes, I use my laptop daily. Technology is very important in my everyday life.*

Poor battery life is a crime now?

**Extended Answer**
Ich verwende fast jeden Tag die modernste Technologie, um mein Leben einfacher zu machen. Wenn ich irgendwohin fahren will, zeigt mir eine App den schnellsten Weg.
*I use the most modern technology almost every day in order to make my life simpler. Whenever I want to go somewhere, an app shows me the quickest way.*

**Grammar (Higher only) — um… zu…**

'Um… zu…' lets you say 'in order to…' or 'to…' do something. 'Um' goes at the start of a clause, usually after a comma, and 'zu' goes at the end with an infinitive verb after it. There's more info on 'um… zu…' on p.132.

Ich benutze mein Handy, **um** meiner Familie SMS **zu** schicken.
*I use my mobile phone **to** send my family texts.*

### Practice Question

Q1 Listen to these teenagers talking about the technology they use and decide whether the statements below are true or false.

LISTENING

Listening Track 13

a) Nadja prefers computers to laptops. [1 mark]
b) Bastian likes using apps in his everyday life. [1 mark]
c) Lisa thinks she spends too much time on her laptop. [1 mark]
d) Hilbert always gets the latest mobile phone. [1 mark]

### A page on mobile phones and more — now that's Handy…

Examiners love asking about technology, so make sure you can talk about what you use it for. If you want to give your revision some technological welly, why not scan one of the QR codes on this page…

# The Internet

The internet is great for finding out important information, like the height of the average giraffe, or the world record for the most cups of tea made in an hour. Email is quite useful too, I suppose...

## Das Internet — *The internet*

### Vocabulary

|  |  |
|---|---|
| die (Web)Seite | *(web) page* |
| das WLAN | *Wi-Fi®* |
| die E-Mail | *e-mail* |
| die Kommunikation | *communication* |
| der Kontakt | *contact* |
| die Nachricht | *news, message* |
| online | *online* |
| streamen | *to stream* |
| einkaufen | *to shop* |
| sich [dat.] ansehen | *to look at, watch* |
| planen | *to plan, design* |
| das Netz (Higher) | *net, network, web* |
| die Verbindung (Higher) | *connection, link* |
| verbinden (Higher) | *to connect, link* |
| sich informieren (über + noun) (Higher) | *to find out (about + noun)* |

Heute kann man fast alles online machen und ich kann mir mein Leben ohne das Internet nicht vorstellen.

*Today you can do almost everything online and I can't imagine my life without the internet.*

Es geht mir auf die Nerven, wenn ich keine Verbindung zum WLAN habe.

*It gets on my nerves when I have no Wi-Fi connection.*

In der Zukunft möchte ich meine eigene Webseite planen.

*In the future I would like to design my own web page.*

### Grammar (Higher only) — dative reflexive pronouns

You need to use dative pronouns with some German verbs, like 'sich vorstellen' *(to imagine)* and 'sich ansehen' *(to look at, watch)*.

**Ich sehe mir Filme an.**
*I watch films.*

**Sie stellt sich das jetzt vor.**
*She imagines it now.*

See p.111 for more pronouns.

## Ich benutze das Internet für... — *I use the internet for...*

**Question**
Wie benutzt du das Internet?
*How do you use the internet?*

**Simple Answer**
Meistens streame ich Musik. Ich kann neue Musik einfach finden und das ist für mich sehr spannend.
*I mostly stream music. I can find new music easily and that's very exciting for me.*

**Extended Answer**
Ich kaufe sehr gern online ein. Die Auswahl an Kleidung ist viel größer als im Geschäft, obwohl es schwierig ist, die richtige Größe zu bestellen.
*I really like to shop online. The choice of clothes is much greater than in the shop, although it's difficult to order the right size.*

Ich verbringe viel Zeit im Internet. Meine Eltern glauben, dass ich davon abhängig bin.

*I spend a lot of time on the internet. My parents think I'm addicted to it.*

waste — verschwende

Durch Online-Videospiele spiele ich mit Leuten auf der ganzen Welt.

*Through online video games, I play with people all over the world.*

In forums, I chat — In Foren chatte ich

Man kann im Internet viel herausfinden. Das finde ich nützlich, wenn ich meine Hausaufgaben mache.

*You can find out a lot on the internet. I find that useful when I do my homework.*

research — erforschen

Um mich über verschiedene Themen zu informieren, besuche ich viele Webseiten.

*In order to inform myself about various topics, I visit lots of web pages.*

I listen to podcasts — höre ich Podcasts

# Sicherheit im Internet — *Internet safety*

## Vocabulary

| | | | | | | |
|---|---|---|---|---|---|---|
| die Sicherheit | *security, safety* | die Quelle | *source* | die Daten | *data* |
| der Schutz | *protection* | sicher | *safe, secure* | das Opfer | *victim* |
| die Information | *information* | fremd | *strange* | stehlen | *to steal* |

(die Daten, das Opfer, stehlen — Higher)

Onlinesicherheit ist sehr wichtig. Man braucht ein starkes Passwort, um seine privaten Informationen zu schützen.

*Online safety is very important. You need a strong password to protect your personal information.* ← to prevent hacking — um das Hacken zu verhindern

Früher war ich Opfer eines Cyberangriffs, weil ich die Quelle einer fremden E-Mail nicht geprüft habe.

*In the past, I was the victim of a cyber attack, because I didn't check the source of a strange email.*

Wenn jemand dein Passwort herausfindet, werden deine Daten schutzlos.

*If someone finds out your password, your data becomes unprotected.* ← they can steal your data — kann er deine Daten stehlen

## Grammar (Higher only) — '-los'

You can add '-los' to the end of some nouns to make an adjective that means 'without' or '-less'.

    der Schutz + los = schutzlos    *without protection / unprotected*
    die Hilfe + los = hilflos    *helpless*

## Practice Questions

**Q1** Answer these questions out loud in German. (SPEAKING)

    **a)** Wie hast du neulich das Internet benutzt?
    **b)** Wie kann man im Internet sicher bleiben?
    **c)** Schickst du oft Nachrichten online? Warum / warum nicht?    [6 marks]

*Top Tip for Higher Students*
✓ Say what someone should do using 'man sollte' and an infinitive.

**Q2** Mia and Hans are writing about how they use the internet. (READING)

> **Mia:** Ich benutze das Internet ab und zu. Auf meinem Laptop mache ich nur meine Hausaufgaben. Ich sorge mich auch um meine Sicherheit im Internet, weil viele Webseiten private Informationen wollen. Mein Vater hat aber eine positive Meinung über das Internet. Er nimmt schon an einem Online-Buchclub teil.

> **Hans:** Jeden Morgen stehe ich auf und gehe auf meine Lieblingsseiten für die Nachrichten. Am Wochenende mag ich Filme auf meinem Laptop streamen. Ich weiß viel über das Internet, deshalb kann ich mich vor Gefahren schützen. Meine Mutter liebt auch das Internet fast so viel wie ich. Sie kauft oft online ein.

Who mentions what? Write **M** for **Mia**, **H** for **Hans** and **M + H** for **Mia** and **Hans**.

    **a)** Who uses the internet every day?    [1 mark]
    **b)** Who uses their laptop to watch movies?    [1 mark]
    **c)** Who is worried about their safety on the internet?    [1 mark]
    **d)** Whose parent is enthusiastic about the internet?    [1 mark]

## Accept cookies? Only if they're chocolate chip...

The internet is changing all the time, so make sure you can use the future tense to say how you might use the web in the future. For example, in a minute I'm going to look up how to knit a cardigan for my pet ferret...

# Social Media

*Social media might be great for procrastination, but unfortunately you do have to revise it as well...*

## Soziale Medien — *Social media*

### Vocabulary

| | | | |
|---|---|---|---|
| der / die Influencer(in) | *influencer* | hochladen | *to upload* |
| das Foto | *photo* | herunterladen | *to download* |
| das Video | *video* | teilen | *to share* |
| das Blog | *blog* | folgen | *to follow* |
| der Post | *(blog) post* | aufnehmen | *to record* |
| das Gespräch | *conversation, talk* | reagieren (auf) | *to react (to)* |

*The thing that is being followed needs to be in the dative case (see p.131).*

So oft wie möglich rede ich online mit meinen Freunden.
*As often as possible, I talk online with my friends.*

Ich bin Blogger(in) und ich gehöre zu mehreren sozialen Netzwerken.
*I am a blogger and I belong to several social networks.*

Ich folge einem Influencer, der Fotos von seinen Ferienreisen teilt.
*I follow an influencer, who shares photos of his travels.*

*I write two posts per week* — ich schreibe zwei Posts pro Woche

*uploads funny videos* — lustige Videos hochlädt

### Question
Verbringst du viel Zeit auf den sozialen Medien?
*Do you spend a lot of time on social media?*

### Simple Answer
Nein. Ich verbringe lieber meine Zeit in der wirklichen Welt, obwohl ich ab und zu Blogs lese.
*No. I prefer to spend my time in the real world, although I read blogs now and then.*

### Extended Answer
Ja. Regelmäßig benutze ich die sozialen Medien. Zum Beispiel sehe ich mir Videos an, die ich mit meinen Freunden teile. Manchmal nehme ich Videos auf und stelle sie online, weil ich selbst Influencerin werden möchte.
*Yes. I regularly use social media. For example, I watch videos which I share with my friends. Sometimes I record videos and put them online, because I would like to be an influencer myself.*

"Does it look like I'm holding it? Be honest."

## Die Vorteile sind... — *The advantages are...*

Meiner Meinung nach sind soziale Medien echt nützlich. Man kann Jugendliche kennenlernen, die die gleichen Interessen teilen.
*In my opinion, social media is really useful. You can get to know young people who share the same interests.*

Es gefällt mir, dass man zu verschiedenen Gruppen gehören kann.
*I like that you can belong to different groups.*

Alle können durch Apps miteinander in Kontakt bleiben. Es ist einfach, sofort einem Freund auf der anderen Seite der Welt eine Nachricht zu schicken.
*Everyone can stay in contact with each other through apps. It is easy to send a message to a friend on the other side of the world immediately.*

*organise an event* — eine Veranstaltung organisieren

*watch interesting videos* — sich interessante Videos ansehen

*react to the newest posts* — auf die neuesten Posts reagieren

# Die Nachteile sind... — *The disadvantages are...*

## Vocabulary

| | | | |
|---|---|---|---|
| die Gefahr | *danger, risk, threat* | privat | *private, personal* |
| das Risiko | *risk, hazard, danger* | die Risiken | *risks, hazards, dangers* |
| das Mobbing | *bullying* | vorsichtig | *cautious, careful, wary* |

Ein Nachteil von sozialen Medien ist, dass es schwierig ist, das Privatleben zu schützen.

*A disadvantage of social media is that it's difficult to protect your private life.*

Solange man vorsichtig ist, kann man die Gefahren von sozialen Medien reduzieren.

*As long as you are cautious, you can reduce the dangers of social media.*

Manche Leute benutzen soziale Netzwerke für Cyber-Mobbing, was schwer zu verhindern ist.

*Some people use social networks for cyber-bullying, which is difficult to prevent.*

to avoid negative conversations — negative Gespräche zu vermeiden

risks — Risiken

## Grammar — linking phrases

You can use linking words and phrases in German to introduce the positive and negative aspects of a topic. Here are just a few useful ones — remember to put the verb as the second idea when you use them.

| auf der einen Seite | *on the one hand* | allerdings | *though, indeed* | jedoch | *however* |
|---|---|---|---|---|---|
| auf der anderen Seite | *on the other hand* | dagegen | *on the other hand* | obwohl | *although* |

**Soziale Medien sind echt praktisch. Dagegen gibt es viele Gefahren.**
*Social media is really useful. On the other hand, there are many dangers.*

'Obwohl' is a subordinating conjunction, so it sends the verb to the end (see p.114).

## Practice Questions

Q1 You are writing an article for a German newsletter about how young people engage with social media. You should aim to write 90 words. Write about:

- how you personally use social media
- the advantages of social media
- the dangers of social media. **[15 marks]**

Top Tips for Higher Students
✓ Explain why you do something with 'um... zu...'.
✓ Use 'das Gute' and 'das Schlechte' to talk about 'the good thing' and 'the bad thing'.

Q2 Read Brigitte's email about her use of social media and then answer the questions below.

> Soziale Medien sind wunderbar. Ich verwende sie abends, aber ich erlaube es mir nie, soziale Medien vor der Schule zu nutzen. Ich sehe gern Videos, die meine Freunde aufgenommen haben. Obwohl ich nur fünfzig Personen auf sozialen Medien folge, ist das genug. Ich rede online nur mit Menschen, die ich persönlich kenne. Meine Eltern vertrauen mir, weil ich nie private Informationen mit Fremden teile.

Fluffy's owner had been liking photos of other cats.

a) When does Brigitte spend most of her time on social media? [1 mark]
b) What does Brigitte like to do on social media? [1 mark]
c) Who does she chat to on social media? [1 mark]
d) How do her parents feel about her using social media? [1 mark]

## Social media platforms — an influencer's going-out shoes...

Social media isn't all funny videos and photos of your grandad's pet rock — it has disadvantages too. Use phrases like 'auf der einen/anderen Seite' to show you've considered all sides of the topic.

# Media and Technology — Vocabulary

Time to scroll through some vocab...

## Technology

| | |
|---|---|
| die Technologie | technology |
| die Technik | technology |
| das System | system |
| das Programm | program |
| der Computer | computer |
| die Kamera | camera |
| der/das Laptop | laptop |
| das Handy | mobile phone |
| das Telefon | telephone |
| die SMS | text message |
| die/das App | app |
| der Ton | sound, tone |
| anrufen | to phone, ring |
| simsen | to text |
| schicken | to send |
| funktionieren | to function, work |
| digital | digital, digitally |

| | |
|---|---|
| modern | modern, up-to-date |
| kompliziert | complicated, complex |
| nützlich | useful |
| schnell | quickly, fast |
| kaputt | broken, ruined |
| neu | new, recent |
| teuer | expensive, dear, costly |
| einfach | simple, easy |
| **Higher:** | |
| das Gerät | appliance, tool |
| telefonieren | to (make a telephone) call |
| aufladen | to charge |
| klingen | to sound, ring |
| sich [dat.] vorstellen | to imagine |
| technisch | technical |
| speziell | specific |

*Some nouns taken from English have two possible genders in German. The one that appears first in the list is the most common.*

## The Internet

| | |
|---|---|
| das Internet | internet |
| die (Web)Seite | (web) page |
| das WLAN | Wi-Fi® |
| die/das E-Mail | e-mail |
| die Kommunikation | communication |
| der Kontakt | contact |
| die Nachricht | news, message |
| online | online |
| streamen | to stream |
| einkaufen | to shop |
| sich [dat.] ansehen | to look at, watch |
| planen | to plan, design |
| die Sicherheit | security, safety |
| der Schutz | protection |
| die Information | information |
| die Quelle | source |

| | |
|---|---|
| das Wort | word |
| sicher | safe, secure |
| fremd | strange |
| **Higher:** | |
| das Netz | net, network, web |
| die Verbindung | connection, link |
| verbinden | to connect, link |
| der / die Leser(in) | reader |
| sich informieren (über + noun) | to find out (about + noun) |
| informieren | to inform |
| die Studie | study, survey |
| die Werbung | advertising, advert(isement) |
| die Daten | data |
| das Opfer | victim, sacrifice, casualty |
| verstecken | to hide |
| stehlen | to steal |

## Social Media

| | |
|---|---|
| Medien | media |
| soziale Medien | social media |
| der / die Influencer(in) | influencer |
| das Video | video |
| das/der Blog | blog |
| der Post | (blog) post |
| das Gespräch | conversation, talk |
| hochladen | to upload |
| herunterladen | to download |
| teilen | to share |
| folgen | to follow |

| | |
|---|---|
| die Gefahr | danger, risk, threat |
| das Risiko | risk, hazard, danger |
| das Mobbing | bullying |
| privat | private, personal |
| persönlich | personal |
| echt | genuine, real, genuinely, really |
| aufnehmen | to record |
| drehen | to film, turn |
| **Higher:** reagieren (auf) | to react (to) |
| die Risiken | risks, hazards, dangers |
| vorsichtig | cautious, careful, wary |

Section Ten — Media and Technology

# Revision Summary Test for Section Ten

Don't switch off just yet — have a go at these questions to close the circuit on this section...
- These questions are **hard**, but they'll really help you see **how well you know your stuff**.
- Tackle the **revision summary test** below, or scan the QR code to do it **online**.
  You can **track your progress** online and see **which areas need more work**.
- There are **sample answers** for the test here: www.cgpbooks.co.uk/BerlinExtras

## Technology

1) Give the German for the following words:  a) system   b) program   c) text message
2) In German, give two things you normally use your mobile phone for.
3) You're chatting to three friends. For each sentence, say which device each friend mentions. Then choose the sentence that mentions a broken device.
   a) 'Wir haben viel Technologie zu Hause. Mein Vater hat eine moderne Kamera gekauft.'
   b) 'Obwohl er nützlich und schnell ist, war mein neuer Laptop sehr teuer.'
   c) 'Mein Computer ist sehr alt und funktioniert nicht mehr. Er ist total kaputt.'
4) Give the two German words for 'technology' that are in this section.
5) How would you say 'Today, digital technology makes life much easier.' in German? Do you agree with this statement? Answer in German.
6) Your Austrian exchange partner says 'Telefone sind praktisch, jedoch geht mir der Ton auf die Nerven, wenn jemand mich anruft.' What did they say?
7) Denk an ein Gerät, das du benutzt. Wie würdest du das Gerät verbessern? [H]

## The Internet

8) In German, describe how you spend your time on the internet.
9) Ömar is trying to use his laptop in a café. He says 'Das WLAN funktioniert hier nicht. Ich muss eine wichtige E-Mail schicken.' Say what the problem is in English.
10) Translate the following words into German:
    a) to design   b) protection   c) communication   d) page   e) contact   f) source
11) Hanna says to you 'Meine Sicherheit ist mir sehr wichtig. Wie kann ich online sicher bleiben?' What is she saying? In German, give her two pieces of advice.
12) Three teenagers give their reasons for using the internet. How would you say them in German?
    a) 'I read the news on the internet because it is cheaper than newspapers.'
    b) 'I rarely go to the cinema. I prefer to stream films at home.'
    c) 'I like to shop online, as I live far away from town.'
13) Give the German for these words:  a) to connect   b) reader   c) to find out about   d) victim [Higher]
14) Translate this into English: 'Die Verbindung zum Netz ist hier sehr schwach. Außerdem gibt es so viele Werbungen auf die Webseite. Ich kann sie kaum verwenden!'

## Social Media

15) What is the opposite of 'herunterladen'? What do these words mean? Now make up two German sentences, each with one of these words.
16) Give the German for these words: a) influencer   b) video   c) blog   d) post   e) personal
17) Niko tells you this: 'Ich benutze oft soziale Medien. Ich lerne gern Leute kennen, die die gleichen Interessen teilen.' Give the English for what he said, then say what you use social media for.
18) In German, describe one advantage and one disadvantage of social media.
19) Translate the following words into English: [H]
    a) aufnehmen   b) drehen   c) reagieren auf   d) die Risiken   e) vorsichtig

# Section Eleven — Where People Live

Quick Quiz

## The Home

Home is where the heart is, there's no place like home... You might not agree with the clichés, but you do need to be able to talk about your abode (humble or otherwise).

Remember there's also lots of online content here: www.cgpbooks.co.uk/Berlin

### Mein Haus — My house

**Vocabulary**

| | | | | | |
|---|---|---|---|---|---|
| wohnen | to live | die Küche | kitchen | der Garten | garden |
| das Haus | house | das Badezimmer | bathroom | der Haushalt | household |
| die Wohnung | apartment, flat | das Büro | office | der Schlüssel | key |
| das Zimmer | room | der Keller | basement | das Dach | roof |
| das Wohnzimmer | living room | der Gang | hallway | besitzen | to own |

(der Haushalt, der Schlüssel, das Dach, besitzen — Higher)

Ich wohne in einem alten Haus. Es hat drei Schlafzimmer und zwei Badezimmer.

*I live in an old house. It has three bedrooms and two bathrooms.*

- modern — modernen
- new — neuen
- a conservatory — einen Wintergarten

Ich habe mein eigenes Schlafzimmer.

*I have my own bedroom.*

Meine Familie wohnt in diesem Haus seit zehn Jahren.

*My family has lived in this house for ten years.*

- on the ground floor — im Erdgeschoss

Unsere Wohnung liegt im dritten Stock. Wir haben freundliche Nachbarn.

*Our flat is on the third floor. We have friendly neighbours.*

- a nice view from the windows — einen schönen Blick aus den Fenstern

### Wie sind die Zimmer? — What are the rooms like?

**Vocabulary**

| | | | | | |
|---|---|---|---|---|---|
| groß | big, great | bequem | comfortable | der Tisch | table |
| klein | small, little | ruhig | quiet, calm | die Tür | door |
| hoch | high, tall | laut | loud, noisy | das Fenster | window |
| schön | lovely, beautiful | das Bett | bed | angenehm (H) | pleasant |

At that moment, Daria realised she had measured up wrong.

Im Wohnzimmer haben wir ein altes Sofa und einen kleinen Tisch.

*In the living room, we have an old sofa and a small table.*

Die Küche sieht schön aus und sie hat blaue Wände. Sie ist auch sehr sauber.

*The kitchen looks lovely and it has blue walls. It is also very clean.*

Ich finde mein Zimmer ziemlich langweilig. Ich möchte bunte Möbel in mein Zimmer stellen.

*I find my room quite boring. I would like to put colourful furniture in my room.*

Wir haben einen Garten mit vielen Pflanzen und einem hohen Tor.

*We have a garden with many plants and a tall gate.*

In meinem Zimmer gibt es ein bequemes Doppelbett.

*In my room, there is a comfortable double bed.*

- single bed — Einzelbett

**Grammar — identifying plurals**

You can use grammatical markers like articles and verb forms to tell whether a noun is plural or not.

**Die** Zimmer **sind** klein.
*The rooms are small.*

**Das** Zimmer **ist** klein.
*The room is small.*

# Ein typischer Tag — *A typical day*

### Vocabulary

| | | | |
|---|---|---|---|
| aufstehen | *to get up* | essen | *to eat* |
| sich anziehen | *to get dressed* | sich kümmern um | *to take care of* |
| machen | *to do, make* | verlassen | *to leave* |
| helfen | *to help* | schlafen | *to sleep* |
| kochen | *to cook* | einschlafen | *to fall asleep* |

Jeden Morgen stehe ich um sieben Uhr auf und ziehe mich an.

*Every morning, I get up at seven o'clock and get dressed.*

clean my teeth — putze mir die Zähne

Wir helfen unserem Vater, ein großes Frühstück zu machen.

*We help our father to make a big breakfast.*

wash up — abzuwaschen

Ich verlasse das Haus und ich gehe mit meinem Hund im Park spazieren.

*I leave my house and I go for a walk with my dog in the park.*

take out the rubbish — bringe den Müll raus

**Q&A Audio**

### Question
Kannst du einen typischen Tag für dich beschreiben?

*Can you describe a typical day for you?*

### Simple Answer
Ich gehe in die Schule und abends mache ich Rugbytraining.

*I go to school and in the evenings I do rugby training.*

### Extended Answer
Ich stehe um halb acht auf. Nach dem Frühstück gehe ich in die Schule. Am Ende des Schultages holt meine Mutter mich ab. Später kochen wir zusammen das Abendessen.

*I get up at half past seven. After breakfast, I go to school. At the end of the school day, my mother picks me up. Later, we cook dinner together.*

## Practice Questions

**Q1** Look at the two photos below. Talk in German about what is in the photos. You should talk for about a minute and say something about both photos.

[5 marks]

**Q2** Translate the following sentences into English.

*Higher*

a) Sie hat den Schlüssel verloren.
b) Das Haus hat ein rotes Dach.
c) Sie besitzt ihre Wohnung nicht.
d) In meinem Haushalt ist es immer leise.
e) Es ist angenehm, im Garten zu sitzen.
f) Ich schlafe um zehn Uhr ein. [12 marks]

---

### I moved into a gingerbread house — home sweet home...

Next time you get the chance, use your own home to practise this vocab — walk around and name the different rooms and objects in German. You could even put labels everywhere if you want to. Go wild...

Find the CGP RevisionHub at cgpbooks.co.uk/Berlin

Section Eleven — Where People Live

# The Local Area

Ah, my local area — the station I'm always running to, the cafés I haunt, the street where I fell on my face... What a place. For the exam, make sure you're also able to talk all about where you live.

## Wo wohnst du? — *Where do you live?*

### Vocabulary

|  |  |
|---|---|
| das Dorf | village |
| die Stadt | town, city |
| der Ort | place |
| die Region | region |
| das Zentrum | centre, middle |
| die Straße | street |
| liegen | to be situated |
| **H** der Bereich | area, region |
| die Bevölkerung | population |
| der / die Bürger(in) | citizen |
| der / die Einwohner(in) | resident |
| aufbauen | to construct |

(Higher: die Bevölkerung, der/die Bürger(in), der/die Einwohner(in), aufbauen)

Wir wohnen **im Stadtzentrum**. Viele Menschen wohnen hier in Wohnungen.
We live **in the town centre**. Many people live in apartments here.

- in the outskirts — am Stadtrand

Ich wohne in **einem beliebten Ort**.
I live in **a popular place**.

- a beautiful area — einer schönen Gegend

Mein Haus **liegt** in einem **Dorf**. **Die Einwohner** kennen sich alle.
My house **is situated** in a **village**. **The residents** all know each other.

**Question**
Wo wohnst du?
*Where do you live?*

**Simple Answer**
Ich wohne im Stadtzentrum.
*I live in the city centre.*

**Extended Answer**
Ich wohne in einem Städtchen, das in der Nähe von der Küste liegt. Ich würde lieber in einem Ort mit einer großen Bevölkerung wohnen.
*I live in a little town that is situated near the coast. I would prefer to live in a place with a big population.*

### Grammar (Higher only) — '-chen' and '-lein'

When you add '-<u>chen</u>' or '-<u>lein</u>' to the end of a noun, it means '<u>little</u>'. Nouns with these endings are always <u>neuter</u>, and you often add an <u>umlaut</u> to the <u>root word</u>.

| die Stadt | → | das Städtchen |
|---|---|---|
| *the town* | | *the little town* |

It can also be used to show <u>endearment</u>.

| meine Schwester | → | mein Schwesterlein |
|---|---|---|
| *my sister* | | *my dear/little sister* |

## Wie ist deine Umgebung? — *What is your neighbourhood like?*

### Vocabulary

|  |  |
|---|---|
| die Umgebung | neighbourhood |
| das Gebäude | building |
| der Bahnhof | railway station |
| die Post | post office |
| das Café | café |
| der Markt | market |
| das Kino | cinema |
| der Strand | beach, shore |
| der Wald | forest, wood |
| die Fabrik | factory |
| die Anlage | facility, complex |
| der Bau | construction |

(Higher: die Fabrik, die Anlage, der Bau)

In meiner Umgebung gibt es **viele Cafés**, **einen Supermarkt** und **eine Bibliothek**.
In my neighbourhood, there are **a lot of cafés**, **a supermarket** and **a library**.

- a chemist's — eine Drogerie

Es gibt interessante Dinge zu tun, aber die Stadt **hat kein Kino**.
There are interesting things to do, but the town **doesn't have a cinema**.

- is not near a big city — liegt nicht in der Nähe von einer Großstadt

Meine Freunde und ich kaufen oft Essen **vom Café** und **sitzen im Park**.
My friends and I often buy food **from the café** and **sit in the park**.

- from the bakery — von der Bäckerei

In meiner Stadt gibt es **ein schönes Schloss**. Viele Touristen besuchen es.
In my city, there is **a beautiful castle**. Many tourists visit it.

- a historical monument — ein historisches Denkmal

Section Eleven — Where People Live

# Magst du einkaufen? — *Do you like shopping?*

## Vocabulary

| | | | |
|---|---|---|---|
| einkaufen | to shop | die Hose (sing.) | trousers |
| bezahlen | to pay | der Rock | skirt |
| ausgeben | to spend (money) | das Kleid | dress |
| verkaufen | to sell | Schuhe (m) | shoes |
| das Geschäft | shop | der Kunde | customer (male) |
| die Kleidung | clothes | die Kundin | customer (female) |
| das Hemd | shirt | der Laden | shop |
| die Jacke | jacket | liefern | to deliver, supply |

## Grammar — viel / viele

'Viel' (a lot of) is used with singular or uncountable nouns. 'Viele' (many) is used with plural nouns.

**Ich brauche viel Kleidung.**
*I need a lot of clothes.*

**Ich möchte viele Röcke.**
*I'd like many skirts.*

---

Wenn ich Kleidung kaufen muss, gehe ich ins Einkaufszentrum. Ich gebe dort viel Geld aus.

*When I have to buy clothes, I go to the shopping centre. I spend a lot of money there.*

— clothes — Klamotten (inf.)

Am Sonntag sind viele Geschäfte in meiner Stadt offen.

*On Sunday, many shops in my town are open.*

— closed — geschlossen

Ich will neue Schuhe kaufen, weil diese Schuhe mir nicht mehr passen.

*I want to buy new shoes because these shoes no longer fit me.*

— pick up — abholen

Als ich das Kleid angezogen habe, hat es mir gefallen, aber der Preis war sehr teuer.

*When I put the dress on, I liked it, but the price was very expensive.*

— I prefer to wear trousers — ich trage lieber Hosen

## Practice Questions

**Q1** You are going to host an exchange student at your home and you are writing an email to them about your local area. You should write about 90 words in German. Describe:

- the places of interest in your local area
- something you recently did in your town
- where you will take the exchange student when they visit.   *[15 marks]*

**Top Tip for Higher Students**
✓ Use the conditional to talk about what you would like to do. E.g. 'Es wäre schön, wenn wir das Museum besuchen würden.'

**Q2** Listen to Jana talking about her trip to the shops. Choose the correct option for each question below.

Listening Track 14

a) Jana wanted to buy...
   **A.** a pair of trousers.   **B.** a new jacket.   **C.** a new skirt.   *[1 mark]*

b) The skirt Jana found in the first shop...
   **A.** didn't fit her.   **B.** was very expensive.   **C.** looked horrible.   *[1 mark]*

c) In another shop, Jana found a skirt that was...
   **A.** just as beautiful.   **B.** more expensive.   **C.** not her style.   *[1 mark]*

## Remember this tiplein and you'll do just fine...

It's a handy one about cases. You need to use the dative case whenever you're talking about where you live — when you use a preposition with 'wohnen', like 'in' or 'auf', the noun after it has to be in the dative case.

*Find the CGP RevisionHub at cgpbooks.co.uk/Berlin*

**Section Eleven — Where People Live**

# Directions and Weather

Feeling like you could do with a little direction? Look no further — learn these pages and you'll be sorted when you need to talk about directions and weather, come rain or shine.

## Wo ist es? — *Where is it?*

### Vocabulary

| | | | | | |
|---|---|---|---|---|---|
| die Richtung | *direction, way* | hier | *here* | hinter | *behind* |
| der Weg | *path, way* | da | *there* | neben | *next to, beside* |
| linke | *left (adj.)* | dort | *there* | gegenüber | *opposite* |
| rechte | *right (adj.)* | weiter | *further, (carry) on* | weg | *gone, away* |
| links | *on / to the left* | oben | *above, up there* | drinnen | *inside* |
| rechts | *on / to the right* | unten | *down, below* | heraus | *outside* |

Entschuldigung, wie komme ich zum Bahnhof? — *Excuse me, how do I get to the train station?*

Du findest die Bäckerei gegenüber der Turnhalle. — *You'll find the bakery opposite the gym.*

Gehen Sie ins Einkaufszentrum und die Post ist auf der linken Seite. — *Go into the shopping centre and the post office is on the left-hand side.*

### Grammar — prepositions and cases

Some prepositions take either the accusative or the dative case.

If movement is involved, use the accusative:
**Gehen Sie in die Stadt.** (accusative)
*Go into town.*

If no movement is involved, use the dative:
**Die Post ist in der Stadt.** (dative)
*The post office is in town.*

## Ist es weit weg? — *Is it far away?*

### Vocabulary

| | | | | | |
|---|---|---|---|---|---|
| die Nähe | *vicinity* | der Norden, Nord- | *north* | die Lage | *location* |
| der Kilometer | *kilometre* | der Osten, Ost- | *east* | die Ecke | *corner* |
| nah | *near(by)* | der Süden, Süd- | *south* | fern | *far, distant* |
| weit | *far* | der Westen, West- | *west* | entfernt | *distant, away* |

(Higher)

Das Krankenhaus liegt im Süden der Stadt. Es ist gar nicht weit weg. — *The hospital is in the south of the city. It's not far away at all.*

Der Supermarkt ist in der Nähe von hier. Sie müssen die erste Straße rechts nehmen, und dann finden Sie den Supermarkt auf dem Platz. — *The supermarket is near here. You have to take the first street on the right, and then you will find the supermarket in the square.*

Die Bank ist nur zwei Kilometer von hier entfernt. — *The bank is only two kilometres from here.*

Die Kirche liegt um die Ecke. Sie werden sie nicht verpassen! — *The church is around the corner. You won't miss it!*

Dieses Restaurant liegt in Ostberlin, also ist es weit von hier. Du solltest die U-Bahn nehmen, um hinzureisen. — *This restaurant is in East Berlin, so it's far from here. You should take the metro to travel there.*

Don't forget to use the polite form 'Sie' for people who are older than you. See p.10 for more about the different forms of 'you'.

over there — drüben

three miles — drei Meilen

Matilda wished she'd updated her satnav.

Section Eleven — Where People Live

# Wie ist das Wetter? — *How is the weather?*

## Vocabulary

|  |  |  |  |  |  |
|---|---|---|---|---|---|
| das Wetter | *weather* | schneien | *to snow* | dunkel | *dark, gloomy* |
| das Klima | *climate* | sonnig | *sunny* | die Sonne | *sun* |
| die Temperatur | *temperature* | heiß | *hot* | der Schnee | *snow* |
| der / das Grad | *degree* | warm | *warm* | der Wind | *wind* |
| regnen | *to rain* | kalt | *cold* | der Himmel | *sky* |

Im Sommer wird es sonnig sein. — *In the summer, it will be sunny.*

Heute ist es heißer als gestern. Ich hoffe, dass es später nicht regnen wird. — *Today it is hotter than yesterday. I hope it won't rain later.*

Im Winter schneit es viel. Die Tage sind auch so kurz. — *In the winter it snows a lot. The days are also so short.*

Mir ist heiß, weil es heute mehr als dreißig Grad ist. — *I feel hot because it's more than thirty degrees today.*

*windy* — windig
*cloudy* — wolkig
*foggy* — neblig

*hails* — hagelt
*thunders* — donnert

You should always use 'mir ist...' to talk about feeling hot or cold.

### Question
Wie ist das Wetter?
*What's the weather like?*

### Simple Answer
Es regnet und es ist ziemlich kalt.
*It is raining and it is quite cold.*

### Extended Answer
Heute Morgen war es sehr heiß, aber am Nachmittag hat es geregnet. Es ist noch zwanzig Grad, also ist es nicht kalt, aber es ist nass. Die Temperatur nimmt allerdings nächste Woche ab.

*This morning it was very hot, but in the afternoon it rained. It is still twenty degrees, so it isn't cold, but it is wet. The temperature will fall next week though.*

## Practice Questions

**Q1** You read next week's weather report. Answer the following questions in English.

> Am Montag wird die Temperatur sehr kalt: nur zwei Grad. Aber am Dienstag wird es noch kälter und Schnee ist überall möglich. Von Mittwoch bis Freitag regnet es viel und die Tage werden sehr dunkel. Jedoch verbessert sich das Wetter am Wochenende. Man kann warme Temperaturen und einen klaren Himmel erwarten. Leider gibt es dann einen starken Wind am Sonntagabend.

a) How many degrees will it be on Monday? [1 mark]
b) What will the weather be like on Tuesday? Give **two** details. [2 marks]
c) Give **one** detail about Thursday's weather. [1 mark]
d) What will happen on Sunday evening? [1 mark]

**Q2** [Higher] Listen to a local person giving directions to a tourist. Complete the sentences in English.

a) The station is in the _____ of the city.
b) Before you reach the church, go _____ .
c) Go right when you are _____ .
d) The station is _____ the park. [4 marks]

## Berlin must be very rainy — the forecast always says 'Wetter'...

If you want to predict what the weather *will* be like, there are two ways to do it. Using 'werden' plus an infinitive is one option, but you can also use the present tense with an adverb, e.g. 'Morgen ist es sonnig'.

# Where People Live — Vocabulary

You're on the home stretch of this section now — to celebrate, take a look at some vocab.

## The Home

|  |  |
|---|---|
| wohnen | to live |
| das Haus | house |
| die Wohnung | apartment, flat |
| der Raum | room, space |
| das Zimmer | room |
| das Wohnzimmer | living room, lounge, sitting room |
| die Küche | kitchen |
| das Badezimmer | bathroom |
| das Bad | bath, bathroom, spa |
| die Toilette | toilet |
| das Büro | office |
| der Keller | cellar, basement |
| der Gang | corridor, hallway |
| der Garten | garden |
| das Bett | bed |
| der Tisch | table |
| der Stuhl | chair |
| die Tür | door |
| das Fenster | window |
| die Wand | wall |
| der Boden | floor, ground |
| das Tor | gate |
| das Blatt | leaf |
| die Pflanze | plant |
| der / die Nachbar(in) | neighbour |
| groß | big, great |
| klein | small, little |
| hoch | high, tall |
| schön | lovely, beautiful |
| bequem | comfortable |
| ruhig | quiet, calm |
| laut | loud, noisy |
| sauber | clean |
| nutzlos | useless |
| die Ordnung | order, tidiness |
| die Ruhe | silence, peace, rest |
| nach Hause | (to) home |
| zu Hause | at home |
| der Müll | rubbish, waste, litter |
| aufstehen | to get up |
| sich anziehen | to get dressed |
| machen | to do, make |
| helfen | to help |
| kochen | to cook, boil |
| essen | to eat |
| sich kümmern um | to take care of |
| verlassen | to leave |
| schlafen | to sleep |

**Higher**

|  |  |
|---|---|
| der Haushalt | household, budget |
| der Schlüssel | key |
| das Dach | roof |
| der Hof | yard |
| die Mauer | wall |
| besitzen | to own, have |
| einschlafen | to fall asleep, doze off |
| angenehm | pleasant |

## The Local Area — Places

|  |  |
|---|---|
| das Dorf | village |
| die Stadt | town, city |
| der Ort | place, town, location |
| die Region | region, area |
| die Gegend | area, region |
| das Gebiet | region, area, territory |
| das Zentrum | centre, middle |
| die Mitte | middle, centre |
| die Straße | street, road |
| die Hauptstraße | main street |
| die Umgebung | surroundings, neighbourhood |
| das Gebäude | building |
| die Gebäude | buildings |
| der Bahnhof | railway station |
| das Krankenhaus | hospital |
| die Polizei | police |
| der Supermarkt | supermarket |
| die Post | post office, post, mail |
| das Café | café, coffee shop |
| der Imbiss | take away, diner, snack bar, snack, refreshment |

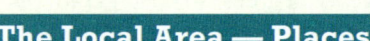

The plural of 'bank' is 'die Banken', whereas the plural of 'bench' is 'die Bänke'.

|  |  |
|---|---|
| der Markt | market |
| die Kirche | church |
| die Moschee | mosque |
| die Synagoge | synagogue |
| der Tempel | temple |
| das Kino | cinema |
| das Theater | theatre |
| die Bank | bank, bench |
| der Park | park |
| das Feld | field, pitch, court (sport) |
| der Platz | place, room, square, seat, pitch (sport) |
| der Strand | beach, shore |
| der Wald | forest, wood |
| das Stadion | stadium |
| das Hotel | hotel |
| die Brücke | bridge |
| die Stelle | place, position |

|  |  |
|---|---|
| bauen | to build, construct |
| liegen | to be situated |
| fehlen | to lack, be absent, be missing |
| es gibt | there is, there are |
| es gab | there was, there were, there used to be |

**Higher**

|  |  |
|---|---|
| der Bereich | area, region, district |
| die Bevölkerung | population, people, members of the public |
| der / die Bürger(in) | citizen |
| der / die Bürgermeister(in) | mayor |
| der / die Einwohner(in) | resident, inhabitant |
| die Fabrik | factory |
| das Werk | work, plant, factory |
| die Industrie | industry |
| die Anlage | facility, complex |
| der Bau | construction, building |
| aufbauen | to build up, construct |
| existieren | to exist |

## The Local Area — Shopping

|  |  |
|---|---|
| einkaufen | to shop |
| bezahlen | to pay |
| akzeptieren | to accept |
| ausgeben | to spend (money) |
| verkaufen | to sell |
| das Geschäft | business, shop |
| die Kleidung | clothes, outfit |
| das Hemd | shirt |
| das T-shirt | T-shirt |
| die Jacke | jacket |
| die Hose (sing.) | trousers |
| der Rock | skirt |
| das Kleid | dress |
| der Schuh | shoe |
| Schuhe (m) | shoes |
| das Paar | pair, couple |
| die Tasche | pocket, bag |
| die Uhr | clock, watch |
| der Preis | price |
| die Rechnung | bill, invoice |
| der Kunde | customer (male) |
| die Kundin | customer (female) |
| passen | to fit, suit |
| tragen | to carry, wear |
| abholen | to get, fetch, pick up |
| öffnen | to open |
| schließen | to close, shut |
| offen | open |
| geschlossen | closed, shut |
| der Laden | shop |
| wechseln | to change, exchange (money) |
| liefern (Higher) | to deliver, supply |
| sich [dat.] anziehen (+ noun) (Higher) | to put on (+ noun) |
| hübsch (Higher) | pretty, cute, lovely |
| hässlich (Higher) | ugly, hideous |

Coco was always happy to fetch some shopping.

## Directions and Weather

|  |  |
|---|---|
| die Richtung | direction, way |
| der Weg | path, way, method |
| linke | left (adj.) |
| rechte | right (adj.) |
| links | on / to the left |
| rechts | on / to the right |
| hier | here |
| da | there |
| dort | there |
| weiter | further, (carry) on |
| oben | upstairs, above, up there |
| unten | downstairs, below, down |
| hinter | behind |
| hinten | at / in the back |
| neben | next to, beside |
| gegenüber | opposite, across from |
| weg | gone, vanished, away |
| die Nähe | vicinity, proximity |
| der Kilometer | kilometre |
| nahe, nah | near(by), close |
| weit | far |
| eng | narrow, close, tight |
| der Norden, Nord- | north |
| der Osten, Ost- | east |
| der Süden, Süd- | south |
| der Westen, West- | west |
| das Wetter | weather |
| das Klima | climate |
| die Temperatur | temperature |
| der / das Grad | degree (temperature) |
| regnen | to rain |
| schneien | to snow |
| sonnig | sunny |
| heiß | hot |
| warm | warm |
| kalt | cold |
| dunkel | dark, gloomy |
| die Sonne | sun |
| der Schnee | snow |
| der Wind | wind |
| der Himmel | sky |
| die Höhe | height, altitude |
| der Frühling | spring |
| der Sommer | summer |
| der Herbst | autumn |
| der Winter | winter |
| die Lage (Higher) | situation, location, position |
| die Ecke (Higher) | corner |
| der Rand (Higher) | edge |
| fern (Higher) | far, distant |
| entfernt (Higher) | distant, away |
| drinnen (Higher) | inside, indoors |
| heraus (Higher) | out, outside |
| hinaus (Higher) | out, beyond |
| der Stern (Higher) | star |
| mir ist... (Higher) | I feel... |

Use 'mir ist...' to talk about the temperature you're feeling, e.g. 'Mir ist kalt' ('I feel cold'). You can also say 'es ist mir...' to mean the same thing.

# Revision Summary Test for Section Eleven

Ding dong, it's another revision summary test — this time, it's all about where you live.
- Yep, these questions are **hard** — they'll really help you see **how well you know your stuff**.
- Tackle the **revision summary test** below, or scan the QR code to do it **online**. Use the CGP RevisionHub to **track your progress** and see **which areas need more work**.
- You can find **sample answers** here: www.cgpbooks.co.uk/BerlinExtras

## The Home

1) Kim says: 'Ich wohne in einem Haus, aber ich will in einer Wohnung wohnen.' What did she say?
2) How do you say the following in German?
   a) corridor  b) window  c) door  d) wall  e) chair  f) table  g) bed  h) floor
3) In German, say what rooms are in your home and describe what they are like.
4) Lara says, 'In meinem Garten gibt es jetzt viele bunte Pflanzen. Es gibt auch viele Blätter an den Bäumen.' In English, write what she has said.
5) Malik describes his morning routine: 'Ich stehe früh auf. Ich ziehe mich an und dann mache ich Frühstück. Ich gehe um zwanzig vor neun zur Schule.' List the activities he mentions in English.
6) Elio asks you, 'Wann verlässt du dein Haus am Morgen?' In English, write what he wants to know.
7) Translate these words into German: a) household  b) key  c) roof  d) yard
8) Wenn du dein eigenes Haus hättest, wie würde es aussehen? Answer in German.

## The Local Area

9) What do the following words mean in English?
   a) das Dorf  b) der Ort  c) das Zentrum  d) die Umgebung  e) die Gegend  f) das Gebiet
10) How many names can you remember for buildings that can be found in a village, town or city? There are 16 you need to know (plus 3 for Higher tier).
11) You are on holiday in a small town in Germany. In German, how would you say that the town has a forest, a large bridge and a park, but there is no beach?
12) Translate these words into German: a) street  b) field  c) square  d) to build  e) to be situated
13) Was ist dein Lieblingsgebäude in deiner Stadt? Warum?
14) In German, list all the names for things you wear in this section. There are 9 you need to know.
15) Jabari says: 'Das Geschäft in der Mitte ist heute geschlossen. Morgen wird es offen sein, also werde ich es dann besuchen.' When is Jabari going to the shop and why?
16) Write this sentence in German: 'I want to wear these shoes, but they don't fit me.'
17) Give the German for: a) bill  b) price  c) to shop  d) to pay  e) to sell  f) to pick up
18) 'Der Bürgermeister der Stadt möchte eine Fabrik in der Nähe vom Strand bauen. Die Bürger sind aber mit diesem Vorschlag nicht zufrieden.' Who is unhappy and what are they unhappy about?
19) Ask the following question in German: 'Will the supermarket deliver the food tomorrow?'

## Directions and Weather

20) Translate these directions into English: 'Das Café ist zehn Minuten von hier. Sie müssen hinter das Krankenhaus und dann durch den Park gehen. Sie werden das Café neben der Post finden.'
21) Write this sentence in English: 'Das Klima ist toll. Die Sonne scheint und der Himmel ist blau.'
22) In German, describe what the weather will be like where you live over the next week.
23) The directions say, 'Die Sportanlage ist um die Ecke. Sie liegt ungefähr zweihundert Meter entfernt.' What does this mean?
24) Imagine somebody asks you 'Wo ist der Supermarkt?' Give them directions in German, using the formal imperative form. Give as much detail as you can.

# Section Twelve — Environmental and Social Issues

## Environmental Problems

Quick Quiz

It's time to talk about a whole world of problems — prepare yourself...

Don't forget you can access your online content here: www.cgpbooks.co.uk/Berlin

### Umweltprobleme — *Environmental problems*

**Vocabulary**

| | | | | | | |
|---|---|---|---|---|---|---|
| die Umwelt | *environment* | zerstören | *to destroy* | der Faktor | *factor* | |
| die Natur | *nature* | schmutzig | *dirty* | menschlich | *human (adj.)* | Higher |
| die Welt | *world* | der Müll | *litter* | der Stoff | *material* | |
| das Problem | *problem* | wegwerfen | *to throw away* | brennen | *to burn* | |
| verschmutzen | *to pollute* | das Fahrzeug | *vehicle* | produzieren | *to produce* | |

Menschliche und natürliche Faktoren führen zu Umweltproblemen.

*Human and natural factors lead to environmental problems.*

Die meisten fossilen Brennstoffe sind umweltschädlich.

*Most fossil fuels are harmful for the environment.*

Die Zerstörung der Wälder ist ein großes Problem. Firmen benutzen oft die Flächen, um Fabriken und Häuser zu bauen.

*The destruction of forests is a big problem. Companies often use the area to build factories and houses.*

Es gibt zu viele Fahrzeuge, die zu Luftverschmutzung führen können.

*There are too many vehicles, which can lead to air pollution.*

Deforestation — Die Abholzung

that produce harmful substances — die Schadstoffe produzieren

Q&A Audio

**Question**

Was für Umweltprobleme gibt es in deiner Gegend?

*What environmental problems are there in your area?*

**Simple Answer**

In meiner Gegend werfen viele Leute ihren Müll nicht richtig weg. Dann landet es im Fluss.

*In my area, lots of people don't throw their rubbish away correctly. Then it lands in the river.*

**Grammar — making verbs into nouns**

In German, you can add the suffix '<u>-ung</u>' to some <u>verb stems</u> to make a <u>noun</u> with a similar meaning. <u>Nouns</u> which <u>end</u> in '<u>-ung</u>' are always <u>feminine</u>.

verschmutz**en** → verschmutz → die Verschmutz**ung**
*to pollute* — *pollution*

zerstör**en** → zerstör → die Zerstör**ung**
*to destroy* — *destruction*

**Extended Answer**

In der Stadt, wo ich wohne, verschwenden einige Leute eine Menge Kleidung. Es ist schlecht für die Umwelt. Meiner Meinung nach verhalten sich diese Menschen unverantwortlich.

*In the town where I live, some people waste a lot of clothes. It is bad for the environment. In my opinion, these people behave irresponsibly.*

### Practice Question

Q1 Translate these sentences about environmental problems into English.

a) Eine Menge Müll verschmutzt die Landschaft. [2 marks]
b) Das Reisen mit dem Flugzeug ist nicht umweltfreundlich. [2 marks]
c) Die Aktionen von einige Leute und Firmen zerstören die Natur. [2 marks]

   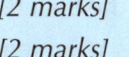 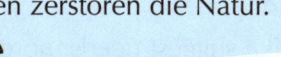

### My noisy neighbour is causing problems in my environment...

Struggling with compound words like 'Umweltprobleme'? Try splitting them up, e.g. 'Umwelt' (environment) + 'probleme' (problems) means 'environmental probl-' \***clang**\* \***crash**\* I SAID KEEP IT DOWN, WILL YOU!

# Environmental Impacts

Now that you can talk about environmental problems, it's time to talk about their impacts. Fun.

## Die Konsequenzen — *The consequences*

### Vocabulary

| | | | | | |
|---|---|---|---|---|---|
| die Konsequenz | *consequence* | die Luft | *air* | der Klimawandel | *climate change* |
| die Sorge | *worry, care* | das Meer | *ocean* | der Zustand | *condition* |
| die Temperatur | *temperature* | der Fluss | *river* | die Folge | *result* |
| steigen | *to increase* | der Wald | *forest* | das Ereignis | *event* |
| das Wetter | *weather* | der Baum | *tree* | verursachen | *to cause* |

(The last three columns marked **Higher**)

### Question
Welches Umweltproblem macht dir Sorgen?
*Which environmental problem worries you?*

### Simple Answer
Ich sorge mich um die Zerstörung von den Wäldern, denn die Tiere werden ihren Lebensraum verlieren.
*I worry about the destruction of the forests because animals will lose their habitat.*

### Grammar — 'Ich habe Angst'
You can use '<u>haben</u>' with <u>some nouns</u> to mean the same as '<u>to be + adjective</u>' in English.

**Er hat <u>Angst</u>.** — He is <u>afraid</u>, <u>anxious</u>.
**Ich habe <u>Hunger</u>.** — I am <u>hungry</u>.
**Sie haben <u>Durst</u>.** — They are <u>thirsty</u>.

### Extended Answer
Ich habe Angst vor den Folgen der Luftverschmutzung für die menschliche Gesundheit. Wahrscheinlich wird die Anzahl von Lungenkrankheiten steigen.
*I'm afraid of the consequences of air pollution on human health. The number of lung diseases will likely increase.*

---

Die Konsequenzen der <u>Wasserverschmutzung</u> können schlimm sein.
*The consequences of <u>water pollution</u> can be serious.*

Als Folge vom Klimawandel wird es mehr extreme Wetterereignisse geben.
*As a result of climate change, there will be more extreme weather events.* ← the ice sheets will melt — werden die Eisschichten schmelzen

Wissenschaftler warnen, dass die Temperaturen steigen und die Gefahr von <u>Waldbränden</u> wächst.
*Scientists warn that temperatures are rising and the threat of <u>forest fires</u> is growing.*

*flooding* — Überschwemmungen
*storms* — Stürmen
*drought* — Dürren

(We're on thin ice...)

## Practice Question

**Q1** Yusuf and Erika are discussing their concerns about the environment. Answer the questions below.

a) What does Erika say there is a lack of in some regions? Name **two** things. [2 marks]
b) Why are the beaches so dirty? [1 mark]
c) Why does Yusuf feel sad? [1 mark]
d) What problem does Erika suggest needs more attention? [1 mark]

Listening Track 16

---

### Ich habe Angst now that I've read this page...
...but learning the vocab is a good distraction. To help you memorise it, make a mind map — in the middle of your paper, put 'Environmental Impacts', then write all the key vocab and German phrases from this page.

# Protecting the Environment

Quick Quiz

After your exams, you could recycle this book — it'd make lovely wallpaper for your bedroom...

## Der Umweltschutz — *Environmental protection*

### Vocabulary

|  |  |
|---|---|
| der Schutz | protection |
| schützen (vor [dat.]) | to protect (from) |
| das Recycling | recycling |
| recyceln | to recycle |
| sauber | clean |
| grün | green |
| die Energie | energy |
| die Quelle | source |
| sparen | to save |
| das Ziel | target |
| die Lösung (Higher) | solution |
| reduzieren | to reduce |
| das Elektroauto | electric car |
| verwenden | to use |

Wir sollten **die Umwelt schützen**. — We should **protect the environment**.

**Sonnenenergie** ist eine mögliche Alternative zu umweltschädlichen Energiequellen wie Öl, Gas und Kohle. — **Solar energy** is a possible alternative to environmentally damaging energy sources, like oil, gas and coal.

Zu Hause recyceln wir viele Stoffe, aber es gibt auch in unserer Stadt **ein Recyclingzentrum**, wohin wir andere Sachen, wie Kleidung, bringen können. — At home, we recycle a lot of materials, but in our town there is also **a recycling centre**, where we can bring other things, like clothes.

Man soll **öffentlichen Verkehrsmitteln** benutzen, statt mit dem Auto fahren. Das würde **Luftverschmutzung** reduzieren. — People should use **public transport** instead of going by car. That would reduce **air pollution**.

- collect litter — Müll aufsammeln
- Renewable energy — Erneuerbare Energie
- Hydroelectric power — Wasserkraft
- Wind energy — Windenergie
- the greenhouse effect — den Treibhauseffekt

Q&A Audio

### Question
Wie kann man umweltfreundlicher sein?
*How can you be more environmentally friendly?*

### Simple Answer
Man soll mehr Energie sparen. Zum Beispiel soll man immer das Licht ausmachen, wenn man einen Raum verlässt.
*People should save more energy. For example, you should always turn lights off when you leave a room.*

### Extended Answer
Man soll so viel wie möglich Obst und Gemüse aus seiner Region kaufen. Jedoch kann es teuer sein und nicht jeder kann es sich leisten. Außerdem kann man weniger Fleisch essen, was besser für die Umwelt wäre.
*You should try as much as possible to buy fruit and vegetables from your region. However, it can be expensive and not everyone can afford it. Furthermore, you can eat less meat, which would be better for the environment.*

## Practice Question

Q1 Write a blog post about protecting the environment. You should aim to write 90 words in German. Write about:
- why it's important to protect the environment
- something you did last week to protect the environment
- what people should do to help in the future.

WRITING

**Top Tip for Higher Students**
✓ Use conditional forms of verbs such as 'wäre' (will be) and 'würde' (would be).

[15 marks]

## I'm environmentally friendly — I always say hello to my plants...

To say what you think people can or should do to care for the environment, use modal verbs like 'können' and 'sollen'. Stick them with an infinitive to talk about actions people can take, e.g. 'recyceln' (to recycle).

# Social Issues

Quick Quiz

There's a lot of doom and gloom in the world, but there are also ways you can make a difference.

## Reich und arm — *Rich and poor*

**Vocabulary**

| | | | | | | |
|---|---|---|---|---|---|---|
| der Nachteil | *disadvantage* | fehlen | *to lack* | | die Krise | *crisis* |
| arbeitslos | *unemployed* | die Gesellschaft | *society* | | die Schuld | *debt* |
| reich | *rich* | die Wirtschaft | *economy* | Higher | knapp | *scarce* |
| arm | *poor* | die Arbeitslosigkeit | *unemployment* | | der Kampf | *struggle* |
| der Hunger | *hunger* | sich [dat.] leisten | *to afford* | | kämpfen | *to struggle* |

(Higher: die Gesellschaft, die Wirtschaft, die Arbeitslosigkeit, sich leisten)

Die Kluft zwischen Arm und Reich nimmt in unserer Gesellschaft zu.
— The gap between poor and rich is increasing in our society.
*Inequality — Ungleichheit*

Die Arbeitslosigkeit kann negative langfristige Effekte auf die Gesundheit haben.
— Unemployment can have negative long-term effects on health.

Einige Familien machen Schulden und sie können sich notwendige Dinge nicht leisten. Als Folge leiden sie unter Hunger.
— Some families get into debt and they can't afford necessary things. As a result, they suffer from hunger.
*poverty — die Armut*

## Gefährliche Situationen — *Dangerous situations*

**Vocabulary**

| | | | | | | |
|---|---|---|---|---|---|---|
| der Krieg | *war* | gefährlich | *dangerous* | H | der Konflikt | *conflict* |
| die Gewalt | *violence, force* | die Situation | *situation* | | der Flüchtling | *refugee* |

Die Gewalt ist ein großes Problem hier.
— Violence is a big problem here.
*Discrimination — Die Diskriminierung*

Flüchtlinge fliehen aus Ländern, die im Krieg oder gefährlich sind.
— Refugees flee from countries that are at war or dangerous.
*which don't protect human rights — die Menschenrechte nicht schützen*

Manchmal gibt es Konflikte zwischen verschiedenen Gruppen in der Gesellschaft.
— Sometimes there are conflicts between different groups in society.
*communities — Gemeinschaften*

## Die Wahlen — *Elections*

**Vocabulary**

| | | | | | | |
|---|---|---|---|---|---|---|
| das Recht | *right, law* | wählen | *to elect, vote* | H | gerecht | *just, fair* |
| die Stimme | *vote* | das Gesetz | *law* | | die Regierung | *government* |

Das Gesetz soll die Menschenrechte schützen.
— The law should protect human rights.

Es ist wichtig zu wählen, damit man fordern kann, dass die Regierung die Lebensbedingungen verbessert.
— It's important to vote so that you can demand that the government improve living conditions.

# Anderen helfen — Helping others

## Vocabulary

| | | | |
|---|---|---|---|
| die Hilfe | help | abnehmen | to reduce |
| freiwillig | voluntary | das Volk *(Higher)* | people |
| retten | to save, rescue | der Fortschritt *(Higher)* | progress |
| verbessern | to improve | sich (freiwillig) melden *(Higher)* | to volunteer |

Ich melde mich freiwillig mit Organisationen, um das Bewusstsein für Obdachlosigkeit zu erhöhen.
*I volunteer with organisations to raise awareness for homelessness.*

Ich habe den Gemeinschaftsgarten in meiner Gegend gegründet, damit Leute ihre psychische und physische Gesundheit verbessern können.
*I founded the community garden in my area so that people can improve their mental and physical health.*

**Q&A Audio**

### Question
Wie hilfst du anderen in deiner Gegend?
*How do you help others in your area?*

### Simple Answer
Jede Woche helfe ich freiwillig in einer Jugendgruppe.
*Every week, I volunteer in a youth group.*

### Extended Answer
Ich glaube, dass psychische Krankheiten ein ernstes Problem sind. Letztes Jahr habe ich an einem Lauf teilgenommen und dadurch habe ich Geld für eine Organisation gesammelt. Diese Organisation unterstützt Menschen mit solchen Krankheiten.

*I think that mental illnesses are a serious problem. Last year, I took part in a race and as a result, I raised money for an organisation. This organisation supports people with such illnesses.*

## Grammar (Higher only) — making nouns from adjectives

You can add 'heit' or 'keit' to some adjectives and adverbs to turn them into nouns that end in -ness or -ty in English. Nouns which end in 'heit' and 'keit' are feminine.

| krank | ill | → | die Krank**heit** | ill**ness** |
| möglich | possible | → | die Möglich**keit** | possibili**ty** |

## Practice Questions

**Q1** Answer these questions out loud in German. *(SPEAKING)*
 a) Wie hast du anderen in der Vergangenheit geholfen?
 b) Warum ist es wichtig, dass wir anderen Menschen helfen?
 c) Was sind die Vorteile, wenn man wählt? [6 marks]

**Top Tip for Higher Students**
✓ Use Higher tier vocab such as 'die Regierung' and 'das Gesetz'.

**Q2** Read this passage written by Annika and answer the questions below in English. *(READING)* *(Higher)*

> Der Konflikt und die Gewalt sind Probleme in meiner Gegend. Jedoch meine ich, dass die Arbeitslosigkeit das größte Problem ist. Viele Menschen sind in Schwierigkeiten, weil sie sich weder Essen noch Energie leisten können. Einige Organisationen helfen ihnen. Meiner Meinung nach wäre es aber besser, wenn die Regierung mehr Unterstützung bieten würde. Eine weitere Lösung wäre bessere Möglichkeiten für Bildung zu schaffen, damit Leute bessere Stellen bekommen können.

 a) According to Annika, what is the biggest issue in her area? [1 mark]
 b) What do many people struggle to afford? Name **two** things. [2 marks]
 c) Why does Annika suggest people should have more opportunities for education? [1 mark]

## I'll need some help coming up with a joke about this stuff...

These pages weren't the cheeriest, but the issues are important and you'll need to be able to talk about them in your exams. Use phrases like 'zum Beispiel' to give examples of issues and solutions in your answers.

# Environmental and Social Issues — Vocabulary

Phew, that was a tough section — well done you for getting this far. As a reward, have some vocab. You're welcome.

## Environmental Problems

|  |  |
|---|---|
| die Umwelt | environment |
| die Natur | nature |
| die Erde | earth, ground, soil, world |
| die Welt | world |
| das Problem | problem |
| verschmutzen | to pollute, contaminate |
| zerstören | to destroy, ruin |
| schmutzig | dirty, filthy |
| der Müll | litter, rubbish, waste |
| werfen | to throw |
| weg | away, gone, vanished |
| wegwerfen | to throw away |
| die Menge | quantity, amount, a lot of, crowd (people) |
| das Fahrzeug | vehicle |
| natürlich | natural, naturally |
| draußen | outside, outdoors |
| überall | everywhere |
| das Klima | climate |
| der Faktor | factor |
| menschlich | human (adj.) |
| der Stoff | material, substance, fabric |
| brennen | to burn |
| produzieren | to produce |
| die Risiken | risks, hazards, dangers |
| riesig | huge, great, tremendous, giant, massive, enormous |
| erschrecken | to frighten, be startled |
| aktuell | current, up-to-date, topical |
| die Fabrik | factory |

(Higher: das Klima … die Fabrik)

## Environmental Impacts

|  |  |
|---|---|
| die Konsequenz | consequence |
| die Sorge | worry, care |
| sorgen | to worry, care |
| die Temperatur | temperature |
| der / das Grad | degree (temperature) |
| steigen | to increase, go up, climb |
| verschwinden | to disappear |
| das Wetter | weather |
| die Luft | air |
| das Meer | sea, ocean |
| der Fluss | river |
| der Lauf | course |
| der Wald | forest, wood |
| der Baum | tree |
| die Pflanze | plant |
| der Himmel | sky |
| der Klimawandel | climate change |
| die Veränderung | change |
| der Zustand | condition, state |
| die Folge | result, consequence |
| der Effekt | effect |
| das Ereignis | event, occurrence, incident |
| die Ursache | cause |
| verursachen | to cause |
| das Feuer | fire |
| wachsen | to grow, increase |
| der / die Wissenschaftler(in) | scientist |
| warnen (vor [dat.]) | to warn (of / about) |

(Higher: der Klimawandel … warnen)

## Protecting the Environment — Actions

|  |  |
|---|---|
| der Schutz | protection, conservation |
| schützen (vor [dat.]) | to protect (from) |
| umweltfreundlich | environmentally friendly |
| das Recycling | recycling |
| recyceln | to recycle |
| sammeln | to collect, gather |
| verboten | forbidden, banned |
| öffentlich | public |
| der Verkehr | traffic, transport |
| das Mittel | means |
| das Ziel | goal, aim, target |
| sauber | clean |
| praktisch | practical, useful |
| die Lösung | solution, answer |
| lösen | to solve, loosen |
| die Verantwortung | responsibility |
| erhalten | to preserve, maintain |
| trennen | to separate |
| reduzieren | to reduce, decrease |
| verbieten | to forbid, prohibit, ban |
| sich [dat.] lassen | to have sth done |
| das Elektroauto | electric car, electric vehicle |
| vorsichtig | cautious, careful, wary |
| die Suche | search |
| die Methode | method, technique |
| die Gegenwart | present |
| künftig | future, from now on |
| langfristig | long-term, in the long run |
| rein | pure, clear, clean, total(ly) |

(H: die Lösung, lösen; Higher: die Verantwortung … rein)

Section Twelve — Environmental and Social Issues

## Protecting the Environment — Energy Sources

| | | |
|---|---|---|
| grün | green | |
| die Energie | energy | |
| sparen | to save | |
| die Quelle | source | |
| das Licht | light | |

*Higher*
- die Sonne — sun
- der Wind — wind
- die Kraft — power
- der Haushalt — household
- verwenden — to use

*Higher*
- das Angebot — offer, supply
- bieten — to offer, provide
- das Gerät — tool, appliance, piece of equipment
- das Projekt — project

## Social Issues

| | |
|---|---|
| die Schwierigkeit | difficulty |
| der Nachteil | disadvantage |
| der Vorteil | advantage, benefit |
| arbeitslos | unemployed |
| der Unterschied | difference |
| reich | rich, wealthy, abundant |
| arm | poor |
| die Kosten | costs, expenses |
| kosten | to cost |
| gleich | equal |
| frei | free |
| der Hunger | hunger |
| leiden (an [dat.]) | to suffer (from) |
| leiden (unter [dat.]) | to suffer (as a result of) |
| fehlen | to lack, be missing |
| der Krieg | war |
| die Gewalt | violence, force |
| die Gefahr | danger, risk, threat |
| gefährlich | dangerous, risky |
| die Situation | situation |
| treiben | to drive |
| brechen | to break |
| die Freiheit | freedom |
| das Recht | right, law |
| die Stimme | vote |
| die Wahl | choice, election, selection |
| die Mehrheit | majority |
| der Aspekt | aspect |
| stimmen (für) | to vote (for) |
| sich erklären | to declare oneself |
| wählen | to choose, elect, vote, select |
| die Leute (pl) | people |
| die Hilfe | help, assistance |
| freiwillig | voluntary, voluntarily |
| retten | to save, rescue |
| verbessern | to improve |
| fallen | to fall, decrease |
| abnehmen | to decrease, reduce |
| breit | wide, broad |
| weit | far, wide, widely |

*Higher*
- die Gesellschaft — society
- die Wirtschaft — economy, commerce
- die Arbeitslosigkeit — unemployment
- sich [dat.] leisten — to afford
- die Bedingung — condition, stipulation, requirement
- die Krise — crisis

| | |
|---|---|
| die Schuld | guilt, blame, debt |
| knapp | scarce, slim |
| der Kampf | fight, struggle, battle |
| kämpfen | to fight, struggle, battle |
| der Konflikt | conflict, dispute |
| der Schaden | damage, harm |
| der Flüchtling | refugee |
| das Opfer | victim, casualty |
| der Gegner | enemy |
| zwingen | to force, compel |
| verhalten | to control |
| die Tat | deed, action |
| stehlen | to steal |
| das Gesetz | law |
| gerecht | just, fair |
| die Einführung | introduction |
| gründen | to establish, found |
| feststellen | to establish, detect, determine, realise |

*Higher*
- die Bundesregierung — federal government
- die Regierung — rule, government
- das Volk — people
- der Bürger — citizen
- der Fortschritt — progress
- das Zeichen — sign, symbol
- die Bildung — education, learning, creation, formation
- bilden — to educate, form
- melden — to report, register
- sich (freiwillig) melden — to volunteer, enlist
- erhöhen — to raise, increase
- die Organisation — organisation
- der Fall — fall, case
- der Bericht — report, record
- die Umfrage — survey
- untersuchen — to examine, investigate, research
- fordern — to demand, claim
- drohen — to threaten
- beweisen — to prove, demonstrate
- aufnehmen — to take in
- lassen — to let, allow
- sich beschäftigen mit — to deal with
- die Erinnerung — memory, reminder
- sinnvoll — sensible, meaningful
- verantwortlich — responsible, in charge

Section Twelve — Environmental and Social Issues

# Revision Summary Test for Section Twelve

I hope you've been saving some energy, because it's time for a revision summary test.
- These questions are **really tricky**, but they'll help you see **how well you know your stuff**.
- Tackle the **revision summary test** below, or scan the QR code to do it **online**.
  You can **keep track of your progress** online and see **which areas need more work**.
- There are **sample answers** here: www.cgpbooks.co.uk/BerlinExtras

## Environmental Problems

1) How would you say the following in English?
   a) draußen   b) die Natur   c) die Erde   d) überall   e) schmutzig
2) Was für Umweltprobleme gibt es? Answer this in German, mentioning at least two things.
3) You hear Chioma talking about environmental problems: 'Environmental problems destroy our natural world. For example, a lot of vehicles pollute the air.' Translate this into German.
4) You hear Finn say: 'Wenn Plastik brennt, produziert es Stoffe, die gar nicht umweltfreundlich sind. Dies ist ein menschlicher Faktor der Klimaveränderung.' What is he saying? *(Higher)*
5) Give the German words for: a) factory   b) enormous   c) current   d) to frighten   e) risks *(Higher)*

## Environmental Impacts

6) List the 7 nouns from this section that are parts of the natural world in German.
7) In German, explain why people should care about rising temperatures.
8) Read this headline: 'Der Klimawandel stellt den Zustand der Umwelt in Gefahr.' What does it say? *(H)*
9) What's the German for: a) result   b) incident   c) cause   d) to cause   e) to grow *(H)*

## Protecting the Environment

10) Give the German words for: a) target   b) conservation   c) to protect   d) clean   e) forbidden
11) Was für eine umweltfreundliche Aktivität hast du letzte Woche gemacht?
12) Which of the following isn't an action people can take to protect the environment?
    a) Man soll grüne Energiequellen benutzen.   c) Man kann Flüsse mit Müll verschmutzen.
    b) Man soll mehr Papier und Glas recyceln.   d) Man muss noch mehr Energie sparen.
13) Give the English words for: a) die Lösung   b) das Elektroauto   c) rein   d) verwenden *(Higher)*
14) Mit welchen drei Methoden kann man die Natur erhalten? Answer this in German. *(Higher)*
15) Your friend Elias tells you: 'Climate change will have long-term effects and it's our responsibility to reduce the damage.' Translate what they said into German. *(Higher)*

## Social Issues

16) Give the English words for: a) die Gewalt   b) der Krieg   c) die Freiheit   d) der Hunger
17) What do these questions want to know?
    a) Haben alle Leute das Wahlrecht?   b) Wie groß ist der Unterschied zwischen Arm und Reich?
18) List the 13 verbs (plus 17 for Higher tier) related to social issues covered in this section.
19) Give the German words for: a) equal   b) voluntarily   c) dangerous   d) wide   e) free
20) Your friend Layla asks you: 'Welche schwierige Situationen gibt es in deiner Gegend? Wie kann man Leuten in Schwierigkeiten Hilfe geben?' How would you respond in German?
21) Give the German words for: a) economy   b) crisis   c) debt   d) struggle   e) society   f) deed *(Higher)*
22) You hear Mika talking about politics: 'Die Regierung hat ein neues Gesetz geschaffen, um die Lebensbedingungen der Bürger zu verbessern.' Translate what she said into English. *(Higher)*
23) Give the English words for: a) das Volk   b) der Fortschritt   c) das Zeichen   d) gerecht   e) fern *(Higher)*
24) Warum gibt es Flüchtlinge? Answer this question in German.

# Section Thirteen — Nouns, Cases and Linking Words

Quick Quiz

# Nouns

Student, meet nouns. Nouns, meet student. I'll let you get acquainted...

## German nouns start with capital letters

In German, absolutely every noun, whether it's a person, place or object, starts with a capital letter.

| der Mann | the man | | die Schule | the school |

## German nouns are either masculine, feminine or neuter

1) Every German noun has a gender. If a noun has 'der' in front, it's masculine (in the nominative case — see p.105). If it has 'die' in front, it's feminine or plural, and if it has 'das' in front, it's neuter.

2) The gender of a noun affects lots of things — the words for 'the' and 'a' change, and so do any adjectives.

eine große Gruppe    a big group

3) You can use these rules to help you recognise whether a noun is masculine, feminine or neuter:

| Gender | Nouns that end in... | And... |
|---|---|---|
| Masculine | -el, -us, -ling, -er | male person nouns, days, months, seasons |
| Feminine | -ie, -heit, -tion, -ung, -ei, -keit, -sion, -tät, -schaft | most female person nouns |
| Neuter | -chen, -um, -lein, -ment | infinitives as nouns, most countries, English words |

4) Words for people often have masculine and feminine versions. You can add '-in' to male person nouns to make them feminine.

der Freund    the (male) friend      die Freundin    the (female) friend

5) Some person nouns also have other changes, like adding umlauts to the vowels.

der Arzt    the (male) doctor      die Ärztin    the (female) doctor

Laughter wasn't the best medicine for Steve's bad back.

## Compound nouns are a combination of two or more words

1) A compound noun is a noun made of two or more words stuck together. The last word in the compound 'decides' what the noun's gender is and how the plural will be formed (see p.104 for more).

die Haustür    front door

2) Compound nouns often have extra letters in between the words.

das Geburtstagsgeschenk    birthday present

*The extra letter(s) in compound words will usually be -e, -s/-es, -n/-en, -ens or -er.*

3) Sometimes the 'e' or 'en' is dropped at the end of the first word, like 'Schwimmbad' (swimming pool).

4) Compound words can also be adjectives or verbs.

hellblau    light blue      aufstehen    to stand up

### Grammar Questions

Look at these German nouns and use the rules on this page to fill in the gaps with 'der', 'die' or 'das'.

1. ...... Freiheit
2. ...... Mittwoch
3. ...... Frühling
4. ...... Mädchen
5. ...... Meinung
6. ...... Polizei
7. ...... Sängerin
8. ...... Schwimmen

## Geschwindigkeitsbegrenzung — yep, that's a real word...

It means 'speed limit'. I wonder if there's a word for 'number-of-letters-in-a-word limit'... There should be.

# Forming Plurals and Other Nouns

Life would be boring if there was just one of everything. Imagine only having one cupcake. Tragic.

## Making nouns plural

1) There are lots of different ways to make nouns plural in German — it's not just a matter of adding an 's'.

| How to make the word plural | Example | |
|---|---|---|
| No change — many nouns ending in '-el', '-en', '-er' | der Keller (the cellar) | → die Keller (the cellars) |
| Add '-e' — most masculine and neuter nouns. They sometimes add an umlaut as well. | der Schuh (the shoe)<br>der Baum (the tree) | → die Schuhe (the shoes)<br>→ die Bäume (the trees) |
| Add '-er' — some masculine and neuter nouns. They sometimes add an umlaut as well. | das Lied (the song)<br>der Wald (the forest) | → die Lieder (the songs)<br>→ die Wälder (the forests) |
| Add '-n' or '-en' — most fem. and some neuter nouns | die Pflanze (the plant) | → die Pflanzen (the plants) |
| Add an umlaut and '-e' — some feminine nouns | die Hand (the hand) | → die Hände (the hands) |
| Add '-nen' — female person nouns ending in '-in' | die Chefin (the boss) | → die Chefinnen (the bosses) |
| Add '-se' — fem. and neuter nouns ending in '-nis' | das Zeugnis (the report) | → die Zeugnisse (the reports) |
| Add '-s' — some nouns, especially borrowed nouns | das Hotel (the hotel) | → die Hotels (the hotels) |

**Higher**

2) Some masculine nouns are called weak nouns, and they are mostly words for people and animals. To make weak masculine nouns plural, add either '-n' (if the noun ends in '-e') or '-en' (for all others).

der Junge  *the boy*  →  die Jungen  *the boys*

> Singular weak masculine nouns also add '-n' or '-en' in the accusative, dative and genitive cases.

## You can also use verbs and adjectives as nouns

1) In German, you can turn infinitives of verbs into nouns. These are always neuter.

schwimmen  *to swim*  →  das Schwimmen  *swimming*

When verbs and adjectives work as nouns in German, they need a capital letter.

2) Words for languages are the same as the adjective of the nationality in German, and are always neuter.

englisch  *english*  →  das Englisch  *the English language*

**Higher**

3) Sometimes in English you use adjectives to talk about groups of people — e.g. the homeless. These are called adjectival nouns. In German, you can use adjectival nouns in the same way.

die Arbeitslosen
*the unemployed*

Adjectival nouns have the same endings that they would if they were still adjectives. See p.123.

4) In German, abstract nouns are often made from adjectives too.

das Gute  *the good thing*

5) Abstract nouns can follow words like 'viel' (a lot of), 'wenig' (few), 'etwas' (something) and 'alles' (everything).

etwas Gutes  *something good*

## Grammar Questions

Translate these sentences into **German**. You might need to find some of the words in a dictionary first.

1. He has many sisters.
2. The children are small.
3. The tables are free.
4. The doctors are nice.
5. **H** The rich (ones) buy a lot. **H**
6. The (male) students play basketball.

---

## Single noun seeks very own happy ending — apply within...

If you're not sure how to make a noun plural, have a look in a dictionary. The plural comes after the noun.

# Cases — Nominative and Accusative

Cases might seem like a strange concept at first, but bear with me — they're essential in German.

## Cases mean that you have to change words to fit

1) In German, words are written differently depending on which case they're in.

   Der kleine Hund grüßt den kleinen Hund.   *The small dog greets the small dog.*

   Both these bits mean 'the small dog', but they're written differently. This is because the second bit is in a different case from the first bit.

2) This page and the next page are all about when you use the different cases.

3) Often, you have to change the words to fit the case — see p.103 for nouns, p.107 for articles and p.123-124 for adjectives.

## The nominative and accusative cases

1) The nominative case and the accusative case are the cases you'll need to use the most.

2) The case of a word depends on what the word's doing in the sentence.

   Der Lehrer liest den Brief.   *The teacher reads the letter.*

   The teacher is doing the action. This makes him the subject of the sentence. The subject is always in the nominative case.

   This bit of the sentence is the verb. It tells you what the subject is doing.

   This last bit is what the verb is done to. It's in the accusative case.

## So remember the golden rules...

1) Use the nominative case for who (or what) is doing the action — this is the subject of the sentence. Use the accusative case for who (or what) the action is done to — this is the direct object.

   Ein Mann kauft einen Schuh.   *A man buys a shoe.*   The man is doing the action, so he's in the nominative case. The shoe is being bought, so it's in the accusative case.

   Der Junge sieht den Hund.   *The boy sees the dog.*   The boy is doing the action, so he's in the nominative case. The dog is being seen, so it's in the accusative case.

2) The bit in the nominative case doesn't always have to be the first bit of the sentence.

   Heute fährt Zoe nach Berlin.   *Today Zoe is going to Berlin.*   Zoe is doing the action, so she's in the nominative case. For more on word order, see p.112.

   Magst du singen?   *Do you like to sing?*      Wahrscheinlich ist er krank.   *He is probably ill.*

### Grammar Questions

Read the sentences. Say which words are in the nominative case and which are in the accusative case.
1. Der Mann spricht Deutsch.
2. Die Stadt hat eine Synagoge.
3. Ich habe eine Schwester.
4. Er kauft Pommes.
5. Meine Mutter hat ein Auto.
6. Ich kaufe einen neuen Rock.

### Get a handle on these cases — wheels would help too...

That dictionary will come in handy again here — it'll always tell you what a word is in the nominative case.

# Cases — Dative and Genitive

Here we go — the other two German cases. They're not as scary as they seem, I promise.

## Use the dative case to say 'to someone', 'from someone'…

1) Before you get going on the dative case, make sure you understand the accusative case (p.105) really well. Then have a look at these two sentences:

   **Accusative case**
   Eva schreibt einen Brief.   *Eva writes a letter.*

   **Dative case**
   Eva schreibt einem Freund.   *Eva writes to a friend.*

2) In the first one, Eva is writing a letter. Eva is in the nominative case because she's writing, and the letter is in the accusative case because it's being written.

3) In the second one, Eva is writing to a friend. The friend isn't being written — he is being written to, so he's the indirect object, which means he can't be in the accusative case. Instead, he's in the dative case.

4) You also need to use the dative case with some verbs (see p.131) and some prepositions (see p.116).

   e.g. helfen (*to help*), geben (*to give*), folgen (*to follow*)

   e.g. mit (*with*), von (*from*), zu (*to*)

## Use the genitive case to talk about belongings

**Higher**

1) When you want to say things like 'Sarah's' or 'Obinna's' or 'my dad's', you need the genitive case.

   Das Auto meines Vaters.   *My father's car.* ← Literally, 'the car of my father'.

   See p.107 for the articles you need to form the genitive case.

   Hermann isst das Eis des Mädchens.   *Hermann eats the girl's ice cream.* ← Literally, 'the ice cream of the girl'.

2) Be careful — you don't need the genitive case for phrases like 'my dad's a doctor'. This is short for 'my dad is a doctor', which is very different to saying that a doctor belongs to your dad.

## Nouns sometimes get endings to fit the case

**Higher**

1) Nouns (see p.103) sometimes change depending on what case they're in.

2) Plural nouns add '-n' in the dative.

   Ich schreibe den Kindern.   *I write to the children.*

   Normally, 'children' = 'Kinder', but in the dative, it becomes 'Kindern'. If the noun already ends in '-n', you don't need to add another 'n'. 'Streets' = 'Straßen', so in the plural dative, it's still 'Straßen'.

3) Masculine and neuter nouns add 's' in the genitive case.

   Das Haus meines Onkels.   *My uncle's house.*

   There are some words where you have to add 'es' rather than just 's'. They usually end in '-s', '-ß', '-x' or '-z'.

### Grammar Questions

In the following sentences, identify the nouns in the dative case and in the genitive case (for Higher tier).

1. Ich gebe meinem Bruder das Buch.
2. Du fährst mit einer Freundin in die Stadt.
3. Er ist der Hund meines Vaters. [H]
4. Sie ist die Katze meiner Mutter. [H]

## I always speak indirectly — it's my dative language…

Lots of words change depending on what case they're in, so it's really important you know how they work. 'The', 'a' and 'no' are just some of the words that are affected by cases and are all on the next page. Handy.

# Definite and Indefinite Articles

A tiger cannot change its stripes. German articles are not tigers — they're changing all the time.

## 'The' — start by learning der, die, das, die

'The' is a definite article — 'der,' 'die' and 'das' are just some of the ways to translate 'the' in German.

1) In English, there's just <u>one</u> word for 'the' — simple.
2) In German, you need to know whether to use the <u>masculine</u>, <u>feminine</u> or <u>neuter</u> word for '<u>the</u>' and what <u>case</u> to use (<u>nominative</u>, <u>accusative</u>, <u>dative</u> or <u>genitive</u>).
3) Start by learning the <u>first line</u> of the grid — <u>der</u>, <u>die</u>, <u>das</u>, <u>die</u>. You <u>absolutely</u> have to know those ones.

| Masculine, nominative | → | Der Vogel ist grau. *The bird is grey.* |

| Masculine, dative | → | Ich singe dem Vogel. *I sing to the bird.* |

|            | Masculine | Feminine | Neuter | Plural |
|------------|-----------|----------|--------|--------|
| Nominative | der       | die      | das    | die    |
| Accusative | den       | die      | das    | die    |
| Dative     | dem       | der      | dem    | den    |
| Genitive   | des       | der      | des    | der    |

*Your song was not accepted — the bird demands another offering.*

## 'A' — start by learning ein, eine, ein

'A' and 'an' are indefinite articles in English — in German, these include 'ein' and 'eine'.

1) The word for 'a' is different for <u>masculine</u>, <u>feminine</u> or <u>neuter</u> nouns, and for different <u>cases</u>.
2) Start by learning the <u>first line</u> of the grid — <u>ein</u>, <u>eine</u>, <u>ein</u>. Then, move on to the other ones.

|            | Masculine | Feminine | Neuter |
|------------|-----------|----------|--------|
| Nominative | ein       | eine     | ein    |
| Accusative | einen     | eine     | ein    |
| Dative     | einem     | einer    | einem  |
| Genitive   | eines     | einer    | eines  |

| Masculine, nominative | → | Ein Hund spielt. *A dog plays.* |

| Feminine, accusative | → | Ich habe eine Katze. *I have a cat.* |

## 'No' — start by learning kein, keine, kein

1) '<u>Kein</u>' means '<u>no</u>' — as in '<u>I have no potatoes</u>'.
2) It <u>changes</u> a bit like '<u>ein</u>' changes.

| Plural, nominative | → | Keine Hunde sind grün. *No dogs are green.* |

|            | Masculine | Feminine | Neuter | Plural |
|------------|-----------|----------|--------|--------|
| Nominative | kein      | keine    | kein   | keine  |
| Accusative | keinen    | keine    | kein   | keine  |

| Neuter, accusative | Ich habe kein Buch. *I have no book.* |

## Grammar Questions

Fill in the gaps with the German for the word in brackets.

1. Ich mag ...... Film. *(the)*
2. Ich gebe es ...... Frau. *(the)*
3. Ich habe ...... Wurst. *(a)*
4. Wer hat ...... Onkel? *(a)*
5. Ich habe ...... Karte. *(no)*
6. Sie wird dir ...... Geld geben. *(no)*

## Your fate is definite — the die is cast...

Don't be put off by the amount of ways to say 'the' and 'a' in German. You can draw out the tables in your notes and repeat them all row by row to learn them — then you'll be able to use them perfectly.

# Subject and Object Pronouns

Unfortunately for nouns, they're pretty replaceable — pronouns are often taking their spot.

## You use subject pronouns in the nominative case

*Check p.105 for more on the nominative case.*

Words like 'I', 'you', 'he', etc. are subject pronouns. They replace the subject of a sentence.

| Nominative case | |
|---|---|
| I | ich |
| you (informal, singular) | du |
| he / she / it / one | er / sie / es / man |
| we | wir |
| you (informal, plural) | ihr |
| you (formal singular & plural) | Sie |
| they | sie |

- Use 'du' for talking to one person you know well, or a young person.
- 'Man' means 'one', 'you' or 'people in general'.
- Use 'ihr' for talking to more than one person you know well, or for a group of young people.
- Use 'Sie' for talking to one or more older people you don't know well, or who you should be polite to.

Der Hund liebt den Mann. Er liebt den Mann. *The dog loves the man. He loves the man.*

## There are pronouns for the accusative and dative cases

1) Words like 'me' and 'you' refer to who or what is having the action done to it — this is the direct object.

| Accusative case | | | | | | us | you (inf. plu.) | you (frml. plu.) | them |
|---|---|---|---|---|---|---|---|---|---|
| me | you (inf. sing.) | you (frml. sing.) | him / her / it | one | Higher | us | you (inf. plu.) | you (frml. plu.) | them |
| mich | dich | Sie | ihn / sie / es | einen | | uns | euch | Sie | sie |

Er ruft seinen Bruder an. Er ruft ihn an. *He calls his brother. He calls him.*

'Anrufen' is a separable verb. See p.139.

2) Indirect objects are things that are affected by the action being done, but not directly. They often have 'to' or 'for' before them in English. You need to use the dative case for them (see p.106).

| Dative case | | | | | | us | you (inf. plu.) | you (frml. plu.) | them |
|---|---|---|---|---|---|---|---|---|---|
| me | you (inf. sing.) | you (frml. sing.) | him / her / it | one | Higher | us | you (inf. plu.) | you (frml. plu.) | them |
| mir | dir | Ihnen | ihm / ihr / ihm | einem | | uns | euch | Ihnen | ihnen |

Ich schreibe meiner Schwester einen Brief. Ich schreibe ihr einen Brief.
*I write my sister a letter. I write her a letter.*

## Jemand, niemand — *someone, no one*

*'Jemand' and 'niemand' are both examples of indefinite pronouns.*

1) 'Jemand' means 'someone'. To say 'no one', use 'niemand'.
2) These pronouns don't have an ending in the nominative case, but they add '-en' in the accusative case.

Ist jemand da? *Is someone there?* — 'Jemand' is the subject of this question — it's in the nominative case.

Ich habe niemanden gesehen. *I have seen no one.* — 'Niemand' is the direct object of this sentence — it's in the accusative case.

Section Thirteen — Nouns, Cases and Linking Words

## Objects often go after the verb

1) You'll normally find the direct object or indirect object after the subject and the verb.

Sie besucht das Schloss.  Sie besucht es.
*She visits the castle.  She visits it.*

'Es' is the direct object in this sentence, because it is the thing being visited. It is in the accusative case.

Ich helfe meinem Bruder.  Ich helfe ihm.
*I help my brother.  I help him.*

In German, some verbs always use the dative case for the object that comes after it. See p.131 for more.

2) When there are two verbs, like in clauses with modal verbs or the perfect tense, the direct object or indirect object comes after the first verb and before the second verb.

Ich will das Buch lesen.  Ich will es lesen.
*I want to read the book.  I want to read it.*

Du bist einer Freundin gefolgt.  Du bist ihr gefolgt.
*You have followed a friend.  You have followed her.*

Isabella was shocked to discover that it was, indeed, the butler who did it.

## Objects aren't always in the same position

1) The indirect object usually comes before the direct object if there are two object nouns in a sentence.

Ich gab meinen Lehrern ein Geschenk.    *I gave my teachers a present.*

2) When there is one object pronoun and one object noun, the pronoun usually comes before the noun.

Ich gab es meinen Lehrern.
*I gave it to my teachers.*

Ich gab ihnen ein Geschenk.
*I gave them a present.*

3) Since cases tell you what things do in a sentence, German word order is more flexible than in English.

Dem Hund gab ich ein Ei.    *I gave the dog an egg.*

Ihm gab ich ein Ei.    *I gave him an egg.*

Although 'Dem Hund' and 'Ihm' are at the start of the sentence, you can tell they're the indirect objects — they're receiving the egg and not giving it. This is because they are in the dative case.

Und was soll ich damit machen?

### Grammar Questions

Write these sentences in **German**, using the right case and position for each pronoun or noun.
1. He sees her.
2. They love him.
3. I helped you (inf. sing.).
4. You (frml. sing.) visit me.
5. I send them an e-mail. [H]
6. The boy gave his father the dog. [H]

## Objection, your honour — my client is ihnnocent...

You need the nominative case for subjects, the accusative case for direct objects and the dative case for indirect objects. If you need to, read through these pages again to really get to grips with object pronouns.

# Relative and Interrogative Pronouns

These pronouns are relatively tricky, but they add a little something extra to your sentences.

## Relative pronouns add detail

1) Words like 'that', 'which' and 'who' relate back to the things you're talking about.

2) In German, relative pronouns send the verb to the end of the relative clause.

The pronoun refers back to 'der Mann'. → Der Mann, der in der Ecke sitzt, ist klein. ← The verb goes to the end of the clause.
*The man who sits in the corner is small.*

*The relative clause (the phrase with the relative pronoun in it) is always introduced with a comma.*

3) Relative pronouns can refer to the subject of the relative clause — the things that do the action. They change depending on the noun's gender (p.103) and whether it's singular or plural.

| | Masculine | Feminine | Neuter | Plural |
|---|---|---|---|---|
| Nominative | der | die | das | die |

Ich kaufe die Katze, die weiß ist.
*I buy the cat which is white.*

These relative pronouns are the same as definite articles (p.107) in the nominative.

4) Relative pronouns can also refer to direct objects — the things that have the action done to them.

| | Masculine | Feminine | Neuter | Plural |
|---|---|---|---|---|
| Accusative | den | die | das | die |

Ich kenne den Mann, den ich sah.
*I know the man who I saw.*

**Higher**

5) 'Was' can also be used as a relative pronoun to refer to whole phrases, or after 'alles', 'nichts', 'etwas', 'vieles' and 'weniges'.

Ich kenne alles, was sie sagte. *I know everything that she said.*

Ich weiß nicht, was er denkt.
*I don't know what he thinks.*

6) Use 'wo' to talk about 'where' something is.

Es ist sonnig, wo ich wohne. *It's sunny where I live.*

## Use interrogative pronouns to ask questions

*See p.8-9 for more about questions.*

1) 'Wer' can be used as a question word. This is called an interrogative pronoun.

Wer sitzt auf der Katze? *Who is sitting on the cat?*

2) There are different words for 'wer'. The one you need to use depends on the case.

| Nominative | Accusative | Dative |
|---|---|---|
| wer | wen | wem |

Mit wem spreche ich? *With whom am I speaking?*

Wen hast du gesehen? *Who did you see?*

### Grammar Questions

Translate these sentences into German. Use the right gender and case and remember the commas.
1. I know the woman who wears a shirt.
2. The people who write to me are nice.
3. Who buys the jacket?
4. Who did he go with?
5. Nothing that she does is easy. [H]

---

## The relatives are coming over — I'll pop the kettle on...

I know I keep banging on about it, but it's super important that the pronoun matches the case and gender.

Section Thirteen — Nouns, Cases and Linking Words

# Reflexive Pronouns

Some German verbs need 'myself', 'yourself', etc. Make sure using them becomes, well, a reflex.

## Talking about yourself — 'sich'

*In a dictionary, verbs that need a reflexive pronoun have 'sich' before them.*

1) '<u>Sich</u>' means '<u>oneself</u>'. It changes depending on <u>who's doing the action</u>.

| **Reflexive pronouns** | | | |
|---|---|---|---|
| mich | myself | uns | ourselves |
| dich | yourself (inf. sing.) | euch | yourselves (inf. plu.) |
| sich | himself / herself / itself | sich | yourself / yourselves (frml. sing. & plu.) |
| | | sich | themselves / each other |

2) <u>Reflexive pronouns</u> help you talk about something you do for yourself. They normally go <u>after</u> the <u>verb</u>.

| | | | |
|---|---|---|---|
| ich verbessere mich | I improve myself | wir verbessern uns | we improve ourselves |
| du verbesserst dich | you improve yourself | ihr verbessert euch | you improve yourselves |
| er verbessert sich | he improves himself | Sie verbessern sich | you improve yourself / yourselves |
| sie verbessert sich | she improves herself | sie verbessern sich | they improve themselves |
| es verbessert sich | it improves itself | | |

3) <u>Reflexive pronouns</u> can also mean '<u>each other</u>', e.g. 'sie streiten sich' *(they argue with each other)*.

4) Here are some examples of verbs that need <u>reflexive pronouns</u>. They're called <u>reflexive verbs</u>.

| | | | |
|---|---|---|---|
| sich freuen | to be pleased | sich entschuldigen | to apologise |
| sich fühlen | to feel | sich setzen | to sit down |
| sich bewegen | to exercise | sich entspannen | to relax |

## Ich denke mir — *I imagine*

Some verbs need you to add '<u>to myself</u>' and '<u>to yourself</u>'. This is the dative case.

**Higher**

| | |
|---|---|
| sich [dat.] merken | to remember |
| sich [dat.] leisten | to afford |
| sich [dat.] vorstellen | to imagine |

| **Reflexive pronouns in the dative case** | | | |
|---|---|---|---|
| mir | myself | uns | ourselves |
| dir | yourself (inf. sing.) | euch | yourselves (inf. plu.) |
| sich | himself / herself / itself | sich | yourself / yourselves (frml. sing. & plu.) |
| | | sich | themselves / each other |

Ich merke mir das Wort. *I remember the word.*

## Ich habe mich verbessert — *I have improved myself*

To form the <u>perfect tense</u> of reflexive verbs, follow the usual rules (p.133), but <u>always use 'haben'</u>, not 'sein'.

Er hat sich schlecht gefühlt. *He felt bad (ill).*
Put the 'sich' straight after 'haben'.

### Grammar Questions

Translate these sentences into **German**, making sure to use the right reflexive pronouns.

1. I apologise.
2. We exercise.
3. They get dressed.
4. He is pleased.
5. I felt happy.
6. She exercised.
7. They sit down. **H**
8. You (inf. sing.) remember it. **H**

## Breathe in… Breathe out… It's time to be self-reflexive…

When you revise these pronouns, learn them alongside the correct subject pronoun — you'll thank yourself.

# Word Order

Hear ye, hear ye — I present to you the five golden rules of German word order.

## 1) Put the verb second

The word order for questions and instructions is different. See p.8 and p.138 for more details.

The verb is almost always the second idea in a German sentence.

Ich spiele Fußball.   I play football. ← The word order for simple sentences like this is similar to English. The person or thing doing the action usually goes first, and the verb comes second.

## 2) Keep the verb second

1) As long as you keep the verb second, German word order can be fairly flexible.
2) You can swap the information around as long as the verb is still the second idea in the sentence (although it might not be the second word).
3) So, if you want to say 'I play football on Mondays', you can say:

Ich spiele montags Fußball.
(I play on Mondays football.)

OR

Montags spiele ich Fußball.
(On Mondays, play I football.)

On second thoughts, Sophie might go to a cheaper restaurant.

## 3) If there are two verbs, send one to the end

If you've got two verbs, treat the first one as normal and send the second one to the end of the clause.

Ich werde viel machen.   (I will a lot do).

## 4) Remember — When, How, Where

At school, you might have heard the phrase 'Time, Manner, Place' — it just means that if you want to describe when, how and where you do something, that's exactly the order you have to say it in.

Ich gehe heute mit meinen Freunden ins Kino.   (I am going today with my friends to the cinema).
         WHEN (Time)    HOW (Manner)    WHERE (Place)

## 5) Watch out for 'joining words' — they can change the word order

1) Relative pronouns (p.110) and subordinating conjunctions (p.114) are examples of joining words that send the verb to the end of a clause.

Ich schwimme, weil ich sportlich bin.
(I swim because I sporty am.)

2) If there are two verbs in a subordinate or relative clause, the verb that normally comes first goes right to the end of the clause.

Ich weiß, wo ich wohnen will.
(I know where I to live want.)

### Grammar Questions

Tick the sentences that use word order correctly and cross out the ones that don't.
1. Ich Basketball spiele.   3. Ich werde in den Wald gehen.   5. Ich esse mit meiner Familie heute.
2. Am Montag lese ich.   4. Er lacht, weil er ist glücklich.   6. Wir fahren am Freitag nach Berlin.

## You can take your verb and stick it ~~up~~ in second position...

Be careful when translating into German — you'll likely need to change the word order to get full marks.

Section Thirteen — Nouns, Cases and Linking Words

# Coordinating Conjunctions

Quick Quiz

Can we coordinate outfits for the party? I'm wearing leopard print, so don't wear your polka dots.

## Coordinating conjunctions join phrases and clauses

*Coordinating conjunctions don't affect word order — the verb comes second.*

### Und — And

| Ich habe eine Katze. | und | Er hat einen Hund. | → | Ich habe eine Katze und er hat einen Hund. |
| I have a cat. | and | He has a dog. | | I have a cat and he has a dog. |

Christiane spielt gern Fußball und Rugby. — Christiane likes playing football and rugby.

### Oder — Or

| Ich gehe tanzen. | oder | Ich spiele Tennis. | → | Ich gehe tanzen oder ich spiele Tennis. |
| I go dancing. | or | I play tennis. | | I go dancing or I play tennis. |

Rainer spielt jeden Tag Fußball oder Rugby. — Rainer plays football or rugby every day.

### Aber — But

*You need to use a comma before 'aber' and 'denn'.*

| Otto will draußen gehen. | aber | Es regnet. | → | Otto will draußen gehen, aber es regnet. |
| Otto wants to go outside. | but | It's raining. | | Otto wants go outside, but it's raining. |

### Denn — Because

| Ich will Trainer werden. | denn | Ich mag Sport. | → | Ich will Trainer werden, denn ich mag Sport. |
| I want to be a coach. | because | I like sport. | | I want to be a coach because I like sport. |

### Sondern — (But) Rather

**Higher**

| Ich will keinen Käse. | sondern | Ich will Kuchen. | → | Ich will keinen Käse, sondern Kuchen. |
| I don't want cheese. | but rather | I want cake. | | I don't want cheese, but rather cake. |

When both clauses joined by a coordinating conjunction use the same subject and verb, you don't have to repeat them.

## Grammar Questions

Translate these sentences into **German** using the right conjunction.
1. I go by bus and you go by train.
2. We go to the park because it's sunny.
3. I want to listen to music or watch TV.
4. He's a vegetarian, but she eats meat.

---

## My hand-eye coordination is so bad — I can't even catch a cold...

Remember, coordinating conjunctions don't affect word order — they just join up sentences. Smashing.

Find the CGP RevisionHub at cgpbooks.co.uk/Berlin

# Subordinating Conjunctions

Use a subordinating conjunction and get one fab German sentence. Just watch the word order.

## Subordinating conjunctions add extra information

| weil | *because* | obwohl | *although* | bevor | *before* | | ob | *whether, if* |
|------|-----------|--------|------------|-------|----------|---|------|---------------|
| wenn | *if, when* | dass | *that* | während | *while* | **Higher** | damit | *so that* |
| als | *when* | nachdem | *after* | da | *as, because* | | solange | *as long as* |

## Subordinating conjunctions send the verb to the end

### Weil — *Because*

*All these conjunctions need a comma before them.*

| Ich tanze. | **weil** | Ich bin froh. | → | Ich tanze, weil ich froh bin. |
|---|---|---|---|---|
| *I am dancing.* | ***because*** | *I am happy.* | | *I am dancing because I am happy.* |

Subordinating conjunctions: Weil, Obwohl, Als, Wenn
Types of diagrams: Bar, Pie, Flow

### Wenn — *If, when, whenever*

| Ich spreche mit Faye. | **wenn** | Wir spielen Tennis. | → | Ich spreche mit Faye, wenn wir Tennis spielen. |
|---|---|---|---|---|
| *I speak to Faye.* | ***when*** | *We play tennis.* | | *I speak to Faye when we play tennis.* |

### Als — *When*

'Als' also means 'when', but you only use it to refer to the past.

| Ich habe oft geweint. | **als** | Ich war jünger. | → | Ich habe oft geweint, als ich jünger war. |
|---|---|---|---|---|
| *I often cried.* | ***when*** | *I was younger.* | | *I often cried when I was younger.* |

### Obwohl — *Although*

| Ich werde spielen. | **obwohl** | Ich bin müde. | → | Ich werde spielen, obwohl ich müde bin. |
|---|---|---|---|---|
| *I will play.* | ***although*** | *I am tired.* | | *I will play although I am tired.* |

The clause with the subordinating conjunction can come first in the sentence too.

| Obwohl ich müde bin, werde ich spielen. | *Although I am tired, I will play.* |
|---|---|

*If you put the subordinate clause first, the verb in the main clause needs to go right after the comma.*

### Grammar Questions

Write these sentences in **German** using the conjunctions on this page — pay attention to the word order.
1. He likes to dance because it's relaxing.
2. If I have time, I'll come to your party.
3. We were best friends when we were children.
4. She wants to run although it's very hot.

## Shoving verbs to the end of a clause — what weil behaviour...

Knowing when to send the verb to the end is a big deal in German, so make sure you do it at the right time.

# Compound Conjunctions

Compound conjunctions have two parts, but don't panic — they work quite a lot like they do in English. These ones also don't do anything weird to the word order. Excellent news.

## Entweder ... oder — *either ... or*

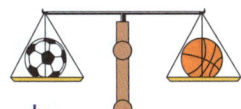

You can use compound conjunctions like 'entweder ... oder' to talk about two nouns or verbs.

| Layla will Fußball spielen. | **entweder ... oder** | Layla will Basketball spielen. | → | Layla will entweder Fußball oder Basketball spielen. |
|---|---|---|---|---|
| *Layla wants to play football.* | *either ... or* | *Layla wants to play basketball.* | | *Layla wants to play either football or basketball.* |

Entweder Yuki gewinnt den Lauf oder sie verliert ihn.    *Either Yuki wins the race or she loses it.*

## Weder ... noch — *neither ... nor*

[Higher]

| Alina trägt Schuhe. | **weder ... noch** | Alina trägt Socken. | → | Alina trägt weder Schuhe noch Socken. |
|---|---|---|---|---|
| *Alina wears shoes.* | *neither ... nor* | *Alina wears socks.* | | *Alina wears neither shoes nor socks.* |

Weder Mila noch Lukas wollen gehen.    *Neither Mila nor Lukas want to go.*

*Alina was starting to get the hint.*

## Sowohl ... als auch — *both ... and*

[Higher]

| Er geht in den Park. | **sowohl ... als auch** | Er geht ins Kino. | → | Er geht sowohl in den Park als auch ins Kino. |
|---|---|---|---|---|
| *He goes to the park.* | *both ... and* | *He goes to the cinema.* | | *He goes both to the park and to the cinema.* |

Sowohl Gizem als auch Elias lesen Liebesromane.    *Both Gizem and Elias read romance novels.*

### Grammar Questions

Translate these sentences into **German**.
1. He reads either a book or the newspaper.
2. Either Jana or Leon play basketball.
3. Neither Felix nor Yasmin want to drive. [H]
4. I want to both climb and swim. [H]

## Sequels are never as good as the original...

...but when you're using compound conjunctions, both parts are just as important as each other. Compound conjunctions are great to sprinkle into your work — they add flare to your language and are sure to impress.

Quick Quiz

# Prepositions

It's time to get prepped for this page on prepositions, which are words that are often used to talk about direction, time and location. They also change the case of the words that come after them.

## Here are the prepositions you need to know

| | | | | | |
|---|---|---|---|---|---|
| durch | *through* | zu | *to* | unter | *under, below, among* |
| für | *for* | ab | *from, as of* | zwischen | *between* |
| ohne | *without* | seit | *since, for* | vor | *in front of, before, ago* |
| bis | *until, up to, by* | an | *on, at* | außer | *except, apart from* |
| gegen | *against* | auf | *on, onto, at, to* | gegenüber | *opposite, across from* |
| um | *at, around* | in | *in, into* | aus | *out, out of, from* |
| mit | *with, by* | hinter | *behind* | bei | *at, with* |
| von | *from, of* | neben | *next to, beside* | pro | *per* |
| nach | *to, towards, after* | über | *about, above, over* | **H** laut | *according to* |

Prepositions affect the <u>case</u> of what comes <u>after</u> them — so read on to find out how to use each one correctly.

## Some prepositions always use the accusative case...

1) You <u>always</u> use the <u>accusative</u> case for '<u>durch</u>', '<u>für</u>', '<u>ohne</u>' and '<u>bis</u>'.

> Er geht nie ohne sein Handy aus.
> *He never goes out without his mobile.*

> ein Geschenk für mich
> *a present for me*

*See p.105 for more on the accusative case.*

**Higher**

2) '<u>Gegen</u>' and '<u>um</u>' also use the accusative case.

> Er steht gegen die Wand. *He stands against the wall.*

> um den Berg *around the mountain*

## ... some always use the dative case...

1) '<u>Mit</u>', '<u>von</u>', '<u>nach</u>', '<u>aus</u>', '<u>zu</u>' and '<u>bei</u>' all always use the <u>dative</u> case.

> mit meiner Katze *with my cat*

> mit dem Bus *by bus*

*For more on the dative case, see p.106.*

> nach der Party *after the party*

> ein Freund von mir *a friend of mine*

> Der Zug ist von der Schweiz gekommen.
> *The train has come from Switzerland.*

Use '<u>von</u>' to say where someone or something has come from <u>recently</u>. For where someone or something is from <u>originally</u>, it's '<u>aus</u>'.

> Sie kommt zu mir.
> *She comes to me.*

> Mila wohnt bei ihren Großeltern.
> *Mila lives with her grandparents.*

> Er kommt aus der Türkei.
> *He comes from Turkey.*

**Higher**

2) '<u>Seit</u>' and '<u>laut</u>' also put the nouns and pronouns after them in the <u>dative case</u>.

> Ich habe sie seit einem Jahr nicht gesehen. *I haven't seen her for a year.*

> Laut meiner Schwester bin ich faul. *According to my sister, I'm lazy.*

Section Thirteen — Nouns, Cases and Linking Words

## ...and some use either the accusative or dative case

*These are also known as dual case prepositions.*

1) '<u>Auf</u>', '<u>an</u>' and '<u>in</u>' can use <u>either</u> the accusative <u>or</u> the dative case. They use the accusative case when what you're talking about is <u>moving</u> and the <u>dative</u> if there's <u>no movement</u>.

2) Use '<u>auf</u>' to say when something is moving '<u>onto</u>' or is '<u>on</u>' something else.

| Die Katze springt auf das Sofa. | The cat jumps onto the sofa. | 'Das Sofa' is in the accusative case because the cat <u>is</u> moving. |
| Die Katze schläft auf dem Sofa. | The cat sleeps on the sofa. | 'Dem Sofa' is in the dative case because the cat <u>isn't</u> moving. |

3) '<u>An</u>' can also be translated as '<u>on</u>' or '<u>at</u>'.

| Ich hänge das Bild an die Wand. | Ich studiere an der Universität. |
| I hang the photo on the wall. | I study at university. |

4) German speakers use '<u>in</u>' where you would say '<u>in</u>' or '<u>into</u>'.

| Sina geht in die Moschee. | Sina steht in der Moschee. |
| Sina goes into the mosque. | Sina stands in the mosque. |

*Josephine couldn't decide which case to use for her weekend away.*

**Higher**
5) '<u>Hinter</u>', '<u>neben</u>', '<u>über</u>', '<u>unter</u>', '<u>zwischen</u>' and '<u>vor</u>' also use the <u>accusative case</u> when there's <u>movement</u>, but use the <u>dative case</u> when there's <u>not</u>.

| Das Kind springt über den Fluss. | The child jumps over the river. |
| Das Buch liegt hinter dem Stuhl. | The book is behind the chair. |

## Zum, am, im — *contracted forms*

1) Some of the words on these pages can be <u>contracted</u> when they go with 'dem', 'das' or 'der'. This happens with '<u>an</u>', '<u>bei</u>', '<u>in</u>', '<u>von</u>' and '<u>zu</u>'.

**Contracted forms**
| an dem → am | bei dem → beim |
| an das → ans | von dem → vom |
| in dem → im | zu der → zur |
| in das → ins | zu dem → zum |

| ans Meer | to the sea | | Ed ist im Bett. | Ed is in bed. |
| am ersten Januar | on the first of January | | zum Bahnhof gehen | to go (by foot) to the station |

**Higher**
2) You can use '<u>beim</u>' before a <u>verb</u> that's being <u>used as a noun</u> (see p.104) to mean '<u>while / when doing something</u>'.

Beim Schwimmen esse ich nie. *While swimming, I never eat.*

3) '<u>Am</u>' can be used to show that someone '<u>is doing</u>' something.

Sie ist am Malen. *She is always painting.*

'Am' is only used in spoken German — you normally just use the present tense (p.130).

### Grammar Questions

Write out these phrases and sentences in **German**, making sure you use the right case.
1. through the wood
2. It is for the woman.
3. from her father
4. without his dog
5. It's in the house.
6. after the film
7. I sing while cooking. [H]
8. I stand under the tree. [H]

## You can make up sentences to remember what case to use...
'**B**rave **O**wls **F**ly **D**aringly' could remind you that '**b**is', '**o**hne', '**f**ür' and '**d**urch' all use the accusative case.

# More Prepositions

Yep, here are more ways to use prepositions — it's the last page on them though, so that's a relief.

## Use the genitive case with these prepositions

*See p.106 for more on the genitive case.*

Some prepositions always put the stuff after them into the genitive case.

| | | | |
|---|---|---|---|
| trotz | in spite of | während | during |
| statt | instead of | wegen | because of |

trotz des Wetters — in spite of the weather

Masculine and neuter nouns usually add '-s' or '-es' (mostly one-syllable words) in the genitive case.

während der Woche — during the week

statt des Zuges — instead of the train

## You can add 'da(r)-' to prepositions

1) When you add 'da-' (or 'dar-' before a vowel) to prepositions, it can mean 'it', 'them', 'that' or 'there'. It turns the preposition into a pronoun so you can avoid repeating the noun.

| darauf | on it/them | dadurch | through it | darin | in it, in there, inside |
| damit | with it/them | dahinter | behind it | darüber | above it, about it |
| dafür | for it/that/them | daneben | next to it, beside it | dazu | to that, for that |
| davon | from it/them | daraus | out of it, from it | darunter | under it, underneath |

Es gibt einen Tisch. Ich stehe darauf.   There is a table. I stand on it.

The pronoun 'darauf' replaces the phrase 'auf einem Tisch'.

Die Katze versteckt sich unter der Brücke. → Die Katze versteckt sich darunter.
The cat hides under the bridge.   The cat hides under it.

Der Vogel sitzt über dem Fenster. → Der Vogel sitzt darüber.
The bird sits above the window.   The bird sits above it.

*You can also add 'wo(r)-' to prepositions to ask questions. See p.8 for more.*

2) 'Da(r)-' pronouns can also be used to refer to whole phrases or ideas.

Er musste den nächsten Zug nehmen, aber er ist dafür zu spät angekommen.
He had to take the next train, but he arrived too late for it.

"I knew I shouldn't have clicked 'next episode'."

3) Some of these prepositions can be translated into English as adverbial phrases. For example, 'dazu' can also mean 'in addition' or 'furthermore'.

Er singt und spielt dazu ein Instrument.   He sings and, in addition, plays an instrument.

## Grammar Questions

Translate these phrases and sentences into **German** using the correct prepositions.

1. He sits on it.
2. They play for it.
3. because of the costs
4. instead of the plants
5. despite the snow
6. during the party
7. She lies under it.
8. They live in there.

## Above it, under it, behind it, beside it... I'm getting dizzy...

Have a go at describing the position of different objects around you to practise using these 'da(r)' pronouns.

# Nouns, Cases and Linking Words — Grammar List

I just got stopped by the grammar police — they said I need to go over these pages. Feel free to join me...

## Nouns

In German, all nouns are masculine, feminine or neuter.
Common endings for masculine nouns are:
-el, -us, -ling, -er

Common endings for feminine nouns are:
-ie, -heit, -tion, -ung, -ei, -keit, -sion, -tät, -schaft

Common endings for neuter nouns are:
-chen, -um, -lein, -ment

Some masculine nouns can be made feminine:
der Journalist → die Journalist**in**
der Arzt → die Ärzt**in**

There are also different ways to make singular nouns plural:
Most masculine and neuter nouns add an '-e'.
der Imbiss → die Imbiss**e**   *snack bar(s)*

*See p.104 for more on plurals and noun endings.*

Most feminine nouns add an '-(e)n'.
die Farbe → die Farbe**n**   *colour(s)*

You can make nouns from some verbs and adjectives:
feiern → das Feiern   *celebrating*
deutsch → das Deutsch   *German*
gut → das Gute   *the good thing* [H]
reich → die Reichen   *the rich (ones)*

## Cases

**Nominative** — who / what does the action.

**Accusative** — who / what the action is done to.

**Dative** — who / what is indirectly affected by the action.

**Genitive** — who / what belongs to someone / something else. [H]

## Subject Pronouns

Subject pronouns replace the person or thing doing the action.

| | |
|---|---|
| ich | *I* |
| du | *you (inf. sing.)* |
| er | *he, it (m)* |
| sie | *she, it (f)* |
| es | *it (nt)* |
| man | *one, you, people in general* |
| wir | *we* |
| ihr | *you (inf. plu.)* |
| Sie | *you (frml. sing. & plu.)* |
| sie | *they* |

'Selbst' or 'selber' can be put after a verb to emphasise who does the action.
selbst, selber   *self*

## Articles

Articles come before a noun. They change depending on the noun's case and gender and whether it's singular or plural.

These are the words for 'the'.

| | Masc. | Fem. | Neut. | Plu. |
|---|---|---|---|---|
| Nom. | der | die | das | die |
| Acc. | den | die | das | die |
| Dat. | dem | der | dem | den |
| Gen. [H] | des | der | des | der |

These are the words for 'a' and 'an'.

| | Masc. | Fem. | Neut. |
|---|---|---|---|
| Nom. | ein | eine | ein |
| Acc. | einen | eine | ein |
| Dat. | einem | einer | einem |
| Gen. [H] | eines | einer | eines |

These are the words for 'not a' and 'no'.

| | Masc. | Fem. | Neut. | Plu. |
|---|---|---|---|---|
| Nom. | kein | keine | kein | keine |
| Acc. | keinen | keine | kein | keine |

## Indefinite Pronouns

These pronouns refer to general or unspecific things.

| | |
|---|---|
| jemand | *someone* |
| niemand | *no one* |
| etwas | *something, some* |
| alles | *everything, all* |
| alle (plu.) | *everyone, everybody* |
| andere | *other, different* |
| beide | *both, the two* |
| einer | *(some)one* |
| irgendein(e) | *some, any* |
| irgendetwas, irgendwas | *something, anything* [Higher] |
| mehrere | *several, multiple, various* |

*In the accusative, you need to add '-en' to 'jemand' and 'niemand'.*

*Some of these indefinite pronouns can go before nouns.*

## Demonstrative Pronouns

These pronouns refer to a specific person or thing.

| | |
|---|---|
| solch | *such* |
| derselbe, dieselbe, dasselbe | *the same (one, ones)* |
| derjenige, diejenige, dasjenige [H] | *the one (who, that)* |

Section Thirteen — Nouns, Cases and Linking Words

# Nouns, Cases and Linking Words — Grammar List

## Direct Object Pronouns

Direct object pronouns replace the person or thing the action is being done to.

| | | | | |
|---|---|---|---|---|
| mich | *me* | | uns | *us* |
| dich | *you (inf. sing.)* | Higher → | euch | *you (inf. plu.)* |
| ihn | *him, it (m)* | | Sie | *you (frml. plu.)* |
| sie | *her, it (f)* | | sie | *them* |
| es | *it (nt)* | | | |
| Sie | *you (frml. sing.)* | | | |
| einen | *one* | | | |

*These pronouns are in the accusative case.*

## Indirect Object Pronouns

Indirect object pronouns replace the person or thing that is being indirectly affected by the action.

| | | | | |
|---|---|---|---|---|
| mir | *me* | | uns | *us* |
| dir | *you (inf. sing.)* | Higher → | euch | *you (inf. plu.)* |
| ihm | *him, it (m)* | | Ihnen | *you (frml. plu.)* |
| ihr | *her, it (f)* | | ihnen | *them* |
| ihm | *it (nt)* | | | |
| Ihnen | *you (frml. sing.)* | | | |
| einem | *one* | | | |

*These pronouns are in the dative case.*

## Relative Pronouns

Relative pronouns relate back to the thing you're talking about. They can mean 'that', 'which', or 'who'. They send the verb to the end of the clause.

| | Masc. | Fem. | Neut. | Plu. |
|---|---|---|---|---|
| Nom. | der | die | das | die |

E.g. Ich sah den Mann, der auf dem Stuhl sitzt.
*I saw the man who sits on the chair.*

| | Masc. | Fem. | Neut. | Plu. |
|---|---|---|---|---|
| Acc. | den | die | das | die |

Higher:
'Was' and 'wo' can also be relative pronouns. 'Was' means 'which' or 'that', and 'wo' means 'where'.

E.g. Er liebt die Stadt, wo er wohnt.
*He loves the town where he lives.*

## Reflexive Pronouns

These pronouns refer back to a person or thing and mean 'self'.

Accusative reflexive pronouns:

| | |
|---|---|
| mich | *myself* |
| dich | *yourself (inf. sing.)* |
| sich | *himself, herself, itself* |
| uns | *ourselves* |
| euch | *yourselves (inf. plu.)* |
| sich | *yourself (frml. sing.)* |
| | *yourselves (frml. plu.), themselves* |

Higher — Dative reflexive pronouns:

| | |
|---|---|
| mir | *myself* |
| dir | *yourself* |
| sich | *himself, herself, itself* |
| uns | *ourselves* |
| euch | *yourselves (inf. plu.)* |
| sich | *yourself (frml. sing.),* |
| | *yourselves (frml. plu.), themselves* |

## Interrogative Pronouns

'Wer' can be used as a question word and means 'who'. It changes depending on the case.

| Nom. | Acc. | Dat. |
|---|---|---|
| wer | wen | wem |

E.g. Wer ist dieser Mann? *Who is this man?*
Wen hast du gesehen? *Who did you see?*

## Subordinating Conjunctions

These conjunctions send the verb to the end of the subordinate clause.

| | |
|---|---|
| weil | *because* |
| wenn | *when, if, whenever* |
| als | *when, as* |
| obwohl | *although* |
| dass | *that* |
| nachdem | *after* |
| bevor | *before* |
| während | *while, whereas* |
| da | *as, because, since, given that* |

Higher:

| | |
|---|---|
| ob | *whether, if* |
| damit | *so that* |
| indem | *while, by* |
| falls | *in case, if* |
| solange | *as long as* |
| sobald | *as soon as* |
| seitdem | *since* |

## Coordinating Conjunctions

| | |
|---|---|
| und | *and* |
| oder | *or* |
| aber | *but, however* |
| denn | *because* |
| H sondern | *(but) rather* |

*See p.113 and p.115 for more on how coordinating and compound conjunctions work in sentences.*

## Compound Conjunctions

| | |
|---|---|
| entweder ... oder | *either ... or* |
| weder ... noch | *neither ... nor* |
| H sowohl ... als auch | *both ... and* |

Section Thirteen — Nouns, Cases and Linking Words

## Accusative Case Prepositions

| | |
|---|---|
| durch | through |
| für | for |
| ohne | without |
| bis | until, till, up to, by |
| gegen | against |
| um | at (o'clock), around |
| pro | per |

*See p.116-118 to find out which prepositions you need to learn the cases for.*

## Dative Case Prepositions

| | |
|---|---|
| mit | with, by |
| von | from, of |
| nach | to, towards, after, according to |
| zu | to |
| ab | from, as of |
| seit | since, for |
| außer | except, apart from |
| gegenüber | opposite, across from |
| aus | out, out of, from |
| bei | at (the house of), with |
| H laut | according to |

## Dual Case Prepositions

These prepositions put the following noun in the accusative when there's movement and in the dative when there's not.

| | |
|---|---|
| an | on, at |
| auf | on, onto, at, to |
| in | in, into |
| hinter | behind |
| neben | next to, beside |
| über | about, above, over |
| unter | under, below, among |
| zwischen | between |
| vor | in front of, before, ago |
| H entlang | along |

Hier!

## Genitive Case Prepositions

| | |
|---|---|
| trotz | in spite of |
| statt | instead of |
| während | during |
| wegen | because of |

*Higher*

## Contracted Forms

| | | | | | | |
|---|---|---|---|---|---|---|
| an dem | → | am | on the, at the | bei dem | → beim | at the, with the |
| an das | → | ans | on(to) the, at the | von dem | → vom | from the, of the |
| in dem | → | im | in the | zu der | → zur | to the |
| in das | → | ins | into the | zu dem | → zum | to the |

*'Beim' or 'am' before an infinitive used as a noun means 'while / when doing something' (Higher tier).*

## Prepositional Pronouns

These pronouns replace a preposition plus a noun.

| | |
|---|---|
| darauf, drauf | on it/them, to it/them |
| damit | with it/them |
| dafür | for it/that/them |
| davon | from it/them, about it/them |
| dadurch | through it, as a result, as a consequence |
| dahinter | behind it |
| daneben | next to it, beside it |
| daraus | out of it, from it |
| darin, drin, drinnen | in it, in there, inside |
| darüber, drüber | above it, about it |
| dazu | to that, for that |
| darunter | under it, underneath |
| dabei | with it, there |
| daran, dran | on it, at it, in the process of it |
| danach | after it, afterwards |
| dagegen | against it, on the other hand |
| darum | around it, therefore |
| davor | before (it), in front of it |
| dazwischen | in between, between (them), among (them) |
| daher | from there, therefore |

These pronouns replace 'was' (what) plus a preposition.

| | |
|---|---|
| worauf | on what, to what |
| womit | with which |
| wofür | for what |
| wovon | from what, about what |
| wodurch | how, through which, as a result of which |
| wohinter | behind what |
| woneben | next to what, beside what |
| woraus | from what, from which |
| worin | in what, into what |
| worüber | what about |
| wozu | on what, onto what, at what, to what |
| worunter | under which, under what |
| wobei | in the process of which, with which, during which |
| woran | on what, at what |
| wonach | what … for, what … of |
| wogegen | against what, whereas |
| worum | about what |
| wovor | what … of, what … in front of |
| wozwischen | between what, between which |

# Revision Summary Test for Section Thirteen

Good golly, that was a chunky grammar section — give these questions a go before you move on.
- These questions are **hard**, but they'll really help you see **how well you know your stuff**.
- Tackle the **revision summary test** below, or scan the QR code to do it **online**. You can **track your progress** online and see **which areas need more work**.
- There are **sample answers** for the test here: www.cgpbooks.co.uk/BerlinExtras

## Nouns, Cases and Articles

1) Write either 'm', 'f' or 'n' to show whether each noun is masculine, feminine or neuter:
   a) Studium   b) Wohnung   c) Himmel   d) Mädchen   e) Herbst   f) Theaterkarte   g) Ärztin
2) Make these nouns feminine: a) der Lehrer   b) der Student   c) der Nachbar   d) der Journalist
3) Make these nouns plural: a) der Fuß   b) der Club   c) die Sängerin   d) das Ei   e) der Fehler
4) Write down whether the words in **bold** are in the nominative, the accusative or the dative case:
   a) Er zeigt es **seinem Freund**.   b) **Meine Mutter** trinkt Kaffee.   c) **Mathe** finde ich interessant.
5) Choose the correct article in **bold**, then translate each phrase into English:
   a) **Keine** / **Keinen** Katzen singen.   c) Du hilfst **den** / **dem** Lehrer.   e) **Das** / **Den** Haus ist groß.
   b) Ich besuche **ein** / **einen** Garten.   d) **Ein** / **Einem** Buch hat Wörter.   f) Ich sehe **die** / **der** Kirche.
6) Fill in each gap by translating the article in brackets into German, using the correct case:
   a) Ich kenne ...... Frau. (a)   c) Heute scheint ...... Sonne. (the)   e) Ich gebe es ...... Kind. (a)
   b) Er hat ...... Geld. (the)   d) Wir sehen ...... Film. (no)   f) ...... Fenster sind offen. (the)
7) Put each noun in the genitive case: a) eine Band   b) der Schüler   c) ein Schloss   d) die Plätze

## Pronouns

8) In German, list the subject pronouns and reflexive pronouns in this section that you need to know.
9) Choose the correct object pronoun in **bold**, then translate each sentence into English:
   a) Ich habe **ihn** / **ihm** gesehen.   c) Sie gibt **mich** / **mir** die Pflanze.
   b) Ich will **dich** / **dir** ein Lied singen.   d) Hast du **sie** / **ihr** heute getroffen?
10) Give these words in German in the nominative and the accusative cases: a) someone   b) no one
11) List the relative and interrogative pronouns in this section. Write a sentence for each type of pronoun.
12) Translate these sentences into German using either 'wo' or 'was'. Watch out for the word order.
    a) I know what he wants.   b) I don't like where I live.   c) We enjoy everything that we do.

## Word Order, Conjunctions and Prepositions

13) Choose the sentences that use correct German word order, then rewrite any that are incorrect:
    a) Den Roman ich liebe.   b) Morgen gehen wir ins Kino.   c) Er möchte fahren mit dem Bus.
14) Translate these conjunctions into English: a) und   b) denn   c) aber   d) entweder ... oder
15) Translate these sentences into German. Use a subordinating conjunction in each case:
    a) I stay at home, because it's raining.   c) Whenever I visit her, we cook together.
    b) When I was young, I had a bird.   d) Although he hates tennis, he watched the match.
16) Say which case these prepositions take, then write a short phrase or sentence for each one:
    a) mit   b) aus   c) ohne   d) bei   e) für   f) von   g) bis   h) nach   i) zu   j) durch
17) Pick the correct option in **bold** so the object is in the right case: a) Er wartet **an die** / **an der** Tür.
    b) Ich stelle es **auf das** / **auf dem** Bett.   c) Der Hund liegt **in den** / **im** Bahnhof.
18) What do these mean in English: a) darauf   b) damit   c) dafür   d) davon?
19) Translate these sentences into German, paying attention to the word order:
    a) Neither Anna nor Yousef like winter.   b) I enjoy both books and video games.
20) Give the English for each of these prepositions, then say which case they use:
    a) laut   b) wegen   c) gegen   d) trotz   e) um   f) während   g) seit   h) statt

Section Thirteen — Nouns, Cases and Linking Words

# Section Fourteen — Adjectives and Adverbs

## Adjective Agreement

Adjectives let you describe things, like all these lovely, helpful, not-overwhelming-at-all tables.

### Adjectives that go after the noun don't change

When the adjective is somewhere after the word it's describing (e.g. shirt), it doesn't change at all. You just use the basic adjective, without any endings.

| Das Hemd ist klein. | *The shirt is small.* | Das Haus ist rot. | *The house is red.* |

### Adjectives after 'the' end in '-e' or '-en'

You've got to add these endings if the adjective comes after 'the' (der, die, das etc.), 'dieser' (*this*), 'jeder' (*each / every*), 'welcher' (*which*), 'letzter' (*last*), 'nächster' (*next*), or 'alle' (*all*).

|  | Masculine | Feminine | Neuter | Plural |
|---|---|---|---|---|
| **Nominative** | rote | rote | rote | roten |
| **Accusative** | roten | rote | rote | roten |
| **Dative** | roten | roten | roten | roten |

Neuter nominative

das rote Hemd — *the red shirt*

Dieses schöne Hemd ist bequem.
*This lovely shirt is comfortable.*

### Some endings after 'a' and possessive adjectives are different

You need these endings when the adjective comes after 'ein' (*a*, or *one*) or 'kein' (*no*, or *none*), or after the possessive adjectives 'mein', 'dein', 'sein', 'ihr', 'unser', 'euer' and 'Ihr'.

|  | Masculine | Feminine | Neuter | Plural |
|---|---|---|---|---|
| **Nominative** | roter | rote | rotes | roten |
| **Accusative** | roten | rote | rotes | roten |
| **Dative** | roten | roten | roten | roten |

Neuter nominative

Mein rotes Hemd ist schön.
*My red shirt is lovely.*

### These are the endings for when there's no article

1) These are the plural adjective endings for when an adjective appears on its own before a noun.

|  | Plural |
|---|---|
| **Nominative** | rote |
| **Accusative** | rote |
| **Dative** | roten |

*You only need to know the plural endings for these types of adjectives for the exam.*

Plural accusative

Ich habe neue Hemden.
*I have new shirts.*

2) You also use these endings if the adjective comes after a number bigger than one, or after 'viele' (*many*), 'wenige' (*few*) or 'einige' (*some*).

Er hat viele alte Hemden.
*He has many old shirts.*

### Grammar Questions

Translate these sentences into **German**, making sure the adjectives agree.
1. The horse is grey.
2. I see three grey horses.
3. He has some grey horses.
4. She likes the grey horses.
5. I have a grey horse.
6. I sit on this grey horse.

### I love adjectives that go before nouns — they're so agreeable...

Adjectives that go after nouns, not so much. Lots of adjectives that go before nouns end in '-en', so when you're memorising adjective endings, focus on the ones that don't end in '-en' — it'll make it a lot easier.

# More Adjectives

My, my, my... a page on how to say things like 'my', 'her' and 'their' — what a treat.

## My, your, our — *possessive adjectives*

1) You have to be able to use these words to say that something belongs to you ('mein') or to someone else.

2) But watch out — they need the right ending to go with the object you're talking about.

|  | Masculine | Feminine | Neuter | Plural |
|---|---|---|---|---|
| Nominative | mein | meine | mein | meine |
| Accusative | meinen | meine | mein | meine |
| Dative | meinem | meiner | meinem | meinen |
| Genitive | meines | meiner | meines | meiner |

Meine Tasche ist blau.
*My bag is blue.*

Ich mag mein Fahrrad.
*I like my bike.*

3) The other possessive words are pretty neat — all of them use the same endings as 'mein' does.

**The Possessive Adjectives**

| mein | my | unser | our |
|---|---|---|---|
| dein | your (inf. sing.) | euer | your (inf. plu.) |
| sein | his | Ihr | your (frml. sing. & plu.) |
| ihr | her | | |
| sein | its | ihr | their |

Unsere Lehrer sind hilfsbereit.
*Our teachers are helpful.*

Seine Tasche ist blau.   *His bag is blue.*

## Some words have the same endings as 'the'

1) 'Welcher' (which), 'dieser' (this), 'jeder' (every), 'letzter' (last) and 'nächster' (next) are all examples of indefinite adjectives.

2) The endings of these words follow the same pattern as 'der'. Look at the last letter for each word in the first table on p.107 — the last line would be diesem, dieser, diesem, diesen.

Welches Fahrrad ist schnell?
*Which bike is fast?*

## 'Wenig', 'viel' — *little, a lot of*

Use the words 'wenig' (little) and 'viel' (a lot of) with uncountable nouns to say how much of it there is.

Ich trinke wenig Kaffee.   *I drink little coffee.*

Ich esse viel Käse.   *I eat a lot of cheese.*

> Don't confuse 'wenig' and 'viel' with 'wenige' and 'viele' on the previous page — those words are only used with plural nouns.

### Grammar Questions

Rewrite these sentences in **German**. Use the tables on this page, p.107 and p.123 for the right endings.
1. Our house is big.
2. Her sister is happy.
3. There's a bird in every tree.
4. Who has my new bag?
5. This music is great.
6. The woman has little money.

## Ihr we go again — more word endings to learn...

Jot down the table for possessive adjective endings and stick it in the inside cover of your exercise book so you can quickly look back at it. After checking it a few times, the endings will soon start to sink in.

Section Fourteen — Adjectives and Adverbs

# Comparative and Superlative Adjectives

Quick Quiz

My sibling often cuts cake so their piece is bigger than mine — in fact, theirs is always the biggest...

## Add '-er' to adjectives to compare things

1) In German, comparative adjectives are made up of a normal adjective and the ending '-er'.

   Anna ist klein.  *Anna is small.*  →  Omar ist kleiner.  *Omar is smaller.*

2) You can't add 'mehr' (more) before the adjective in German like you can in English.

   Tina ist ernster.  *Tina is more serious.*

3) Some comparative adjectives have more changes — and others are just completely different.

   | nah | near | → | näher | nearer |
   | groß | big | → | größer | bigger |
   | dunkel | dark | → | dunkler | darker |

   Lots of short adjectives add an umlaut.
   If an adjective already ends in '-el' or '-er', it drops the 'e'.

   | gut | good | → | besser | better |
   | hoch | high | → | höher | higher |
   | viel | a lot | → | mehr | more |

4) Use 'als' (than) to compare something to something else.

   Meine Katzen sind intelligenter als deine Hunde.  *My cats are more intelligent than your dogs.*

5) 'So... wie' (as... as) lets you show how two things are the same.

   Jo ist so alt wie Li.  *Jo is as old as Li.*

   You just need to use the regular adjective with 'so... wie'.

## Use the ending '-ste' to say 'the ...est'

1) To form a superlative adjective, you normally add '-ste' to the stem of the adjective.

2) When you put the superlative before a noun, you need to use the definite article ('der', 'die', 'das' etc.) and use the correct adjective ending.

   You add '-este' instead when an adjective ends in '-t', '-d', '-sch', '-ß', '-s', '-x', '-z' or '-e'.

   Ich lese die längsten Bücher.
   *I read the longest books.*

   Like comparatives, superlatives sometimes get an umlaut.

   Das lauteste Auto ist blau.
   *The loudest car is blue.*

3) Some superlatives look different to the normal adjective.

   | gut | good | → | der / die / das beste | the best |
   | hoch | high | → | der / die / das höchste | the highest |
   | viel | a lot | → | der / die / das meiste | the most |
   | nah | near | → | der / die / das nächste | the nearest |

   Wo ist das nächste Restaurant?
   *Where is the nearest Restaurant?*

4) When you use the superlative without a noun, you use 'am' and add '-sten' or '-esten' to the stem of the adjective.

   Dieser Ball ist am kleinsten.
   *This ball is the smallest.*

### Grammar Questions

Translate these words, phrases and sentences into **German**.

1. happy, happier
2. slower than Ben
3. This film is sadder.
4. as expensive as
5. We are the quickest. [H]
6. I listen to the best music.
7. They know the most people. [H]

## Never compare yourself to others — except in German...

Using comparatives (and superlatives) in German will make you more impressive — perhaps even the most.

Quick Quiz

# Adverbs

Adverbs describe how you do something. E.g. I eat my chips **quickly** so my brother doesn't nab any.

## Use adverbs to say how you do something

1) In English, you don't say 'We speak strange' — you add '-ly' onto the end to say 'We speak strange<u>ly</u>'.
2) In German, you don't have to do anything — you just stick the describing word in as it is.

| | | | |
|---|---|---|---|
| langsam | *slowly* | freiwillig | *voluntarily* |
| schnell | *quickly* | vielleicht | *possibly* |

Lou singt schrecklich.   *Lou sings terribly.*

3) You can put 'gern' or 'lieber' after the verb to say what you like doing or what you prefer to do.

Sie joggt gern.   *She likes jogging.*     Ich wandere lieber.   *I prefer hiking.*

## Some adverbs describe when you do something

Adverbs can tell you when or how often something happens.

| | | | | | |
|---|---|---|---|---|---|
| immer | *always* | gleich | *right away, immediately* | schon | *already* |
| manchmal | *sometimes* | neulich | *recently, the other day* | nie | *never* |

Wir arbeiten jetzt schnell.   *We work quickly now.*

In German, adverbs follow the order time, manner, place. See p.112 for more about word order.

## Some show where you do something

| | |
|---|---|
| hier | *here* |
| dort | *there* |
| überall | *everywhere* |
| irgendwo | *somewhere* |

Ich wohne dort.   *I live there.*

Er wohnt irgendwo in London.   *He lives somewhere in London.*

"Sir, madam, the camera's this way..."

## Use one of these words to give even more detail

Pop one of these words in front of an adjective or adverb to really impress your teacher.

| | | | |
|---|---|---|---|
| sehr | *very* | viel | *a lot* |
| ganz | *quite* | fast | *almost* |
| etwas | *somewhat* | total | *completely* |

Er spricht ganz langsam.   *He speaks quite slowly.*

Ich bin etwas müde.   *I am somewhat tired.*

### Grammar Questions

Rewrite each of these sentences, adding an adverb. Use more than one adverb where you can.
1. Ich gehe.
2. Sie laufen.
3. Er hat gesprochen.
4. Ich helfe Lukas.
5. Wir werden gewinnen.
6. Die Frau fährt.
7. Stephan kam spät.
8. Es kostet zwei Euro.

## No, TMP does not stand for 'Tickle Me Playfully'...

It stands for 'Time, Manner, Place' — German adverbs go in that order. Remember that and you'll go far.

Section Fourteen — Adjectives and Adverbs

# Comparative and Superlative Adverbs

Quick Quiz

You might do something, but then Günther Graf does it a million times better.* Typical. Still, at least you'll be able to complain about it using comparative adverbs — here's how to use them...

## Comparative adverbs compare actions

You use the nominative case after comparative structures, i.e. 'ich', not 'mich'.

1) To say someone is doing something 'more... than' someone else, add '-er' to the adverb and use 'als'.

> Ida fährt langsamer als ich.   Ida drives more slowly than me.
> Eren singt süßer als du.   Eren sings more sweetly than you.

2) You can say someone is doing something 'less... than' someone else by using 'nicht so... wie'.

> Grace arbeitet nicht so hart wie Ruth.   Grace works less hard than Ruth.

'Nicht so... wie' is also the same as saying 'not as... as'.

3) If you want to say someone or something is doing something 'just as...', or 'just as... as' someone or something else, use 'genauso...' and 'genauso... wie'.

The adverb doesn't change with 'nicht so' and 'genauso'.

> Man kann die Musik genauso gut hier hören.   You can hear the music just as well here.
> Aaron läuft genauso langsam wie Ethel.   Aaron runs just as slowly as Ethel.

## Superlative adverbs say who does something 'the ...est'

If you want to say something's the quickest, the slowest or the craziest, you use 'am' and then add '-(e)sten' to the end of the adverb.

These are examples of the superlative.

Higher

> Dani tanzt am schnellsten.   Dani dances the fastest.
> Der Vogel singt am lautesten.   The bird sings the loudest.

Adverbs ending in '-d' or '-t' add '-esten'.

Always put 'am' before superlative adverbs — never use 'der', 'die' or 'das'.

## Watch out for these odd ones

'Gern', 'gut' and 'viel' are three strange ones that don't follow the rules.

| gern | gladly |
|---|---|
| lieber | rather |
| H am liebsten | most preferably |

| gut | well |
|---|---|
| besser | better |
| H am besten | best |

| viel | a lot |
|---|---|
| mehr | more |
| H am meisten | the most |

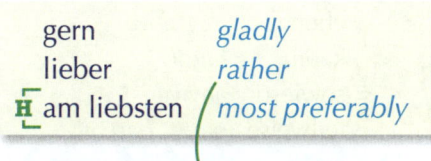
Ich spreche lieber Deutsch.
I prefer speaking German.

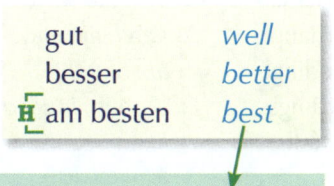
Berlin gefällt mir am besten.
I like Berlin the best.

Er mag die Schuhe am meisten.
He likes the shoes the most.

## Grammar Questions

Translate these phrases into **German**.
1. I run faster than her.
2. We will eat more slowly.
3. She dances better than us.
4. He jumps just as far as me.
5. H He sings the most beautifully. H
6. They play football the best.

*He's so wonderful, though — I can't be annoyed.

## How do you compare actions in German? Errrrrrr...

In English, you sometimes use 'more' with an adverb to make it comparative, but you can't do the same in German. For example, saying 'wir gewinnen mehr oft als sie' would be incorrect — you need to use 'öfter'.

# Adjectives and Adverbs — Grammar List

## Adjective Agreement

### After definite articles

|  | Masc | Fem | Neut | Plu |
|---|---|---|---|---|
| **Nom** | -e | -e | -e | -en |
| **Acc** | -en | -e | -e | -en |
| **Dat** | -en | -en | -en | -en |

### No articles

|  | Plu |
|---|---|
| **Nom** | -e |
| **Acc** | -e |
| **Dat** | -en |

Also after 'welcher' *(which)*, 'dieser' *(this)*, 'jeder' *(each, every)*, 'nächster' *(next)*, 'letzter' *(last)* and 'alle' *(all)*.

Also after 'einige' *(a few, some)*, 'wenige' *(few)* and 'viele' *(many)*.

### After indefinite articles

|  | Masc | Fem | Neut | Plu |
|---|---|---|---|---|
| **Nom** | -er | -e | -es | -en |
| **Acc** | -en | -e | -es | -en |
| **Dat** | -en | -en | -en | -en |

You use 'wenig' and 'viel' without endings for uncountable nouns.

Also after 'kein' *(no)* and possessive adjectives.

## Possessive Adjectives

|  | Masc | Fem | Neut | Plu |
|---|---|---|---|---|
| **Nom** | mein | meine | mein | meine |
| **Acc** | mein**en** | meine | mein | meine |
| **Dat** | mein**em** | mein**er** | mein**em** | mein**en** |
| **Gen** | mein**es** | mein**er** | mein**es** | mein**er** |

Here are all the possessive adjectives. They all use the same endings.

| mein | my | unser | our |
|---|---|---|---|
| dein | your (inf. sing.) | euer | your (inf. plu.) |
| sein | his | Ihr | your (frml. sing. & plu.) |
| ihr | her | | |
| sein | its | ihr | their |

Milo had nearly learned all the German adjective endings.

## Adverbs

| schon | already, yet |
| gern, gerne | gladly |
| selbst | even |
| so | so, in this way, thus, such |
| sehr | very, very much |
| ganz | quite |
| etwas | somewhat |
| viel | a lot |
| meistens | mostly |
| mindestens | at least, minimum |
| wenigstens | at least |
| leider | unfortunately, sadly |
| vorher | beforehand, earlier, previously |
| bereits | already |
| nun | now, well |
| je | ever, each |
| vorbei | past, over |

(Higher: vorher, bereits, nun, je, vorbei)

| seitdem | since then |
| zunächst | first, at first, to begin with, for now, for the time being |
| eher | earlier, sooner, rather |
| erst | first, only, not until |
| bisher | until now, up to now, yet, so far |
| glücklicherweise | fortunately, luckily |
| stattdessen | instead |
| überhaupt | at all, anyway |
| unbedingt | absolutely |
| allerdings | though, indeed, certainly |
| ebenfalls | likewise, also, as well, too |
| jedenfalls | in any case, at any rate, anyhow |
| zumindest | at least |
| außerdem | besides, in addition, furthermore |

(Higher: stattdessen through außerdem)

'Seitdem' can also be a conjunction meaning 'since'.

Adverbs usually go in the order **time, manner, place**.

| dazu | in addition, furthermore, besides |
| zwar | admittedly, to be precise, indeed |
| etwa | about, approximately |
| eben | just, now |
| kaum | hardly |
| sowieso | anyway |
| teilweise | partly, partially |
| sogar | even, in fact, actually |
| doch | however, but |
| sonst | otherwise, else |
| übrigens | by the way |
| hin | there |
| her | from something, ago |

(Higher: sowieso through her)

## Comparative and Superlative Adjectives and Adverbs

| als | than |
| so... wie | as... as |
| genauso... wie | just as... as |
| mehr | more |
| besser | better |
| höher | higher, taller |
| lieber | more gladly, rather |

(Higher: mehr, besser, höher, lieber)

Superlative adjectives before nouns need the correct definite article and ending.

| der beste | the best |
| der höchste | the highest |
| der meiste | the most |
| der nächste | the next, nearest |

Superlative adverbs begin with 'am'.

| am besten | (the) best |
| am höchsten | (the) highest |
| am liebsten | (the) most preferred, most preferably, rather |
| am meisten | (the) most |
| am nächsten | (the) next, nearest |

Section Fourteen — Adjectives and Adverbs

# Revision Summary Test for Section Fourteen

If adjectives and adverbs make things more interesting, then this is the most interesting page of all.
- Yep, these questions are **hard** — they'll really help you see **how well you know your stuff**.
- Tackle the **revision summary test** below, or scan the QR code to do it **online**.
  Use the CGP RevisionHub to **track your progress** and see **which areas need more work**.
- You can find **sample answers** here: www.cgpbooks.co.uk/BerlinExtras

## Adjectives ☐

1) Choose the correct adjective in brackets, then translate each sentence into English.
   a) Ein (bekannten / bekannter) Spieler kommt.
   b) Der Film war (langweilig / langweilige).
   c) Wir besuchen eine (gute / guter) Freundin.
   d) Welches (großes / große) Schloss siehst du?
   e) Sie hat keine (kleine / kleinen) Pflanzen mehr.
   f) Ich helfe jedem (kranken / krank) Tier.

2) Fill in each gap by translating the adjective in brackets into German, using the correct ending.
   a) Der ............... Junge läuft. (tall)
   b) Hast du kein ............... Handy? (new)
   c) Die Straße ist ................ (wide)
   d) Wir tragen einige ............... Jacken. (colourful)
   e) Das Auto gehört einer ............... Frau. (nice)
   f) Diese ............... Hunde spielen. (loud)

3) Give the German for:  a) Happy people dance.  b) I eat blue eggs.  c) She goes to big parties.

4) Find the possessive adjective in each sentence, then translate the word and give its case and gender:
   a) Euer Lieblingslied spielt jetzt.
   b) Julia bleibt bei ihrer Oma.
   c) Er verliert seinen Laptop.
   d) Darf ich Ihre Karte sehen, bitte?

5) Add the correct ending to each possessive adjective, then translate each sentence into English.
   a) Sie helfen ihr.... Eltern.
   b) Sind unser.... Taschen hier?
   c) Dein.... Schule hat einen Tennisclub.
   d) Ich gehe mit mein.... Bruder.

6) Choose the correct option to complete each sentence, then translate each sentence into English.
   a) Ich habe **viel / viele** Liebe für dich.
   b) Es gibt **wenig / wenige** Bücher zu Hause.
   c) Du hast **wenig / wenige** Wasser getrunken.
   d) Ich genieße **viel / viele** Aktivitäten.

7) [H] Add the correct ending to each possessive adjective so that it's in the genitive case.
   a) das Haus mein.... Vaters    b) die Freunde dein.... Kinder    c) die Brille unser.... Schwester

## Adverbs ☑

8) Find the adverb in each of these sentences, then translate each sentence into English.
   a) Otto und Defne singen schön.
   b) Ihr seid endlich angekommen.
   c) Gestern war sie in einem Theaterstück.
   d) Bist du überall in der Schweiz gereist?

9) Decide whether the word in **bold** is an adverb of time, manner or place.
   Then rewrite the sentence, replacing the adverb with a new one of a different type.
   a) Es gab eine Party **hier**.
   b) Ich esse **oft** im Restaurant.
   c) Sie spielt **regelmäßig** ein Instrument.
   d) Er arbeitet **freiwillig** für sie.

10) How would you say these sentences in German?
    a) I'll arrive somewhat late tomorrow.
    b) We were unfortunately quite tired.
    c) He already knows me well.
    d) I almost always play football there.

## Comparatives and Superlatives ☐

11) How do you say the following in German? 'I am younger than Malik, but as old as Franz.'

12) Give the comparative forms of these adverbs:  a) gut  b) viel  c) hoch  d) gern

13) Eli says: 'Lili geht öfter als ich ins Fitness-Studio, aber ich laufe genauso schnell.' What did he say?

14) [Higher] How would you say these superlative phrases in German?
    a) the best film    b) the highest wall    c) the most expensive gift    d) the shortest days

15) Change these German phrases and sentences so that the adverb is superlative:
    a) Wir klettern viel.    b) Sie malt gern.    c) Dieser Strand ist nah.    d) Der Garten ist groß.

16) Translate this sentence into German: 'Dae-hyun studies the most, but Birgitte has the best grades.'

# Section Fifteen — Verbs and Tenses

## Verbs in the Present Tense

Verbs are action words. Present tense verbs say what's happening now, e.g. 'I **tell** a joke. You **laugh**'.

### Use the present tense for what's happening now

1) The present tense is used to say 'I do' and 'I am doing' — German doesn't have a separate '-ing' form.

2) To use a verb, you need to know its infinitive (the form you find in a dictionary), e.g. 'reisen' *(to travel)*.

3) For regular verbs, you take off the '-en' from the infinitive — this leaves you with the stem of the verb.

4) Then add the correct ending to the stem. 'Machen' is regular, so here it is with its endings:

| machen — to do or make | | | |
|---|---|---|---|
| ich mache | *I make* | wir machen | *we make* |
| du machst | *you (inf. sing.) make* | ihr macht | *you (inf. plu.) make* |
| er macht | *he makes* | Sie machen | *you (frml. sing.* |
| sie macht | *she makes* | | *& plu.) make* |
| es macht | *it makes* | sie machen | *they make* |

The first bit ('mach') doesn't change.

For the different forms of 'you' and when to use them, see p.10.

The verb endings change to match the pronoun.

5) The present tense is sometimes used in written German to talk about past events, e.g. in news articles.

*Die deutsche Mannschaft spielt ein historisches Spiel.*
*The German team plays a historic match.*

### Verbs that end in '-rn' or '-ln' work differently

Some regular verbs don't end in '-en' — they end in '-rn' or '-ln'.

For '-ln' verbs, miss out the 'e' before the 'l' for ich.

| lächeln — to smile | |
|---|---|
| ich | lächle |
| du | lächelst |
| er / sie / es | lächelt |
| wir | lächeln |
| ihr | lächelt |
| Sie / sie | lächeln |

For '-rn' verbs, you can miss out the 'e' before the 'r' for ich.

Add '-n' not '-en' for wir, Sie and sie.

| wandern — to hike | |
|---|---|
| ich | wand(e)re |
| du | wanderst |
| er / sie / es | wandert |
| wir | wandern |
| ihr | wandert |
| Sie / sie | wandern |

*Eduardo is in his happy place.*

### Use 'seit' to say how long you've been doing something

**Higher**

Use 'seit' with the present tense for actions that began in the past, but are still continuing today.

*Ich lerne seit drei Jahren Deutsch.*    *I have been learning German for three years.*

Use the dative case after 'seit' (see p.106).

### Grammar Questions

Write these sentences in **German**. Use the endings for 'machen' unless the verb ends in '-rn' or '-ln'.
1. She collects.
2. We believe.
3. You (inf. sing.) ask.
4. You (frml. plu.) dance.
5. I celebrate.
6. They recycle.
7. I play.
8. Jan cooks.
9. I've been living here for a year. [H]

### There's an 'ing' in English — but not in German...

'Ich trinke Wasser' can mean both 'I **drink** water' and 'I **am drink**ing water' — you just need this one form.

# More About the Present Tense

Irregular verbs were born to stand out — unlike regular verbs, they play by different rules.

## Some common verbs are irregular

1) Verbs that don't follow the same pattern as regular verbs are called 'irregular verbs'. These four come up a lot:

**haben — to have**

| | |
|---|---|
| ich habe | I have |
| du hast | you have |
| er / sie / es hat | he / she / it has |
| wir haben | we have |
| ihr habt | you have |
| Sie / sie haben | you / they have |

**sein — to be**

| | |
|---|---|
| ich bin | I am |
| du bist | you are |
| er / sie / es ist | he / she / it is |
| wir sind | we are |
| ihr seid | you are |
| Sie / sie sind | you / they are |

**werden — to become**

| | |
|---|---|
| ich werde | I become |
| du wirst | you become |
| er / sie / es wird | he / she / it becomes |
| wir werden | we become |
| ihr werdet | you become |
| Sie / sie werden | you / they become |

**wissen — to know**

| | |
|---|---|
| ich weiß | I know |
| du weißt | you know |
| er / sie / es weiß | he / she / it knows |
| wir wissen | we know |
| ihr wisst | you know |
| Sie / sie wissen | you / they know |

2) All of these verbs are irregular in the 'du' and 'er' / 'sie' / 'es' forms too, so watch out for them:

| | | | | |
|---|---|---|---|---|
| lesen (er liest) | to read (he reads) | finden (er findet) | to find (he finds) | If the stem ends in 'd', 't', 'm', or 'n', add an 'e' before the 'du' and 'er' / 'sie' / 'es' endings. |
| geben (du gibst) | to give (you give) | fahren (sie fährt) | to go (she goes) | |

## Some verbs make you use the dative case

1) You normally only need the dative case when you're saying 'to something or someone'. See p.106.

2) But some German verbs always need the dative case, like 'helfen' ('to help').

Ich helfe dem Kind.    I help the child.
You use 'dem' because 'Kind' is neuter and 'helfen' needs the dative.

3) These verbs all need the dative case — make sure you learn them:

| | | | | | | | |
|---|---|---|---|---|---|---|---|
| geben | to give | glauben | to believe | antworten | to answer | vertrauen | to trust |
| folgen | to follow | gehören | to belong | empfehlen | to recommend | danken | to thank |

## Grammar Questions

Translate these sentences into **German**. Watch out for any irregular verbs.
1. She has a cat.
2. We are teachers.
3. He becomes independent.
4. You (inf. sing.) follow the man.
5. Do you (frml. plu.) believe me?
6. The dog belongs to my sister.

### I just opened up my parents' dative case — never again...

You'll have to use 'haben' and 'sein' loads in your GCSEs, so it's a good idea to learn their verb forms off by heart. When you can say all of their present tense forms without looking, move onto 'werden' and 'wissen'.

Quick Quiz

# More Ways to Use Verbs

Time to turn up the heat — here are some verb constructions that can really spice up your German.

## Use reflexive verbs to talk about 'myself', 'yourself'...

Use reflexive verbs when you want to talk about what people do to themselves. See p.111 for how to say 'myself', 'yourself' etc. in German in the accusative and dative cases.

Er zieht sich um.   *He gets changed.*    Ich fühle mich krank.   *I feel sick.*

## Impersonal forms with 'es'

Some German phrases have 'es' as the subject. Learn these common examples:

Es geht mir gut.   *I am well.*    Es regnet.   *It's raining.*    Es gefällt mir.   *I like it.*

Es tut mir leid.   *I'm sorry.*    Es gibt keinen Kuchen.   *There is no cake.*

## You can use 'man' instead of the passive

**Higher**

In German, you can use the subject pronoun 'man' with an active verb to avoid using the passive voice.

Man hat das Haus im Jahr 1998 gebaut.   *One built the house in 1998. / The house was built in 1998.*

'Man' has the same verb endings as 'er', 'sie' and 'es'.

## Infinitive phrases can add extra information

**Higher**

1) You can use infinitive constructions to say things like 'in order to', 'without' and 'instead of'.

   Ich habe es gemacht, um Geld zu sparen.   *I did it in order to save money.*

   Sie fährt nie nach Italien, ohne Eis zu essen.   *She never travels to Italy without eating ice cream.*

   Ich sehe oft fern, statt ins Kino zu gehen.   *I often watch TV instead of going to the cinema.*

2) When you use verbs like 'versuchen' and 'hoffen' with a second verb, the second verb is in the infinitive and needs 'zu' before it.

   Ich versuche, ein Buch zu schreiben.   *I'm trying to write a book.*

3) Leave the 'zu' out if the first verb is a modal verb. See p.140.

   Ich muss nach Hause gehen.   *I must go home.*

   'Müssen' is a modal verb, so you don't need a 'zu'.

### Grammar Questions

Translate these sentences into **German**.
1. She gets dressed.
2. It's snowing.
3. I should say something.
4. We feel very well.
5. I study lots in order to get good grades. [H]
6. I often go out without closing the door. [H]

## Imparsleynal forms — a great herb construction...

I see that slight smirk of yours — I know that wasn't one of my best jokes, but you can't blame me for trying.

Section Fifteen — Verbs and Tenses

# Talking About the Past

If you want to describe something that happened in the past, I've got the perfect tense for you.

## Use the perfect tense for things that have finished

*See p.131 for all the endings for 'haben'.*

1) The perfect tense usually starts with 'haben' ('to have') and ends with a past participle.

   *Ich habe ein Fahrrad gekauft.* — *I have bought a bike.*

2) To form the past participle (the past tense bit) of regular verbs, follow these steps:

   | kaufen *to buy* | kaufen - en = kauf | gekauft *bought* |
   |---|---|---|
   | Begin with the verb in the infinitive. | Remove '-en' from the end of the infinitive to get the verb stem. | Add 'ge-' to the start and add '-t' to the end. |

   *If a verb stem ends in 'd', 't', 'm' or 'n', add '-et' to get the past participle.*

3) You don't always need the 'have' part in English.

   *Ich habe auf ihn gewartet.* — *I (have) waited for him.*

4) Use time phrases like 'früher' with the perfect tense to talk about what you used to do regularly.

## Some past participles are formed differently

1) There are quite a few other ways that past participles can be made:

   *Inseparable prefixes include 'be-', 'ent-', 'er-', 'über-', 'ge-' and 'ver-'.*

   | Type of verbs | What to do | Example |
   |---|---|---|
   | Some verbs with inseparable prefixes | Add '-t' to verb stem | erzählen (*to tell*) → erzählt (*told*) |
   | Infinitives ending in 'ieren' | | studieren (*to study*) → studiert (*studied*) |
   | Other verbs with inseparable prefixes | No change | vergessen (*to forget*) → vergessen (*forgotten*) |
   | Some irregular verbs | Add 'ge-' to infinitive | schlafen (*to sleep*) → geschlafen (*slept*) |

2) Some verb stems also have a vowel change and end in '-en' to form the past participle.

   | Change | Example | Other verbs |
   |---|---|---|
   | ei → ie | treiben (*to do*) → getrieben | steigen, schreiben |
   | i → u | trinken (*to drink*) → getrunken | finden, singen |
   | e → o | helfen (*to help*) → geholfen | treffen, sprechen |
   | ie → o | fliegen (*to fly*) → geflogen | verlieren |

   Verbs with prefixes form the past participle the same way as the main verb, e.g. 'beschreiben' becomes 'beschrieben' because 'schreiben' has a vowel change.

## Ist sie gegangen? — *Has she gone?*

*See p.131 for the different forms of 'sein'.*

1) Some verbs need 'sein' ('to be') and not 'haben' in the perfect tense.

   *Ich bin gegangen.* — *I have gone.*

2) It's mostly movement verbs that need 'sein'. Here's a list of some common ones:

   | to go, drive | fahren → gefahren | to stay | bleiben → geblieben |
   |---|---|---|---|
   | to come | kommen → gekommen | to be | sein → gewesen |

### Grammar Questions

Write these sentences in **German**. Remember to check whether you need 'haben' or 'sein'.
1. I have drunk coffee.   2. We have stayed here.   3. She has asked.   4. He has found me.

## What's a time-traveller's favourite food? Past-a...

Try writing down the 'sein' verbs on this page from memory. For an extra challenge, give each past participle.

*Find the CGP RevisionHub at cgpbooks.co.uk/Berlin*

**Section Fifteen — Verbs and Tenses**

# The Simple Past

Boy, oh boy. Two whole pages about the simple past — I'm so excited, I could cry.

## Ich hatte — *I had* / Ich war — *I was*

*You might hear the simple past referred to as the 'imperfect', too.*

1) Use the simple past to talk about the past without using 'haben' or 'sein' with the past participle.
2) You'll use the simple past forms of 'haben' and 'sein' loads — so it's well worth learning them.

**Ich hatte** — *I had*

| | |
|---|---|
| ich hatte | *I had* |
| du hattest | *you (inf. sing.) had* |
| er / sie / es hatte | *he / she / it had* |
| wir hatten | *we had* |
| ihr hattet | *you (inf. plu.) had* |
| Sie hatten | *you (frml. sing. & plu.) had* |
| sie hatten | *they had* |

Sie hatten vier Brüder. *They had four brothers.*

Sie hatte ein blaues Kleid. *She had a blue dress.*

**Ich war** — *I was*

| | |
|---|---|
| ich war | *I was* |
| du warst | *you (inf. sing.) were* |
| er / sie / es war | *he / she / it was* |
| wir waren | *we were* |
| ihr wart | *you (inf. plu.) were* |
| Sie waren | *you (frml. sing. & plu.) were* |
| sie waren | *they were* |

Wir waren sehr müde. *We were very tired.*

Ich war ein komisches Kind. *I was a strange child.*

3) Another phrase you need to know is 'es gab', which is the simple past tense form of 'es gibt'. It means 'there was' or 'there were' — it stays the same regardless of whether the noun is singular or plural.

Es gab ein Konzert. *There was a concert.*   Es gab viele Lichter. *There were lots of lights.*

4) You also need to learn the simple past forms of modal verbs (see p.140).

## Regular verbs in the simple past

1) Other forms of the simple past are used more in written German.
2) This is how you form the simple past form of a regular verb:

| kaufen *to buy* | → | kaufen - en = kauf | → | ich kaufte *I bought* |
|---|---|---|---|---|
| Begin with the verb in the infinitive. | | Remove '-en' from the end of the infinitive. | | Add the correct simple past ending for the person. |

**machen** — to make

| | | | |
|---|---|---|---|
| ich machte | *I made* | wir machten | *we made* |
| du machtest | *you made* | ihr machtet | *you made* |
| er / sie / es machte | *he / she / it made* | Sie / sie machten | *you / they made* |

**spielen** — to play

| | | | |
|---|---|---|---|
| ich spielte | *I played* | wir spielten | *we played* |
| du spieltest | *you played* | ihr spieltet | *you played* |
| er / sie / es spielte | *he / she / it played* | Sie / sie spielten | *you / they played* |

Amelia and her mum liked to jazz things up.

| Er hasste mich. | Wir lernten Deutsch. | Ihr kochtet zusammen. | Ich spielte Saxophon. |
|---|---|---|---|
| *He hated me.* | *We learned German.* | *You cooked together.* | *I played the saxophone.* |

# Common irregular verbs in the simple past

Some verbs are irregular in the simple past. Here are some examples you need to learn.

**gehen — to go**

| | |
|---|---|
| ich ging | I went |
| du gingst | you (inf. sing.) went |
| er / sie / es ging | he / she / it went |
| wir gingen | we went |
| ihr gingt | you (inf. plu.) went |
| Sie gingen | you (frml. sing. & plu.) went |
| sie gingen | they went |

**fahren — to go / drive**

| | |
|---|---|
| ich fuhr | I went / drove |
| du fuhrst | you (inf. sing.) went / drove |
| er / sie / es fuhr | he / she / it went / drove |
| wir fuhren | we went / drove |
| ihr fuhrt | you (inf. plu.) went / drove |
| Sie fuhren | you (frml. sing. & plu.) went / drove |
| sie fuhren | they went / drove |

Er ging nach Hause.
He went home.

← Use 'gehen' when you mean 'to go by foot'.

Wir fuhren nach Wien.
We went / drove to Vienna.

← Use 'fahren' for going somewhere in a vehicle, even if you're not the one doing the driving.

**wissen — to know**

| | |
|---|---|
| ich wusste | I knew |
| du wusstest | you (inf. sing.) knew |
| er / sie / es wusste | he / she / it knew |
| wir wussten | we knew |
| ihr wusstet | you (inf. plu.) knew |
| Sie wussten | you (frml. sing. & plu.) knew |
| sie wussten | they knew |

**kommen — to come**

| | |
|---|---|
| ich kam | I came |
| du kamst | you (inf. sing.) came |
| er / sie / es kam | he / she / it came |
| wir kamen | we came |
| ihr kamt | you (inf. plu.) came |
| Sie kamen | you (frml. sing. & plu.) came |
| sie kamen | they came |

# Learn these irregular verbs in the simple past too

Here are some other verbs which are also irregular in the simple past — there are some more on p.146.

| | | | | | | | | | |
|---|---|---|---|---|---|---|---|---|---|
| denken | ich dachte | I thought | bleiben | ich blieb | I stayed | essen | ich aß | I ate |
| helfen | ich half | I helped | sprechen | ich sprach | I spoke | sehen | ich sah | I saw |
| finden | ich fand | I found | schreiben | ich schrieb | I wrote | lesen | ich las | I read |
| nehmen | ich nahm | I took | beginnen | ich begann | I began | geben | ich gab | I gave |
| laufen | ich lief | I ran | ziehen | ich zog | I moved | setzen | ich saß | I sat |

Er lief durch den Wald.
He ran through the wood.

Wir sprachen viel zusammen.
We spoke together a lot.

Ich fand die Brücke.
I found the bridge.

## Grammar Questions

Translate the sentences below into **German** using the simple past tense.

1. I had a dog.
2. We were happy.
3. He was young.
4. They had a good idea.
5. They ate there.
6. You (inf. sing.) helped me.
7. You (frml. sing.) thought a lot.
8. You (inf. plu.) began late.
9. We saw him.
10. They played tennis.
11. Mila wrote a book.
12. I moved to Greece.

## My fridge is always sad — it misses the good cold days...

Time to repair it — I'm sick of my food going off. Anyway, the simple past forms of 'haben' and 'sein' are used more than their perfect tense forms, so get those 'hatte' and 'war' forms learnt — you'll thank me later.

# Talking About the Future

You've got not one, but two ways to talk about the future in German — spoiled for choice, I'd say.

## 1) You can use the present tense to talk about the future

1) To say something is going to happen in the future, say it happens and then say when it's going to happen.

| **Happening now** → | Ich fahre nach Spanien. | *I am going to Spain.* |
|---|---|---|
| **Going to happen** → | Ich fahre nächstes Jahr nach Spanien. | *I am going to Spain next year.* |

*See p.130-131 for more on the present tense.*

This tells you when it's going to happen.

2) The time bit can go anywhere in the sentence, as long as you keep to the rules of word order — see p.112.

Nächstes Jahr fahre ich nach Spanien.    *Next year, I'm going to Spain.*

| nächste Woche | *next week* | am Montag | *on Monday* | im Mai | *in May* |
| morgen | *tomorrow* | diesen Sommer | *this summer* | in der Zukunft | *in the future* |

## 2) You can use 'werden' to say 'will' or 'to be going to...'

1) This part's slightly trickier. 'Ich werde' means 'I will' or 'I am going to'. To form the future tense with 'werden', you need the right form of 'werden' and the infinitive of the other verb.

| **Ich werde** Use the right form of the verb 'werden'. | **+** | **bald nach Köln** Add in any extra information here. | **+** | **fahren** Use the infinitive of the other verb here. | **=** | **Ich werde bald nach Köln fahren.** *I will go to Cologne soon.* This is the future tense. |

Ich werde mehr für die Umwelt tun.    *I am going to do more for the environment.*

2) 'Werden' is an irregular verb, so you'll have to learn its endings.

*'Werden' also means 'to become'.*

**werden — will / to be going to**

| ich werde | *I will* | wir werden | *we will* |
| du wirst | *you (inf. sing.) will* | ihr werdet | *you (inf. plu.) will* |
| er / sie / es wird | *he / she / it will* | Sie / sie werden | *you (frml. sing. & plu.) / they will* |

Wir werden unsere Hausaufgaben machen.    *We will do our homework.*

Nächstes Jahr wirst du in die Schule gehen.    *Next year, you will go to school.*

### Grammar Questions

Write these sentences in **German** using both ways of making the future tense.
1. I'll go to the park on Monday.
2. Anna will meet us next week.
3. He will explain it soon.
4. They will visit us next year.
5. I'll eat chips tomorrow.
6. Next time, we'll buy the car.

---

**Don't get Zukunft-able using one way to talk about the future...**
Switch up your German with both forms of the future on this page — it'll show you really know your stuff.

Section Fifteen — Verbs and Tenses

# Negative Forms

Quick Quiz

Sorry to bring the mood down, but you were going to have to learn about negatives at some point.

## Use negative forms to say what's not happening

1) To say what doesn't happen, you can add a negative word to the sentence.

   | nicht | *not* | nichts | *nothing* | nie | *never* |

2) The negative word usually goes towards the end of the main clause. This includes going after direct and indirect objects, reflexive pronouns and time phrases.

   Der Mann bewegt sich nie.
   *The man never exercises.*

   Ich gebe meinem Bruder das Buch heute nicht.
   *I'm not giving my brother the book today.*

3) However, it comes before adjectives, adverbs, separable prefixes and phrases of manner and place.

   Ich bin nicht groß.
   *I am not tall.*

   Ich bereite nichts schnell vor.
   *I prepare nothing quickly.*

   Ich fahre nie mit dem Bus zur Schule.
   *I never travel to school by bus.*

4) In main clauses with two verbs, e.g. with modal verbs or the perfect tense, the negative word goes between the two verbs.

   Er kann nichts tun.  *He can do nothing.*

   Ich bin letzte Woche nicht nach Griechenland geflogen.  *I did not fly to Greece last week.*

5) After subordinating conjunctions (p.114), the negative word comes before the verb.

   Ich gehe nie ins Kino, weil ich Filme nicht mag.  *I never go to the cinema because I don't like films.*

## Use 'nicht' in different places for emphasis

**Higher**

1) You can change where the 'nicht' goes to emphasise different parts of the sentence.

   Er schwimmt nicht am Sonntag im Meer.  *He doesn't swim in the sea on Sunday.*  — But he might swim on another day.

   Er schwimmt am Sonntag nicht im Meer.  *He doesn't swim in the sea on Sunday.*  — But he might swim somewhere else.

   Nicht er schwimmt am Sonntag im Meer.  *He doesn't swim in the sea on Sunday.*  — But someone else might swim in the sea on Sunday.

2) Use 'sondern' after saying what you don't do to say what is happening instead.

   Sie ist nicht böse, sondern geduldig.  *She is not angry, but (rather) patient.*

Do you want to go in, then?

### Grammar Questions

Translate these sentences and phrases into **German**.
1. She doesn't fly.
2. He isn't sporty.
3. She gives him nothing.
4. If I don't cook today...
5. I will never eat meat.
6. They don't travel by train, but by bus. [H]

## Only dwell on the negatives when you're doing it in German...

Go through all of the rules on this page and have a go at writing an appropriate sentence for each one.

# Giving Orders

I'm not bossy, I just like telling people what to do. With German imperatives, you can too.

## Use the imperative to give orders

1) <u>Imperatives</u> are used to give instructions. They tell people what to do, e.g. '<u>sit still</u>'.

2) To form the <u>imperative</u>, use the <u>present tense</u> of the verb for 'du', 'ihr' or 'Sie'. The <u>only</u> form that ends differently from the <u>normal present tense</u> is the '<u>du</u>' form. It loses its ending (the '-st').

3) Here's how to turn a verb into an imperative — p.10 has more on which form of 'you' to use.

**Example** — telling people to go

| Verb | Imperative | English |
|---|---|---|
| du gehst | Geh! | Go! (inf. sing.) |
| ihr geht | Geht! | Go! (inf. plu.) |
| Sie gehen | Gehen Sie! | Go! (frml. sing. & plu.) |

Esst mehr!
*Eat more! (inf. plu.)* — The pronouns 'du' and 'ihr' aren't used at all.

Bleiben Sie hier!
*Stay here! (frml. sing. & plu.)* — 'Sie' imperatives use the pronoun — it goes after the verb.

4) Lots of verbs have an optional '<u>e</u>' on the '<u>du</u>' form of the imperative, like 'fragen' *(to ask)*: Frag(e)! *(Ask!)*.

## There are some irregular imperatives

1) Some imperatives <u>don't follow the rules</u> in the '<u>du</u>' form, e.g. '<u>lesen</u>' only loses the 't' from 'du liest'.

Lies die Zeitung!     *Read the newspaper! (inf. sing.)*

2) '<u>Haben</u>' and '<u>werden</u>' also have a different stem in the 'du' form.

| Verb | Imperative | English |
|---|---|---|
| du hast | Hab! | Have! (inf. sing.) |

| Verb | Imperative | English |
|---|---|---|
| du wirst | Werde! | Become! (inf. sing.) |

3) The stem of '<u>sein</u>' is '<u>sei</u>' in <u>all the imperative forms</u>.

| Verb | Imperative | English |
|---|---|---|
| du bist | Sei! | Be! (inf. sing.) |
| ihr seid | Seid! | Be! (inf. plu.) |
| Sie sind | Seien Sie! | Be! (frml. sing. & plu.) |

Seid leise!     *Be quiet! (inf. plu.)*

Sei geduldig!     *Be patient! (inf. sing.)*

## Imperatives can be used with negatives and reflexive verbs

1) To form <u>negative imperatives</u>, use '<u>nicht</u>'.

Weint nicht!     *Don't cry! (inf. plu.)*

2) <u>Reflexive pronouns</u> go <u>straight after</u> the <u>verb</u>. They go <u>after</u> the <u>pronoun</u> if you use '<u>Sie</u>'.

Zieh dich an!     *Get yourself dressed! (inf. sing.)*

### Grammar Questions

Translate these sentences into **German**. The bit in brackets tells you who you're talking to.

1. Dance! (inf. sing.)
2. Be friendly! (inf. plu.)
3. Sit down! (inf. plu.)
4. Follow me! (frml. plu.)
5. Don't leave us! (inf. sing.)
6. Don't be sad! (frml. sing.)

---

### Brush off the *dust* to give orders using 'du'...

Remember, to get the 'du' imperative, you can drop the 'du' and '-st' ending from the present tense verb.

Section Fifteen — Verbs and Tenses

# Separable Verbs

Oh great, some more weird things that German verbs do — why am I not surprised.

## Separable verbs sometimes  split up...

1) <u>Separable verbs</u> are made up of two bits: the <u>main verb</u> and a <u>bit on the front</u> that can be taken off.

   ausgehen (*to go out*) = aus + gehen

2) In the <u>present tense</u>, change the verb for the <u>right person</u> and send the '<u>aus</u>' bit to the <u>end of the clause</u>.

   Ich gehe gern aus.   *I like going out.*

3) Here are some examples of <u>separable verbs</u>. The bits that can be taken off are underlined.

   | <u>an</u>kommen | *to arrive* | <u>an</u>ziehen | *to attract* | <u>mit</u>nehmen | *to take along* |
   |---|---|---|---|---|---|
   | <u>aus</u>sehen | *to appear* | <u>auf</u>stehen | *to get up* | <u>zurück</u>kommen | *to return* |

**Higher**

4) In the <u>simple past</u> (see p.134-135), send the <u>front bit</u> to the <u>end</u> and put the <u>main verb</u> in the <u>simple past</u>.

   ankommen (*to arrive*) = an + kommen → kam ... an (*arrived*) → Ich kam spät an. *I arrived late.*

5) You might want to use separable verbs as <u>imperatives</u>, but you'll need to <u>split them up</u> first.

   Ruf mich an, Bernhard!   *Call me, Bernhard!*   Passen Sie auf, bitte!   *Pay attention, please!*

## ...but other times they stay together

1) To use a separable verb in the <u>perfect tense</u> (see p.133), keep the <u>front bit</u> the same, but put the <u>main verb</u> in the <u>perfect tense</u>.

   aufhören (*to stop*) = auf + hören → aufgehört (*stopped*) → Er hat endlich aufgehört. *He has finally stopped.*

   *The main verb decides whether you use 'haben' or 'sein'.*

2) When you use separable verbs in the <u>future tense</u> with '<u>werden</u>' (see p.136) or with <u>modal verbs</u> (p.140), you use them in their <u>infinitive</u> form.

   Sie wird zurückkommen.   *She will return.*   Ich will ausgehen.   *I want to go out.*

3) In <u>subordinate clauses</u> (see p.114), the main verb and the front bit stick together.

   Ich bin nie früh, da ich spät aufstehe.   *I'm never early because I get up late.*   ← The separable verb has to agree with the subject.

### Grammar Questions

Translate these sentences and phrases into **German** using separable verbs.

1. She goes out.
2. I arrive today.
3. He has called his brother.
4. You (inf. sing.) have got up.
5. I will come back.
6. If we watch television...
7. He took part. **H**
8. Stop it, Eric! **H**

## This relationship isn't prefixable — we should break up...

It looks like there's a lot to remember about separable verbs, but it basically comes back to this one rule — whenever the separable verb is sent to the end of a sentence or a clause, the two pieces stick together.

Quick Quiz

# Modal Verbs

Modal verbs let you express opinions, certainty and ability. Well, they must be useful.

## Learn these modal verbs in the present tense

1) Here are <u>six really handy</u> modal verbs:

| **wollen** — to want | |
|---|---|
| ich will | wir wollen |
| du willst | ihr wollt |
| er will | Sie wollen |
| sie will | sie wollen |
| es will | |

| **mögen** — to like | |
|---|---|
| ich mag | wir mögen |
| du magst | ihr mögt |
| er mag | Sie mögen |
| sie mag | sie mögen |
| es mag | |

For 'I would like', use 'ich möchte' — see p.141.

| **dürfen** — may | |
|---|---|
| ich darf | wir dürfen |
| du darfst | ihr dürft |
| er darf | Sie dürfen |
| sie darf | sie dürfen |
| es darf | |

| **können** — can, to be able to | |
|---|---|
| ich kann | wir können |
| du kannst | ihr könnt |
| er kann | Sie können |
| sie kann | sie können |
| es kann | |

| **sollen** — to be supposed to | |
|---|---|
| ich soll | wir sollen |
| du sollst | ihr sollt |
| er soll | Sie sollen |
| sie soll | sie sollen |
| es soll | |

| **müssen** — must, to have to | |
|---|---|
| ich muss | wir müssen |
| du musst | ihr müsst |
| er muss | Sie müssen |
| sie muss | sie müssen |
| es muss | |

2) This is how you use them:

**Ich muss** (Use the right form of the modal verb.) **+** **einen Brief** (Add extra info in here.) **+** **schreiben** (Use the infinitive of the other verb at the end.) **=** **Ich muss einen Brief schreiben.** *I must write a letter.*

## You can use modal verbs in the past tense too

1) To say something like 'I wanted to wash the car', you have to use the <u>past tense</u> of the <u>modal verb</u>.

2) For the simple past, <u>take off</u> the '<u>-en</u>' and the <u>umlaut</u> if there is one, and then <u>add the endings</u> in bold.

| **können** — can | |
|---|---|
| ich konn**te** | wir konn**ten** |
| du konn**test** | ihr konn**tet** |
| er / sie / es konn**te** | Sie / sie konn**ten** |

[Higher] wir konnten, ihr konntet, Sie / sie konnten

Follow the same pattern for 'wollen', 'dürfen', 'sollen' and 'müssen' too.

**WATCH OUT**
'Mögen' is a bit different. It changes to 'mochten' in the past tense. It takes the same endings as all the others though.

Er konnte seine Tasche nicht finden.
*He couldn't find his bag.*

Ich mochte in der Band spielen.
*I liked playing in the band.*

### Grammar Questions

Write these sentences in **German**.
1. You (inf. sing.) may stay.
2. We like to play tennis.
3. Jane can sing.
4. He was supposed to go.
5. She had to play.
6. I wanted a new bicycle.

## What do you *mean* I used my modal verbs joke in Section Three?

I'll have to think of another one to go here. Er... leave it with me — where there's a will, there's a wollen...

# Conditional Forms

Quick Quiz

I would now like to introduce you to the conditional in German — you should read this page well.

## Ich möchte Deutsch sprechen — *I would like to speak German*

1) '<u>Ich möchte</u>' means '<u>I would like</u>'. It's the conditional form of '<u>mögen</u>' and really handy for asking for things.

*See p.10-11 for more on how to ask for things politely.*

**Ich möchte** — I would like

| ich möchte | wir möchten |
| du möchtest | ihr möchtet |
| er / sie / es möchte | Sie / sie möchten |

Was möchten Sie?
*What would you like?*

Ich möchte Eis, bitte.
*I would like ice, please.*

2) If you're adding <u>another verb</u> to say what you'd like to do, that verb has to go to the <u>end</u>.

Ich möchte
Use the right form of 'möchten'. **+** Französisch
Add extra info in here. **+** lernen
Use the infinitive of the other verb at the end. **=** Ich möchte Französisch lernen.
*I would like to learn French.*
This is in the conditional.

Ich möchte bitte das Hemd kaufen.
*I would like to buy the shirt, please.*

Wir möchten bitte in die Stadtmitte fahren.
*We would like to go into the city centre, please.*

## Ich würde — *I would*

1) You can say '<u>I would</u>...' in German by using the conditional form of '<u>werden</u>' and an <u>infinitive</u> at the end.
2) Make sure you learn the different conditional forms of '<u>werden</u>':

**Ich würde...** — I would

| ich würde | wir würden |
| du würdest | ihr würdet |
| er / sie / es würde | Sie / sie würden |

Was würdest du ihm sagen?
*What would you say to him?*

Wir würden nichts tun.
*We would do nothing.*

## Ich sollte — *I should*

You need to know how to use '<u>sollten</u>' (*should*) too.

Gerhard really should learn to drive.

**Ich sollte** — I should

| ich sollte | wir sollten |
| du solltest | ihr solltet |
| er / sie / es sollte | Sie / sie sollten |

Ich sollte mehr Gemüse essen.    *I should eat more vegetables.*

Wir sollten das Haus verlassen.    *We should leave the house.*

### Grammar Questions

Translate these sentences into **German** using the conditional.
1. We would like cheese.
2. Shreya would like to sing.
3. They would not visit me.
4. I would drink a lot.
5. You (inf. sing.) should wait.
6. We should ask our teacher.

## Using conditionals won't make your hair shinier and softer...

...but it will impress the examiner. Have a go now — grab a friend, imagine you're on holiday in a German-speaking country and practise ordering something in a restaurant with them using 'ich möchte'.

# The Subjunctive

Woohoo — here's the last page of grammar to learn. It's tricky stuff, though, so hold onto your celebratory jig for a bit longer. The subjunctive is super impressive so it's well worth learning it.

## Use the subjunctive for things that aren't true now

1) The subjunctive in German is used to talk about things that could be true, but aren't.
2) Subjunctive phrases in English are things like 'if I were you'. 'Were' is in the subjunctive because it's talking about something that isn't true.
3) The subjunctive is often introduced by 'wenn' (if):

Wenn ich im Urlaub wäre... *If I were on holiday...*

'Wenn' sends the verb to the end of the clause.

In Tina's mind, she was always on the Costa del Sol.

## Learn the different forms of 'wäre' and 'hätte'

You need to know the forms of 'ich wäre' *(I would be / I were)* and 'ich hätte' *(I would have / I had)*.

**Ich wäre** — I would be / I were

| | |
|---|---|
| ich wäre | wir wären |
| du wärst | ihr wärt |
| er / sie / es wäre | Sie / sie wären |

Du wärst ein guter Lehrer.
*You would be a good teacher.*

**Ich hätte** — I would have / I had

| | |
|---|---|
| ich hätte | wir hätten |
| du hättest | ihr hättet |
| er / sie / es hätte | Sie / sie hätten |

Er hätte das beste Auto.
*He would have the best car.*

## Use the subjunctive to extend your sentences

1) In English, you can use 'if' to talk about a possible situation. In German, you can use 'wenn' plus the subjunctive — this is called a conditional clause.

Wenn ich fünf Millionen Euro hätte, wäre ich reich.
*If I had five million euros, I would be rich.*

'Hätte' refers to something that might happen, but isn't happening now — it's in the subjunctive.

2) You can also follow a conditional clause with 'würde' *(would)* and an infinitive.

Wenn ich älter wäre, würde ich im Ausland wohnen. *If I were older, I would live abroad.*

### Grammar Questions

Translate the following phrases and sentences into **German**.

1. If we were hungry...
2. I would have a dog.
3. They would be very sad.
4. If you (inf. sing.) were an actor...
5. If he had a car, it would be red.
6. If I had the time, I'd paint more.

## I came down with subjunctivitis — I had to take an antiwärel...

To make sure the subjunctive really sinks in, practise using it by writing a few sentences in German about what you would do if you didn't have any more exams. After that, treat yourself to something nice.

# Verbs and Tenses — Grammar List

## Regular Verbs

Regular verbs end in '-en' — they follow the pattern of 'spielen'.

### spielen (to play)

**Present**
ich spiel**e**
du spiel**st**
er / sie / es spiel**t**
wir spiel**en**
ihr spiel**t**
Sie / sie spiel**en**

**Past Participle**
(haben) **ge**spiel**t**

**Imperative** (Higher)
Spiel! (du)
Spiel**t**! (ihr)
Spiel**en** Sie!

**Simple Past** (Higher)
ich spiel**te**
du spiel**test**
er / sie / es spiel**te**
wir spiel**ten**
ihr spiel**tet**
Sie / sie spiel**ten**

*See p.130 for how to form verbs ending in '-ln' or '-rn'.*

*You also need to know how to use negative words in sentences — see p.137 for more.*

## Important Irregular Verbs

### sein (to be)

**Present**
ich bin
du bist
er / sie / es ist
wir sind
ihr seid
Sie / sie sind

**Past Participle**
(sein) gewesen

**Imperative** (Higher)
Sei! (du)
Seid! (ihr)
Seien Sie!

**Simple Past**
ich war
du warst
er / sie / es war
wir waren
ihr wart
Sie / sie waren

**Subjunctive** (Higher)
ich wäre
du wärst
er / sie / es wäre
wir wären
ihr wärt
Sie / sie wären

### haben (to have)

**Present**
ich habe
du hast
er / sie / es hat
wir haben
ihr habt
Sie / sie haben

**Past Participle**
(haben) gehabt

**Simple Past**
ich hatte
du hattest
er / sie / es hatte
wir hatten
ihr hattet
Sie / sie hatten

**Subjunctive** (Higher)
ich hätte
du hättest
er / sie / es hätte
wir hätten
ihr hättet
Sie / sie hätten

### wissen (to know)

**Present**
ich weiß
du weißt
er / sie / es weiß
wir wissen
ihr wisst
Sie / sie wissen

**Past Participle** (H)
(haben) gewusst

**Simple Past** (Higher)
ich wusste
du wusstest
er / sie / es wusste
wir wussten
ihr wusstet
Sie / sie wussten

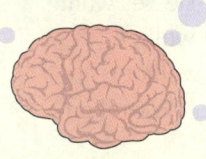

## Vowel Changes in the Present Tense

Some verbs are irregular in the 'du' and 'er' / 'sie' / 'es' forms.

**'e' → 'i'** e.g. 'essen' *(to eat)*

du isst
er / sie / es isst

Other verbs include 'helfen' *(to help)*, 'sprechen' *(to speak)* and 'geben' *(to give)*.

**'a' → 'ä'** e.g. 'fahren' *(to go, drive)*

du fährst
er / sie / es fährt

Other verbs include 'lassen' *(to let, allow)*, 'fallen' *(to fall)* and 'laufen' *(to run)*.

**'e' → 'ie'** e.g. 'sehen' *(to see)*

du siehst
er / sie / es sieht

Other verbs include 'lesen' *(to read)* and geschehen (H) *(to happen)*.

## The Future

The verb 'werden' means 'to become'. You can also use it in the present tense with an infinitive to form the future tense.

### werden (to become, will)

**Present**
ich werde
du wirst
er / sie / es wird
wir werden
ihr werdet
Sie / sie werden

**Conditional** (Higher)
ich würde
du würdest
er / sie / es würde
wir würden
ihr würdet
Sie / sie würden

**Past participle**
(sein) geworden

*You can use 'werden' in the conditional with an infinitive to say what you 'would do'.*

# Verbs and Tenses — Grammar List

## Modal Verbs

### mögen (to like)

**Present**
ich mag
du magst
er / sie / es mag
wir mögen
ihr mögt
Sie / sie mögen

**Simple Past**
ich mochte
du mochtest
er / sie / es mochte
wir mochten
ihr mochtet (H)
Sie / sie mochten

**Conditional**
ich möchte
du möchtest
er / sie / es möchte
wir möchten
ihr möchtet
Sie / sie möchten

**Past Participle** (H)
(haben) gemocht

### müssen (must, to have to)

**Present**
ich muss
du musst
er / sie / es muss
wir müssen
ihr müsst
Sie / sie müssen

**Simple Past**
ich musste
du musstest
er / sie / es musste
wir mussten
ihr musstet (H)
Sie / sie mussten

*The conditional form of 'sollen' is the same as the simple past.*

### sollen (to be supposed to, ought to, should)

**Present**
ich soll
du sollst
er / sie / es soll
wir sollen
ihr sollt
Sie / sie sollen

**Simple Past**
ich sollte
du solltest
er / sie / es sollte
wir sollten
ihr solltet (H)
Sie / sie sollten

**Conditional** (Higher)
ich sollte
du solltest
er / sie / es sollte
wir sollten
ihr solltet
Sie / sie sollten

### können (can, to be able to)

**Present**
ich kann
du kannst
er / sie / es kann
wir können
ihr könnt
Sie / sie können

**Simple Past**
ich konnte
du konntest
er / sie / es konnte
wir konnten
ihr konntet (H)
Sie / sie konnten

### wollen (to want)

**Present**
ich will
du willst
er / sie / es will
wir wollen
ihr wollt
Sie / sie wollen

**Simple Past**
ich wollte
du wolltest
er / sie / es wollte
wir wollten
ihr wolltet (H)
Sie / sie wollten

### dürfen (may, to be allowed to)

**Present**
ich darf
du darfst
er / sie / es darf
wir dürfen
ihr dürft
Sie / sie dürfen

**Simple Past**
ich durfte
du durftest
er / sie / es durfte
wir durften
ihr durftet (H)
Sie / sie durften

*Chris found out the hard way that he shouldn't fall asleep around Emily.*

## Separable Verbs

Separable verbs have a front bit that sometimes comes apart from the main verb, like in 'aussehen'.

### aussehen (to appear)

**Present**
ich sehe aus
du siehst aus
er / sie / es sieht aus
wir sehen aus
ihr seht aus
Sie / sie sehen aus

**Past Participle**
(haben) ausgesehen

**Imperative** (Higher)
Sieh aus! (du)
Seht aus! (ihr)
Sehen Sie aus!

**Simple Past** (Higher)
ich sah aus
du sahst aus
er / sie / es sah aus
wir sahen aus
ihr saht aus
Sie / sie sahen aus

### Separable Prefixes

| Prefix | Example | |
|---|---|---|
| ab | abnehmen | *to reduce* |
| zu | zunehmen | *to increase* |
| aus | ausgehen | *to go out* |
| ein | einladen | *to invite* |
| an | anfangen | *to start* |
| teil | teilnehmen | *to take part* |
| auf | aufstehen | *to get up* |
| zurück | zurückkommen | *to come back* |
| mit | mitnehmen | *to take along* |
| vor | vorbereiten | *to prepare* |
| fern | fernsehen | *to watch television* |

Section Fifteen — Verbs and Tenses

## Past Participles

Regular verbs follow the same pattern as 'spielen', but some verbs form past participles differently.

### 'i' → 'u'

| Infinitive | Past Participle | |
|---|---|---|
| springen | (sein) gesprungen | jumped |
| finden | (haben) gefunden | found |
| trinken | (haben) getrunken | drunk |
| singen | (haben) gesungen | sung |
| zwingen | (haben) gezwungen | forced |
| klingen | (haben) geklungen | sounded |
| verbinden | (haben) verbunden | connected |
| gelingen | (sein) gelungen | succeeded |

*Higher:* zwingen, klingen, verbinden, gelingen

### 'e' → 'o'

| Infinitive | Past Participle | |
|---|---|---|
| empfehlen | (haben) empfohlen | recommended |
| sprechen | (haben) gesprochen | spoken |
| treffen | (haben) getroffen | met |
| helfen | (haben) geholfen | helped |
| werfen | (haben) geworfen | thrown |
| stehlen | (haben) gestohlen | stolen |
| gelten | (haben) gegolten | applied |

*H:* stehlen, gelten

### 'ie' → 'o'

| Infinitive | Past Participle | |
|---|---|---|
| genießen | (haben) genossen | enjoyed |
| bieten | (haben) geboten | offered |
| fliegen | (sein) geflogen | flown |
| schießen | (haben) geschossen | shot |

*H:* schießen

Most past participles use 'haben', but some use 'sein'. 'Sein' verbs are usually the ones which involve movement.

### 'ei' → 'ie'

| Infinitive | Past Participle | |
|---|---|---|
| schreiben | (haben) geschrieben | written |
| beschreiben | (haben) beschrieben | described |
| scheinen | (haben) geschienen | seemed |
| treiben | (haben) getrieben | pursued |
| entscheiden | (haben) entschieden | decided |
| bleiben | (sein) geblieben | stayed |
| steigen | (sein) gestiegen | increased |

See p.133 for more on how past participles are formed.

## Other Irregular Past Participles

| Infinitive | Past Participle | |
|---|---|---|
| gehen | (sein) gegangen | gone |
| bringen | (haben) gebracht | brought |
| gewinnen | (haben) gewonnen | won |
| beginnen | (haben) begonnen | begun |
| schwimmen | (sein) geschwommen | swum |
| essen | (haben) gegessen | eaten |
| nehmen | (haben) genommen | taken |
| stehen | (haben) gestanden | stood |
| öffnen | (haben) geöffnet | opened |
| schließen | (haben) geschlossen | closed |

| Infinitive | Past Participle | |
|---|---|---|
| verlieren | (haben) verloren | lost |
| brechen | (haben) gebrochen | broken |
| sterben | (sein) gestorben | died |
| denken | (haben) gedacht | thought |
| kennen | (haben) gekannt | known |
| tun | (haben) getan | done |
| ziehen | (haben) gezogen | pulled, moved |
| nennen | (haben) genannt | named |
| sitzen | (haben) gesessen | sat down |

*Higher:* denken, kennen, tun, ziehen, nennen, sitzen

## Saying 'used to'

You can use the past tense with 'früher' to talk about what you 'used to do' on a regular basis.

früher — *previously, in the past, in former times*

E.g. Früher bist du viel geschwommen.
*You used to swim a lot.*

This could be you after your GCSE exams — just 563,856 more verb conjugations to go.

Find the CGP RevisionHub at cgpbooks.co.uk/Berlin

Section Fifteen — Verbs and Tenses

# Verbs and Tenses — Grammar List

## The Simple Past

Regular verbs form the simple past like 'spielen', but some verbs don't follow the same pattern.

| Infinitive | Simple Past Stem | |
|---|---|---|
| gehen | ging | went |
| bleiben | blieb | stayed |
| entscheiden | entschied | decided |
| schreiben | schrieb | wrote |
| finden | fand | found |
| beginnen | begann | began |
| gewinnen | gewann | won |
| fallen | fiel | fell, decreased |
| schlafen | schlief | slept |
| lassen | ließ | allowed, let |
| laufen | lief | ran, walked |
| geben | gab | gave |
| helfen | half | helped |
| sehen | sah | saw, watched |
| lesen | las | read |
| sprechen | sprach | spoke, talked |
| sterben | starb | died |
| essen | aß | ate |
| sitzen | saß | sat |
| liegen | lag | lay, was situated |
| nehmen | nahm | took |
| kommen | kam | came |
| fahren | fuhr | went, drove |
| ziehen | zog | pulled, moved |
| bringen | brachte | brought |
| denken | dachte | thought |

The stem is used for the 'ich' and 'er / sie / es' forms. For all other pronouns you use the correct present tense ending.

## Useful Verb Constructions

### Impersonal Verbs

| | |
|---|---|
| es regnet | it's raining |
| es gibt | there is / are |
| es gab | there was / were / used to be |
| es gefällt mir | I like it |
| es geht mir gut | I am well |
| es tut mir leid | I'm sorry |

### Using 'seit'

When talking about how long you've been doing something for, you use the present tense + 'seit'.

seit + time period + present tense — to have been + -ing + for + time period

E.g. Ich gehe seit zwei Jahren ins Fitness-Studio.
*I've been going to the gym for two years.*

### Using 'man'

The pronoun 'man' + a verb can be used instead of the passive.

man — one, you, people in general

E.g. Man sammelt den Müll.
*The rubbish is collected.*

### Infinitive Constructions

Use these constructions with an infinitive to introduce extra information to your sentence.

| | |
|---|---|
| zu ... | to ... |
| um ... zu | in order to ... |
| ohne ... zu | without ... |
| statt ... zu | instead of ... |

## Reflexive Verbs

Reflexive verbs let you talk about something you do to yourself — they need a reflexive pronoun (p.111).

### Accusative Reflexive Verbs

| | |
|---|---|
| sich freuen | to be happy, pleased |
| sich fühlen | to feel |
| sich bewegen | to exercise |
| sich entschuldigen | to apologise |
| sich anziehen | to get dressed |
| sich treffen | to get together, meet up |
| sich setzen | to sit down |
| sich entspannen | to relax, chill out |

The verb changes in the same way as verbs without reflexive pronouns.

### Dative Reflexive Verbs

| | |
|---|---|
| sich denken | to imagine |
| sich merken | to remember |
| sich leisten | to afford |
| sich vorstellen | to imagine |
| sich ... lassen | to have ... done |

Section Fifteen — Verbs and Tenses

# Revision Summary Test for Section Fifteen

You made it — the last revision summary. I can't believe this is auf Wiedersehen... *Grabs tissues*
- These questions are **really tricky**, but they'll help you see **how well you know your stuff**.
- Tackle the **revision summary test** below, or scan the QR code to do it **online**.
  You can **keep track of your progress** online and see **which areas need more work**.
- There are **sample answers** here: www.cgpbooks.co.uk/BerlinExtras

## The Present Tense and Ways to Use Verbs

1) Give all the present tense forms of these verbs: a) sagen   b) haben   c) sein   d) wissen
2) Translate these verb phrases into German:
   a) it lasts   b) I recycle   c) he allows   d) they collect   e) we improve   f) you (inf. sing.) wait
3) Write a sentence in the present tense using these verbs: a) folgen   b) helfen   c) glauben
4) How would you say 'It's snowing and there is a lot of traffic.' in German?
5) Karin says: 'Seit elf Monaten wohne ich in Frankreich.' What did she say?
6) Using 'man' (*one*) and an active verb, how would you say 'The door is opened slowly.' in German?
7) Write three sentences using each of these constructions: a) um ... zu   b) ohne ... zu   c) statt ... zu

## The Perfect, Simple Past and Future Tenses

8) How would you say 'I have learned a new language.' in German?
9) Translate these phrases into German: a) I have gone   b) He has stayed   c) They have run
10) Give the past participles for these verbs, then say whether each one uses 'haben' or 'sein'.
    a) diskutieren   b) steigen   c) singen   d) fliegen   e) nehmen   f) beginnen   g) verstehen
11) List all the forms of 'haben' and 'sein' in the simple past, then write a sentence using each verb.
12) Write down all the present tense forms of 'werden', then write down three
    sentences in the future tense using a different form of 'werden' each time.
13) Give the correct simple past tense form for each verb below. The subject is given in brackets.
    a) kochen (ihr)   b) kommen (wir)   c) fragen (du)   d) gehen (ich)   e) helfen (er)

## Negative Forms, Imperatives and Separable Verbs

14) How would you say 'There was a nice bag in the shop, but I did not buy it this time.' in German?
15) Write three sentences in German, each using one of these words: a) nie   b) nichts   c) nicht
16) Translate the following sentence into German: 'I prepare dinner for my family.'
    Now rewrite it in the perfect tense and then again in the future tense.
17) 'Although I'm not going out, I put my jacket on.' How would you say this in German?
18) Give the imperative forms of these verbs, using the pronoun in brackets.
    a) sein (Sie)   b) lachen (ihr)   c) essen (du)   d) einschlafen (du)   e) sich entschuldigen (ihr)

## Modal Verbs, the Conditional and the Subjunctive

19) List all the modal verbs in this section. There are 6 you need to know.
20) Translate these sentences into German:
    a) She had to do the homework.   b) He wasn't supposed to disappear.   c) I was allowed to play.
21) Joe tells you: 'Ich möchte nach Spanien fahren.' What did he say in English?
22) Translate these sentences into German: a) How would you (inf. sing.) solve the problem?
    b) They should go shopping.   c) I would say something.   d) What would you (inf. plu.) eat?
23) Explain when you would use the subjunctive in German.
24) List all the forms of 'wäre' and 'hätte'. Write two sentences, one with 'wäre' and one with 'hätte'.
25) 'Wenn ich das Geld hätte, würde ich um die Welt reisen.' Translate this into English.

Find the CGP RevisionHub at cgpbooks.co.uk/Berlin

Section Fifteen — Verbs and Tenses

# Pronunciation in German

## Spelling and Pronunciation

German pronunciation can be quite different from English — so here is a handy guide for you. Go ahead and scan the QR code to hear the sounds and words in the tables spoken aloud.

*Listening Track 17*

### There are lots of vowel sounds in German

The table below shows the different ways that common vowel sounds are spelt in German.

*Listen to the audio and practise pronouncing each sound out loud as you hear it.*

| Spelling | Example 1 | Example 2 |
|---|---|---|
| a, ah, aa | Haar | Abend |
| a | Katze | lassen |
| e, eh, ee | leben | mehr |
| e | essen | nett |
| i, ih | Linie | ihr |
| i | Mitte | finden |
| o, oh | also | wohnen |
| o | von | sonnig |
| u, uh | Buch | Uhr |
| u | um | Grund |
| ei, ai | drei | Mai |
| ie | viel | schwierig |
| au | genau | Baum |
| eu | deutsch | heute |
| er | erste | Herbst |

Lots of vowels have two ways of pronouncing them — one sounds long and the other sounds short.

The short form of a vowel is often followed by two consonants.

The '-y' at the end of words borrowed from English, like 'Party', sounds the same as 'ie' in German.

In German, you'll often come across two dots above the vowels 'a', 'o' and 'u' — this mark is called an umlaut and it changes how these vowels are pronounced.

| Spelling | Example 1 | Example 2 |
|---|---|---|
| ä, äh | spät | Hähnchen |
| ä | verändern | Sänger |
| ö, öh | hören | Höhe |
| ö | zwölf | öffnen |
| ü, üh | Gemüse | fühlen |
| ü | Müll | glücklich |
| äu | Verkäufer | träumen |

*Dom does a great impression of the letter 'ö'.*

Vowels with umlauts also have long and short forms.

The letter 'y' in German often has the same sound as 'ü', e.g. 'typisch' and 'Physik'.

The 'äu' sound is the same as the 'eu' sound.

## Learn how to pronounce these German consonants

Here are some of the main ways of spelling common consonants and letter combinations in German:

| Spelling | Example 1 | Example 2 |
|---|---|---|
| z | Zeit | kurz |
| w | deswegen | Woche |
| v | vor | Vater |
| ch | jedoch | brauchen |
| ch | lächeln | ich |
| sch | Schule | frisch |
| sp- | Spiel | sprechen |
| st- | stehen | streng |
| s-/-s- | singen | Reise |
| ß/ss/-s | Fuß | besser |
| r | rot | Beruf |
| r | sportlich | Ohr |
| th | Thema | Mathe |
| j | Jahr | jetzt |
| qu | Quelle | bequem |

The hard 'ch' sound comes after 'a', 'o', 'u' and 'au'.

The soft 'ch' sound comes after 'e', 'i', 'ei/ai', 'eu' and all vowels with an umlaut.

'r' sounds more like a consonant when it's at the beginning of a syllable or before a vowel.

'r' sounds more like a vowel when it's not at the beginning of a syllable and comes after a vowel.

Some letters and letter combinations change their sound when they come at the end of a word.

| Spelling | Example 1 | Example 2 |
|---|---|---|
| -er | sicher | unter |
| -b | gelb | Urlaub |
| -d | Strand | und |
| -g | Tag | Zug |
| -ig | lustig | wichtig |
| -tion | Aktion | Information |

'-er' has an 'uh' sound, like the '-er' in 'mother'.

'-ig' sounds the same as '-ich'.

'-b' has a 'p' sound.

'-d' has a 't' sound.

'-g' has a 'k' sound.

## Äu! Jü! Jeß jü! Tesst aud johr Tschömann ßaunds...

There are lots of ways to get yourself used to hearing German sounds — boogying along to German songs, watching German films, listening to German podcasts... It's all in the name of revision, so get creative with it.

*Find the CGP RevisionHub at cgpbooks.co.uk/Berlin*

**Pronunciation in German**

# Exam Advice

## The Listening and Speaking Exams

There are four separate exams for AQA GCSE German and each one is worth 25% of your final mark. But never mind the maths — these pages are crammed full of advice to help you tackle the exams head on.

### The listening exam has two sections

1) For the listening paper, you'll listen to various recordings of people speaking in German.

2) The paper is 45 minutes long for Higher-tier students and 35 minutes long for Foundation-tier students. It's split into Section A and Section B.

*DISCLAIMER*
You probably won't be this happy during your listening exam.

> Section A is the longer section — it's worth 40 marks at Higher tier and 32 marks at Foundation tier. It contains comprehension questions in English, and you'll write your answers in English.

> Section B is a shorter dictation section — it's worth 10 marks at Higher tier and 8 marks at Foundation tier. You'll hear some short sentences and write them down in German.

3) Read the paper thoroughly before the recording begins — the questions will give you a good idea of the topics you'll be asked about. This should help you predict what to listen out for.

4) Make notes while listening to the recordings, and listen to the end, even if you think you have the answer.

5) Don't worry if you can't understand every word — just listen carefully and try to pick out the key vocab.

### The speaking exam has three parts

1) Your speaking exam will be conducted and recorded by your teacher.

2) The exam is in three parts. Before you start, you'll get 15 minutes of preparation time. The time allowed for the exam is 10-12 minutes at Higher tier and 7-9 minutes at Foundation tier.

*During your preparation time, you can make notes to use at any point during the exam.*

> **① Role-play**
> You'll get a card with a scenario on it. It'll have five tasks — four will be notes on what you should talk about. The '?' shows you have to ask a question.

> **② Reading aloud task**
> You'll get a card with several sentences in German. You'll read them aloud, then your teacher will ask you four questions related to the topic of the sentences.

> **③ Photo card discussion**
> You'll receive a card with two photos on it. Your teacher will ask you to talk about them and then ask you questions related to the same theme.

### Try to be imaginative with your answers

You need to find ways to show off the full extent of your German knowledge. You should try to:

1) Use a range of tenses — e.g. for a question on daily routine, think of when something different happens.

> Aber morgen werde ich Fußball spielen.   *But tomorrow I will play football.*

2) Talk about other people, as well as yourself — it's fine to make people up if it helps.

> Ich mag Sport, aber meine Oma hasst ihn.   *I like sport, but my grandma hates it.*

*You can use non-binary or gender-neutral pronouns in the exams — just make sure you're consistent and your adjectives agree.*

3) Give loads of opinions and reasons for your opinions.

> Meiner Meinung nach soll man mehr recyceln.   *In my opinion, people should recycle more.*

---

### Silence please! I'm taking my sneaking exam...

Don't panic if you make a mistake in the speaking exam — what's important is how you deal with it. You won't lose marks for correcting yourself, so show the examiner that you know where you went wrong.

# The Reading and Writing Exams

The writing exam is a great way of showing off what you can do — try to use varied vocabulary, include a range of tenses, and pack in any clever expressions that you've learnt over the years. First up, though...

## The reading exam has two sections

1) The Higher-tier reading paper is 1 hour long, and the Foundation-tier paper is 45 minutes. Both are worth 50 marks and have two sections.

2) In Section A, you'll be given a variety of German texts and then asked questions about them. The questions and answers will be in English.

   - Scan through each text first to get an idea of what it's about. Then read the questions that go with it carefully, making sure you understand what information you should be looking out for.
   - Next, go back through the text, focusing on finding the information you need. If you're having trouble with a particular question, you might want to move on and come back to it later.

3) Section B will ask you to translate several short German sentences (between 35-50 words in total) into English. The sentences will be on topics you've studied, so the vocabulary should be familiar. Here are some top tips for doing your translations:

   - Translate a whole sentence at a time, rather than word by word — this will avoid any of the German word order being carried into the English.
   - Keep an eye out for different tenses — there will be a variety.
   - Read through your translations to make sure they sound natural.

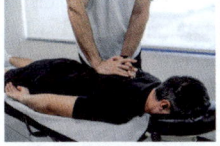

Marvin knew how to deal with one kind of tense.

## There are various types of questions in the writing exam

1) The Higher-tier writing paper is 1 hour and 15 minutes long and the Foundation-tier paper is 1 hour and 10 minutes long. Some tasks are only for one tier, but others appear in both — these are explained below.

2) Each task is worth a different number of marks, so you should spend more time on the higher-mark tasks. For longer answers, make a quick plan before you start and remember to leave time to check your work.

**Foundation**

**Photo Response Task (10 marks)**
You'll be asked to write five short sentences in German to describe a black and white photo.

**Grammar Task (5 marks)**
You'll need to complete five short sentences by choosing the correct option, using your grammar knowledge.

**50-word Writing Task (10 marks)**
You'll be asked to produce a short piece of writing in response to five bullet points. You'll be expected to write about 50 words in total.

**Translation Task (10 marks)**
You'll translate sentences from English into German. The sentences could be on any topic you've studied. See above for some top tips for translation tasks.

**90-word Writing Task (15 marks)**
You'll be asked to write about 90 words in response to three bullet points. You'll have a choice between two questions. Make sure you write about each bullet point.

**Higher**

**150-word Writing Task (25 marks)**
You'll need to write about 150 words in German, based on two bullet points. There will be two questions to choose from. This task is more creative — so don't forget to include some opinions with reasons.

## And lastly, don't forget your pen...

When you're nervous and stressed, it's easy to misread a question or skip question parts. For writing questions with bullet points, make sure you talk about each bullet in turn — tick them off as you go along.

Find the CGP RevisionHub at cgpbooks.co.uk/Berlin

# Answers

*The answers to the translation questions are sample answers only, just to give you an idea of one way to translate them. There may be different ways to translate these sentences that are also correct.*

*For dictation and translation questions, this symbol ( | ) shows where to divide the marks. There is 1 mark awarded for the first part of the text, and 1 mark awarded for the second.*

## Section One — General Stuff

### Page 5: Numbers and Time

1) a) fifteen   b) his sister's third birthday   c) twenty
2) a) B   b) B   c) A

### Page 7: Times and Dates

1) a) Saturday
   b) yesterday
   c) 12th September
   d) in the evening

### Page 9: Questions

2) a) Worüber bist | du glücklich?
   b) Womit kann ich | dir helfen?
   c) Wofür brauchst | du das?
   d) Wohinter versteckt | sie das Geschenk?
   e) Worauf | warten wir?

### Page 11: Being Polite

1) a) She forgot Eric's birthday.
   b) by paying for dinner
   c) a present
   d) He has an exam tomorrow.

### Page 13: Opinions

1) a) True   b) True   c) False   d) True

## Section Two — Identity and Relationships with Others

### Page 21: My Family and Friends

2) a) three
   b) to look after the cat
   c) chat
      play video games
   d) through mutual friends

### Page 23: Describing People

1) a) They are nice people.
   b) their hair colour
   c) She has short hair.
      She has a thin face.
   d) Because his brother is younger than him.

### Page 25: Relationships and Partnerships

2) a) five years ago
   b) They didn't get along anymore.
   c) more independent
   d) They are important to her. /
      She spends more time with them.
   e) to get married
      to have children

## Section Three — Healthy Living and Lifestyle

### Page 29: Food

1) a) C   b) B   c) A   d) B

### Page 31: Healthy and Unhealthy Living

2) a) She often ate fast food.
      She smoked a lot of cigarettes.
   b) She has started going to the gym regularly.
      She doesn't smoke any more.
   c) She feels healthier.
      She is happy with her progress.

### Page 33: Illnesses and Treatments

2) a) False   b) False   c) False   d) True

## Section Four — Education

### Page 39: School Life

1) a) N   b) P   c) P
2) a) A, C   b) B, C

### Page 41: School Pressures and Difficulties

2) a) Sie wird im Sommer | ihr Schulzeugnis bekommen.
   b) Ich arbeite hart, | um erfolgreich zu sein.
   c) Wir wissen nicht, | ob wir gute Noten erreichen werden.
   d) Ich bereite mich | auf meine Prüfungen vor.

## Section Five — Future Study and Work

### Page 47: Career Choices and Ambitions

2) a) To earn money for his year abroad.
   b) He had lots of tasks to do.
   c) He doesn't want a full-time job.
      He wants to work for himself.

## Section Six — Free-time Activities

### Page 51: Cinema and TV

2) a) They entertain her.
   b) the news
      sports programmes
   c) She leaves the living room.
   d) She sits for hours in front of the TV.

### Page 52: Music

1) a) Preethi — F
   b) Jürgen — A
   c) Frieda — E

### Page 53: Sport

1) a) I enjoy football | but tennis is better.
   b) The team wins | almost every match.
   c) Next year I will | take part in a contest.

### Page 55: Going Out and Other Hobbies

2) a) the newspaper
   b) She wants to be an artist.
   c) satisfied / happy / content
   d) The games can be really expensive.

## Section Seven — Customs, Festivals and Celebrations

### Page 59: Celebrations

1) a) B, C   b) A, B

### Page 61: Customs and Festivals

1) a) Ostern ist eine wichtige | Zeit für Christen.
   b) Jedes Jahr feiern Muslime | mit ihren Familien Eid.
   c) Religionen haben oft | interessante und historische Feste.
2) a) hanging the lights on the Christmas tree (with her family)
   b) on Three Kings' Day (Twelfth Night)
   c) on Christmas Eve
   d) She felt a connection with the others in the church.

## Section Eight — Celebrity Culture

### Page 65: Favourite Celebrities

1) a) She is an author.
   b) three times
   c) in a shop
   d) Because she writes very well.
   e) as famous as Niko

### Page 67: Celebrity Life

2) a) performing in front of an audience
   b) well-known, famous / her role model
   c) working long hours
      receiving criticism
   d) She is worthy despite the criticism.

## Section Nine — Travel and Tourism

### Page 71: Where to Go

1) a) Austria
      Switzerland
   b) three days
   c) sunny
      warm
   d) travel abroad (to Turkey)

### Page 73: Accommodation and Travel

1) a) Unser Zimmer | war sehr sauber.
   b) Wir haben in einer | günstigen Wohnung gewohnt.
   c) Sie sind mit dem Bus | nach Frankreich gefahren.
   d) Mein Bett war | bequem und warm.
   e) Ich bin im Hotel | angekommen.
2) a) very exhausting / tiring / strenuous
   b) She left her house very late.
   c) It was a lot more expensive than the old one.
   d) twelve hours
   e) colourful boats
      white houses

### Page 75: What to Do

2) a) relaxed
   b) bought cheap drinks / went swimming
   c) museums
      the capital city
   d) to go on a trip to a famous castle

## Section Ten — Media and Technology

### Page 79: Technology

1) a) False   b) True   c) True   d) False

### Page 81: The Internet

2) a) H   b) H   c) M   d) M + H

### Page 83: Social Media

2) a) in the evenings
   b) watch videos (that her friends have recorded)
   c) only people she knows personally
   d) They trust her.

## Section Eleven — Where People Live

### Page 87: The Home

2) a) She lost | the key.
   b) The house has | a red roof.
   c) She does not | own her apartment.
   d) In my household, | it is always quiet.
   e) It is pleasant | to sit in the garden.
   f) I fall asleep | at ten o'clock.

### Page 89: The Local Area

2) a) C   b) B   c) A

### Page 91: Directions and Weather

1) a) two degrees
   b) It will be colder.
      There might be a lot of snow.
   c) It will rain a lot. / It will be dark/gloomy.
   d) There will be strong wind.
2) a) south
   b) left
   c) next to the factory
   d) opposite

## Section Twelve — Environmental and Social Issues

### Page 95: Environmental Problems

1) a) A lot of rubbish | pollutes the countryside.
   b) Travelling by plane | is not environmentally friendly.
   c) The actions of some people | and companies destroy nature.

### Page 96: Environmental Impacts

1) a) water
      food
   b) People throw their litter on the beach.
   c) Nature is suffering everywhere.
   d) sea / water pollution

### Page 99: Social Issues

2) a) unemployment
   b) food
      energy
   c) So that people can get better jobs.

## Section Thirteen — Nouns, Cases and Linking Words

### Page 103: Nouns

1) die Freiheit      5) die Meinung
2) der Mittwoch      6) die Polizei
3) der Frühling      7) die Sängerin
4) das Mädchen       8) das Schwimmen

### Page 104: Forming Plurals and Other Nouns

1) Er hat viele Schwestern.
2) Die Kinder sind klein.
3) Die Tische sind frei.
4) Die Ärzte / Die Ärztinnen sind nett.
5) Die Reichen kaufen viel.
6) Die Studenten spielen Basketball.

## Page 105: Cases — Nominative and Accusative

1) nom. — Der Mann  acc. — Deutsch
2) nom. — Die Stadt  acc. — eine Synagoge
3) nom. — Ich  acc. — eine Schwester
4) nom. — Er  acc. — Pommes
5) nom. — Meine Mutter  acc. — ein Auto
6) nom. — Ich  acc. — einen neuen Rock

## Page 106: Cases — Dative and Genitive

1) dat. — meinem Bruder
2) dat. — einer Freundin
3) gen. — meines Vaters
4) gen. — meiner Mutter

## Page 107: Definite and Indefinite Articles

1) den
2) der
3) eine
4) einen
5) keine
6) kein

## Page 109: Subject and Object Pronouns

1) Er sieht sie.
2) Sie lieben ihn.
3) Ich habe dir geholfen.
4) Sie besuchen mich.
5) Ich schicke ihnen einen E-mail.
6) Der Junge gab seinem Vater den Hund.

## Page 110: Relative and Interrogative Pronouns

1) Ich kenne die Frau, die ein Hemd trägt.
2) Die Leute, die mir schreiben, sind nett.
3) Wer kauft die Jacke?
4) Mit wem ist er gegangen / gefahren?
5) Nichts, was sie macht, ist einfach.

## Page 111: Reflexive Pronouns

1) Ich entschuldige mich.
2) Wir bewegen uns.
3) Sie ziehen sich an.
4) Er freut sich.
5) Ich habe mich froh gefühlt.
6) Sie hat sich bewegt.
7) Sie setzen sich.
8) Du merkst es dir.

## Page 112: Word Order

You should have ticked: 2, 3 and 6.
You should have crossed: 1, 4 and 5.

## Page 113: Coordinating Conjunctions

1) Ich fahre mit dem Bus und du fährst mit dem Zug.
2) Wir gehen in den Park, denn es ist sonnig.
3) Ich will Musik hören oder fernsehen.
4) Er ist Vegetarier, aber sie isst Fleisch.

## Page 114: Subordinating Conjunctions

1) Er mag tanzen, weil es entspannend ist.
2) Wenn ich Zeit habe, werde ich zu deiner Party kommen.
3) Wir waren beste Freunde, als wir Kinder waren.
4) Sie will laufen, obwohl es sehr heiß ist.

## Page 115: Compound Conjunctions

1) Er liest entweder ein Buch oder die Zeitung.
2) Entweder Jana oder Leon spielen Basketball.
3) Weder Felix noch Yasmin wollen fahren.
4) Ich will sowohl klettern als auch schwimmen.

## Page 117: Prepositions

1) durch den Wald
2) Es ist für die Frau.
3) von ihrem Vater
4) ohne seinen Hund
5) Es ist im Haus.
6) nach dem Film
7) Ich singe beim Kochen.
8) Ich stehe unter dem Baum.

## Page 118: More Prepositions

1) Er sitzt darauf.
2) Sie spielen dafür.
3) wegen der Kosten
4) statt der Pflanzen
5) trotz des Schnees
6) während der Party
7) Sie liegt darunter.
8) Sie wohnen darin.

## Section Fourteen — Adjectives and Adverbs

## Page 123: Adjective Agreement

1) Das Pferd ist grau.
2) Ich sehe drei graue Pferde.
3) Er hat einige graue Pferde.
4) Sie mag die grauen Pferde.
5) Ich habe ein graues Pferd.
6) Ich sitze auf diesem grauen Pferd.

## Page 124: More Adjectives

1) Unser Haus ist groß.
2) Ihre Schwester ist glücklich.
3) Es gibt einen Vogel in jedem Baum.
4) Wer hat meine neue Tasche?
5) Diese Musik ist toll.
6) Die Frau hat wenig Geld.

## Page 125: Comparative and Superlative Adjectives

1) glücklich / froh, glücklicher / froher
2) langsamer als Ben
3) Dieser Film ist trauriger.
4) so teuer wie
5) Wir sind am schnellsten.
6) Ich höre die beste Musik.
7) Sie kennen die meisten Leute.

## Page 126: Adverbs

1) Ich gehe sehr schnell.
2) Sie laufen oft weit.
3) Er hat kaum gesprochen.
4) Normalerweise helfe ich Lukas viel.
5) Wir werden bestimmt gewinnen.
6) Die Frau fährt immer überall.
7) Leider kam Stephan etwas spät.
8) Es kostet ungefähr zwei Euro.

## Page 127: Comparative and Superlative Adverbs

1) Ich laufe schneller als sie.
2) Wir werden langsamer essen.
3) Sie tanzt besser als wir.
4) Er springt genauso weit wie ich.
5) Er singt am schönsten.
6) Sie spielen Fußball am besten.

## Section Fifteen — Verbs and Tenses

### Page 130: Verbs in the Present Tense
1) Sie sammelt.
2) Wir glauben.
3) Du fragst.
4) Sie tanzen.
5) Ich fei(e)re.
6) Sie recyceln.
7) Ich spiele.
8) Jan kocht.
9) Ich wohne hier seit einem Jahr.

### Page 131: More About the Present Tense
1) Sie hat eine Katze.
2) Wir sind Lehrer / Lehrerinnen.
3) Er wird unabhängig.
4) Du folgst dem Mann.
5) Glauben Sie mir?
6) Der Hund gehört meiner Schwester.

### Page 132: More Ways to Use Verbs
1) Sie zieht sich an.
2) Es schneit.
3) Ich sollte etwas sagen.
4) Wir fühlen uns sehr gut.
5) Ich studiere viel, um gute Noten zu bekommen.
6) Ich gehe oft aus, ohne die Tür zu schließen.

### Page 133: Talking About the Past
1) Ich habe Kaffee getrunken.
2) Wir sind hier geblieben.
3) Sie hat gefragt.
4) Er hat mich gefunden.

### Page 135: The Simple Past
1) Ich hatte einen Hund.
2) Wir waren froh.
3) Er war jung.
4) Sie hatten eine gute Idee.
5) Sie aßen da / dort.
6) Du halfst mir.
7) Sie dachten viel.
8) Ihr begannt spät.
9) Wir sahen ihn.
10) Sie spielten Tennis.
11) Mila schrieb ein Buch.
12) Ich zog nach Griechenland.

### Page 136: Talking About the Future
1) Ich gehe am Montag in den Park. / Ich werde am Montag in den Park gehen.
2) Anna trifft uns nächste Woche. / Anna wird uns nächste Woche treffen.
3) Er erklärt es bald. / Er wird es bald erklären.
4) Nächstes Jahr besuchen sie uns. / Nächstes Jahr werden sie uns besuchen.
5) Morgen esse ich Pommes. / Morgen werde ich Pommes essen.
6) Nächstes Mal kaufen wir das Auto. / Nächstes Mal werden wir das Auto kaufen.

### Page 137: Negative Forms
1) Sie fliegt nicht.
2) Er ist nicht sportlich.
3) Sie gibt ihm nichts.
4) Wenn ich heute nicht koche...
5) Ich werde nie Fleisch essen.
6) Sie fahren nicht mit dem Zug, sondern mit dem Bus.

### Page 138: Giving Orders
1) Tanz!
2) Seid freundlich!
3) Setzt euch!
4) Folgen Sie mir!
5) Verlass uns nicht!
6) Seien Sie nicht traurig!

### Page 139: Separable Verbs
1) Sie geht aus.
2) Ich komme heute an.
3) Er hat seinen Bruder angerufen.
4) Du bist aufgestanden.
5) Ich werde zurückkommen.
6) Wenn wir fernsehen...
7) Er nahm teil. / Er hat teilgenommen.
8) Hör auf, Eric!

### Page 140: Modal Verbs
1) Du darfst bleiben.
2) Wir mögen Tennis spielen.
3) Jane kann singen.
4) Er sollte gehen.
5) Sie musste spielen.
6) Ich wollte ein neues Fahrrad.

### Page 141: Conditional Forms
1) Wir möchten Käse.
2) Shreya möchte singen.
3) Sie würden mich nicht besuchen.
4) Ich würde viel trinken.
5) Du solltest warten.
6) Wir sollten unseren Lehrer / unsere Lehrerin fragen.

### Page 142: The Subjunctive
1) Wenn wir Hunger hätten...
2) Ich hätte einen Hund.
3) Sie wären sehr traurig.
4) Wenn du Schauspieler / Schauspielerin wärst...
5) Wenn er ein Auto hätte, wäre es rot.
6) Wenn ich die Zeit hätte, würde ich mehr malen.

# Index

## A
accommodation 72
adjectives 13, 22, 23, 81, 123-125
  agreement 123
  comparative 125
  indefinite 124
  possessive 124
  superlative 125
  used as nouns 104
adverbs 23, 126, 127
  comparative 127
  superlative 127
'alle', 'alles' 110, 123
articles 86, 105, 107, 123

## B
buildings 72, 74, 86, 88

## C
careers 46, 47
cases 4, 12, 50, 72, 90, 105-109, 111, 116-118, 123, 124
celebrations 59
celebrities 64-67
cinema 50
clothes 89
comparatives 75, 127
compound words 20, 32, 33, 95, 103
conditional 31, 141
conjunctions 53
  compound 115
  coordinating 113
  subordinating 112, 114, 137
countries 70

## D
dates 6
days of the week 6
der, die, das... 107
describing people 22, 23
dieser, diese... 123, 124
direct objects 105, 109
directions 90

## E
eating out 54
ein, eine... 107
environment 95-97
'etwas' 104, 110, 126
exam advice 150, 151

## F
family and friends 20-25
festivals 60, 61
films 50
food 29, 54
free time 50-55
'Freund', 'Freundin' 24
further education 45
future tenses 25, 46, 136, 139

## G
'gefallen' 12
gender 46, 103, 104, 107
'gern' 52, 126, 127
greetings 10

## H
'haben' 96, 131, 133, 134
health 30-33
hobbies 50-55
holidays 70-75
home 86

## I
'ich möchte' 10, 141
illnesses 32
imperatives 138, 139
imperfect tense (simple past) 134, 135, 139, 140
indirect objects 106, 109
infinitives 31, 40, 54, 130, 132, 136, 139, 140
internet 80, 81

## J
jeder, jede... 123, 124
'jemand' 108
jobs 46, 47

## K
Karneval 60
kein, keine... 123

## L
'lieber' 12, 126, 127
listening exam 150

## M
'man' 40, 108, 132
marriage 25
may I... ? 11
mein, meine... 124
mich, dich... 108, 111
mir, dir... 108, 111
months of the year 6
music 52
myself, yourself... 111, 132

## N
nationalities 19
negatives 137, 138
'nichts' 110, 137
'niemand' 108
nouns 88, 99, 103-106
  compound 20, 32, 103
  from verbs 74, 95, 104
  weak 104
numbers 4

## O
opinions 12, 13

## P
partnership 24
passive voice 132
past participles 133
perfect tense 52, 109, 111, 133, 137, 139
personalities 23
plurals 22, 86, 104, 106, 123
polite phrases 10, 11
pollution 95, 96
prefixes 65, 67, 137
prepositions 8, 50, 70, 90, 116-118
present tense 130, 131, 136
pronouns 108
  interrogative 110
  object 108
  prepositional 118
  reflexive 24, 80, 111, 137
  relative 110
  subject 108
pronunciation 148, 149

## Q
questions — how to ask them 8, 9, 110

## R
reading exam 151
relationships 24, 25
restaurants 54
rooms 86
routines 38, 87

## S
school
  life 38, 39
  pressures 40, 41
  subjects 37
seasons 6, 91
'sein' 131, 133, 134
'seit' 116, 130
shopping 54, 89
simple past 134, 135, 139, 140
social issues 98, 99
social media 82, 83
speaking exam 150
sport 30, 53
study 37, 45
subjunctive 142
superlatives 125, 127

## T
technology 79
'Time, Manner, Place' 112, 126, 137
times of day 5, 6
town 74, 88, 90
transport 72
TV 51

## U
umlauts 88, 103, 104, 125, 148
'um... zu...' 79, 132
unemployment 98
'used to' 52, 133

## V
verbs 132
  dative case 12, 106, 131
  impersonal 132
  irregular 29, 131, 133-136, 138
  modal 31, 40, 132, 140
  reflexive 24, 59, 111, 132, 138
  separable 51, 139
'viel', 'viele' 4, 89, 123, 124

## W
weather 91
'weil' 112, 114
welcher, welche... 123, 124
'wenig', 'wenige' 123, 124
'werden' 25, 136, 139
where is... ? 90
word order 31, 38, 40, 53, 83, 109, 112-115, 136
  questions 8
would (conditional) 141
writing exam 151

## Y
'you' 10, 108, 138